Bourgeois to Buddha

My Trials & Errors Across Four Continents

A Memoir

Laurel Ann Francis

Interior design: Saloff Enterprises
Cover design: Mark Saloff Designs
Front cover tapestry: Laurel Ann Francis, "Removing the Veils."

Print ISBN: 978-1-7370937-0-1
E-book ISBN: 978-1-7370937-1-8
Library of Congress Number: 2021912060

Published in the United States of America
Copyright information available upon request. v. 1.0
First Edition

Acknowledgments

Thank God for the privilege of living this life and having time to finish this memoir.

I am most grateful to my three children who, as adults, confidently left the nest to study and begin their careers just as I was falling apart and ready to fly the coop myself.

Mahalo to my dear middle child Michelle who urged me to write this memoir because of her eagerness to have it shared in print: "Just start talking and I will write it down," she said, "I have friends who want their mothers to read your story."

Gratitude for Merllyn Liggett and Sylvia Partridge who took over from there, typing and suggesting revisions to my baby-stepped script.

Muchas gracias to North Shore and Westside writers' clubs on Kaua'i who kept me going until I was confident enough to sit down at the computer and compose later chapters.

Danke schoen to Susan Barozzi who seemed to enjoy being my first chapter-by-chapter "change agent" editor over a two-year period, and to Vigil for checking me on the spiritual stuff.

Merci to librarians for loving books and to my favorite librarian, Kat Bengston, for offering encouraging and professional advice when I needed it most, and even going so far as to suggest that a couple of chapters should be sent to *The New Yorker* for possible publication.

Tak dear Sally Tomiko, a friend who reads five books a week and declared my efforts worthy to publish (after slowing down her reading pace to correct my punctuation).

Great appreciation to the numerous others who nudged me along the way (believing my personal fiction was OK to tell) as well as to my brother, Captain Greg, who contributed to getting my Doc into a paperback, and to Uncle Sam-ulus for assistance in balancing the books.

Kudos to Isa Maria who meticulously brought this project to the threshold of fruition. I am also grateful to have Jamie Saloff as my layout and publishing guide. Loving blessings out to Marguerite Pawlick and Sarah Zoglio who shared countless cups of tea with me as we played with photos and fonts maneuvering the world of cover design before turning it over to Mark Saloff to pull it all together.

Most obliged to the teachers on my guru shopping trip whose wise spoken and written words have served as guidance for this journey and beyond.

Even those of you who stepped on my toes in this earth dance, thanks for being the impetus for me to glide more gently on our globe.

◁ Act One ▷

Departure From the Status Quo

One

Beginning of the End

I t was a simple suggestion by the minister in a sweet ceremony: "Would the married couples here please rise and join our beloved bride and groom, and renew your vows as Justin and Judith recite theirs." My reaction shocked me.

This sunny day had started without a hint of the dark cloud that would color my sky that day. We parked by the split rail fence which was spilling over with roses and entered the old clapboard Cape Cod church for the long-anticipated ceremony. Justin, a bachelor and Jerry's longtime friend from his Frankfurt, Germany Foreign Service days, was marrying his South Shore sweetheart. This horsewoman was a good match for this Yankee Jack of all trades.

I was happy for them as they stood on the altar steps surrounded by six different varieties of hydrangeas which were just coming into bloom. The sun was streaming through the west facing stained glass window. It was all so perfect and loving until the three little words "renew your vows" startled every cell of who I thought I was.

My body froze. *"No way"* was my first, second and third visceral response as my mind raced to the unthinkable: I was deeply and profoundly not interested or willing to repeat those promises made long before. Whatever was going on in my husband's head at the time I do not know, but he made no attempt to act on the suggestion either. We didn't look at each other or even touch hands. Red light for sure. We had a problem which neither of us brought up at that opportune moment or at any time in the near future. Our friends' marriage began that day as our two-decade-long vow of togetherness slid into a deeper, more dramatic divide. The tied knot would steadily unravel scene by scene in a perfectly imperfect play of opposites.

The action changes as actors exit. What goes down must come up; what was here goes there; looking out becomes going within. There is peace and there is war. Would duality ever give way to non-duality?

Here follows a story of falling and rising again in four acts, with names changed when necessary to protect accomplices in my fledgling enterprise of a life. I often quote and credit the loquacious Lamas, Rams, Gurus, Babajis (and teachers without the "ji") whose wise words helped deliver my darkness to the light. My conditioning makes it impossible to be 100% original regardless of how unique I play at being as the curtain rises...

"Don't you love your wife?" Dr. Martinez asked after diagnosing my husband as having a prostate problem, the "priests' disease," he called it. Jerry's affirmative answer didn't include having sex with me, his wife of 20 years, however; so the urologist gave us an Rx spelled S-E-X, to stimulate our libidos. He recommended a dose of "explicit literature" and sex toys as a method to arouse renewed interest in his marital duties and the release of all that backed-up semen. (Had this medical checkup and diagnosis taken place in the 21st Century, a trip to the pharmacy might well have ended this memoir before it began.)

The following Saturday night, Jerry and I set out to fill the prescription. We headed an hour down the highway to Boston's red light district, the Beantown Downtown Crossing where tourists are advised not to go at night. But we weren't tourists; we were on a mission.

As our first stop, we ducked into a venue promising "Special -Today Only: New Xciting Stars / Private Viewing Booths."

After changing dollars into quarters, we slide into separate dark, solitary, "hots" smelly, curtained cubicles with an inviting peep hole in one wall. I for my luggage. I responded in kind as Jerry drove home in a sulk which I was not motivated to break. Having resisted an affair and having fantasized being welcomed home with passion, I was furious and full of regret about both non-events.

I continued to beat on myself with the realization that my husband didn't love me and I didn't love him. The next day, I purchased the most outrageously suggestive "peek-a-boo" card I could find and mailed it from the office to the one man who was interested in me and my body. The slippery slope began with an erotic pen to paper correspondence with Parker, using snail mail in those days before we all had computers. It's a wonder that the letters didn't catch fire as they crossed the country between our New England and Missouri professional buildings.

How I got so far away from the self I thought I was called for a review of our early married life. I offer the Reality TV version (before there was such a thing), revealing the cracks in the pedestal of our "perfect American family."

It started out as a "male-breadwinner, stay-at-home-wife" kind of household (roles which were rewarding to Jerry and me at the time): first renting, then buying the three bedroom ranch; wife barefoot and pregnant; happy husband with only his career to think about.

We started a cooperative nursery school with friends, which was fulfilling and creative as well as a happy place for daughter Michelle. Jerry took up golfing with his boss and joined the Lion's Club. I went back to teaching high school as soon as all three children were enrolled in elementary school, which changed some expectations, but nary a dent in our *you know who's boss* conditioning. Perhaps that is where the tension took birth.

It's no surprise that I got more uppity as I earned more money, even though there barely seemed to be enough when we sat down to pay the bills. Our teenagers, given their Yankee work ethic and desire to fit in, were extra busy with part-time jobs delivering papers, babysitting, doing yard work, catering, housekeeping, and factory jobs. In no time, they were wearing Levis and Timberland Boots just like their peers. Even with all that, our children excelled at sports and their studies as they stretched their wings. Jerry expected it of them and offered consistent encouragement and support. I respected that trait of his, but I fumed when he stressed to them how superior they were to anyone else. My comeback was: Let's be OK with being some-where in the middle, since it was obvious that we could be better at some things than others, while having less success than many in different areas. I so appreciated how resourceful Dianna, Michelle and Christopher were, but didn't want them to be snobs. We loved our children and hopefully they felt it in spite of how we couldn't always protect them from the challenges of their adolescent and teen years.

Jerry professed idealism whenever he described our family, which took a bit of denial because, in spite of our children being high achievers, there was a shadow side: our eldest daughter suffered panic attacks, our middle child was battling an addiction, and our 17-year-old son was developing an ulcer. They were fortunate to outgrow these distresses (or trade them in as I did as an adult).

Their teen years were not the best of times (but not as bad as previous years when we relocated three times after Jerry's job losses and a failed fran-chise attempt). I shared the dysfunction as I poured most of my energy into my profession, which paid half the mortgage as we recovered enough finan-cially to move into a two-story colonial with a barn and an income rental apartment. Motivated to stay relevant and to increase my income, I also earned my master's degree while teaching full time. Looking back, I know that was hard on us (except for snow days when we were all free from school and took off for the White Mountains to ski, I even managed not to freak out when ticketed after my sweet little two door red Toyota Corolla with skis on the roof was picked up for speeding by radar). It would have been nice to have had a housecleaner or a cook. Somehow I made time to keep up with the laundry and host holiday dinners for the in-laws, all the things that came with the territory...

◇ ◇ ◇

As the years passed, Jerry kept having to change jobs as his temper flared and his thirst for scotch increased. I came to dread parties or any outing where drinks were served because after his third, there was no reasoning with him. He would buy most of the rounds and fight me over the car keys for the drive home.

◇ ◇ ◇

He was less adamant about my taking the steering wheel after getting a DWI following his usual post service club meeting. It was embarrassing to have his wife talk to him behind a screen at the police station before bailing him out and driving him home. Later on, when he refused to go anywhere that the hosts did not offer him a beer as soon as we walked in the door, I went alone.

Soon our separate ways became the norm. I gave up drinking and that ended our so-called lovemaking because I only tolerated sex when I was tipsy.

Even though my knuckles started to swell with arthritis, I held onto my own particular love, peace and apple pie family story until our son, as a senior in high school, applied for Air Force ROTC. This was a shock to me. How could this happen to "Another Mother for Peace," a *Beyond War* facilitator and fervent campaigner for all the presidential peace candidates? How was it possible that I could have an offspring who would even consider becoming a cog in the wheel of the military complex? But Christopher was accepted, put on the USAF Reserve uniform, and managed to get his college education paid for by Uncle Sam. My son chose not to be "without" anymore. He was not going to graduate with huge debts as his sisters had in spite of all their scholarships and the help we could not afford. I began to realize that Jerry wasn't the only one in denial.

By this time, with a Master's degree to my name, I got a new job as a volunteer coordinator with the local college. It felt great to buy my first car and commute to a professional office. I appreciated the more flexible schedule after being controlled by school bells for seven years, and even welcomed that it often meant working nights and weekends. Planning events was fun and I felt creative as I trained, managed and rewarded volunteers who ran clubs for youth. In-service training on campus felt special, and I undertook making the required five-year plans with gusto. Married life may not have been satisfying, but my career was.

◊ ◊ ◊

It was in the late 1980's that Jerry declared, "I'm putting the house on the market."

I gasped in horror. "Not our home! You want to sell our family home and move to a condo!?"

I sighed. Even with our two daughters launched on their careers and our son away at his senior year in college, I found this idea of leaving our one-of-a-kind historic home (even if it didn't have a plaque) deplorable. This 100-year-old Victorian on a large lot in the North End was my familiar comfort zone which gave me a façade of family respectability and stability. I felt it being pulled out from under me. Perhaps the children did also. "Where are we going to bring our children home for the holidays?" Michelle asked.

Since it was not my style to confront my husband openly, I reverted to passive-aggressive behavior. We would go to a showing of magazine-perfect condos and I would pick them apart and be sour with the realtors. I couldn't have been less cooperative as I became more and more depressed and angry with each real estate viewing. I was a real bitch. Even at top-of-the-line town-house showings, I sulked. I could and would not see myself living in a cookie cutter development. Newly intractable, I wasn't going to move to dead-end Gloomsville.

Fate stepped in once again with a temporary escape valve and the panacea I sought. I put in a proposal and got approval to attend a second out-of-town conference, just two years after my first outing. With a firm commitment to give a presentation at a professional development conference in Austin (with a fringe benefit), I wrote to my secret pen-pal, the one-kiss hunk from my past.

"I'll meet you there," Parker replied, as we made plans to rendezvous again after 24 months of bonding with lascivious letter writing.

Within an hour of meeting at the Hilton, we were in bed together and this iceberg melted from the bottom up. I was alert as a workshop presenter, which justified my attendance, although a bit blurry-eyed as a participant later in the week, due to my after-hours activity.

Parker and I had nothing in common but our jobs and PhD level chemistry. It was more than enough to make me fast forward here and spare you the details of how much fun we had as the "all-man" part of him and the "just like a virgin" part of me. One other important turning point was that never again would alcohol be a necessary part of the equation.

It was also a new beginning for me because after that week of sex, I was not planning on waiting another two years for more. I resonated with the wording of that famous song *"Enjoy yourself, it's later than you think...".*

I rationalized a new reality with a different sense of right and wrong. Since my husband didn't share the influence of arousal, I felt justified to find someone who did. I was in heat and plotted how to keep the fire ignited with a new flame. I may have been an amateur at this cheater's game, but I was a quick study at becoming a woman "on the make." This involved a new interest in items from Victoria's Secret and a premeditated decision as to which events offered the most possibilities. I focused on a man's response to me and an analysis of his availability. I surreptitiously auditioned him for a part in the next scene change in my drama, all settings being in drug-and-alcohol-free zones. (Needy I may have been, but not quite that desperate.)

I was living out my passionate lustful side while keeping up a professional woman, wife and mother front. (Well, not that much mothering as the children were no longer living under our roof – visiting my daughters in Boston was always so much fun as I felt more like a girlfriend.)

One part of my mind believed that novel-worthy affairs were making me as happy as my fantasies, and they did for a while. After an "outing" I would go home and gleefully play love songs and dance around the living room, into the kitchen, up and down the stairs, and out onto the porch.

Breaking Up Is Hard to Do

Darn if the freestyle was not without angst and guilt about the adultery I engaged in and desired. Jerry and I continued to go to the Universalist-Unitarian Church, the service my local lover also attended (you know the bit about meeting a mate at church). At a coffee hour one Sunday, I was standing with my tall, slim, French-looking husband on my right and my cute, brown-eyed, fire-fighting lover-hunk on the left. I flushed as I felt his fireman energy, which so often fanned my flames before cooling my fiery passion. It could have been tantalizing but it wasn't. I credit it as a defining moment when I knew I had to change: there had to be another way.

◇ ◇ ◇

The church we attended was quite liberal and the Reverend was an intellectual atheist-humanist. He had recently completed a series of sermons on World Religions, with emphasis on the "Golden Rule" as practiced by them all (without my noticing that I wasn't doing the "onto others..." bit).

I became interested in Buddhism. It was that "end of suffering" teaching that perked up my ears. And, I wondered, when dipping my nose into Hinduism (not yet my toes into the Ganges), what all this Kundalini rising was about. Could I pretend that my intense sexual arousal had something to do with root chakra awakening? In an effort to find out what was going on, I registered for a yoga class and a private session with an instructor named Maureen.

"That's it, continue. Keeping your back on the floor with your arms stretched out at shoulder level, lift your right leg over to the left side of your body. Now, left leg to the right side. Keep the rotation going; repeat."

Maureen, my super-slim Houdini-flexible yoga instructor and psycho-therapist, was directing me in a cross-body posture while I was stretched out on a mat at her sunny studio.

"I'm so stiff," said this body, resistant to the unfamiliar movements. It was work to keep going. "Ouch."

Just when I was ready to give up, something strange happened that scared me. I felt a shift and tears welled up. I started to shake and to whimper, then sobbed. Was this a so-called release? It was a small crack in my armor. Small maybe, but isn't that where the light comes in?

"Good, very good," Maureen encouraged, handing me tissues for my snotty nose. "Let go."

That was the movement and the moment. I began recognizing, albeit reluctantly, the reality that my life and my marriage weren't working and that they hadn't been for years. I couldn't change my husband; he couldn't keep me from changing. Where did couples come up with the illusion that we could tweak the other into our ideal fantasy?

◊ ◊ ◊

I wanted out, but I was scared. After so much pent-up repression and passiveness held for so long in my arthritic joints, stooped posture and tight face, I acknowledged it was time to end the charade of my marriage. I stopped denying the guilt that I felt about my extracurricular behaviors. It didn't matter that Jerry wasn't aware of what was going on, or just choosing not to know. I started reading more spiritual books, hoping somewhere to get courage without having to go to Oz. Standing up for myself was not familiar territory, but I found strength to at least lie down in a different bed. I moved out of the master double to a single.

◊ ◊ ◊

"What's with you? What the hell has happened to you?" Jerry asked the morning after I spent my first night sleeping in our daughters' bedroom.

My only answer was, "Maybe because of what menopause does to women sometimes, a hormonal thing."

"Yes, that and those crazy ideas you get at the Unitarian-Universalist Church, isn't it?"

He's right there, I admitted to myself, grateful to daughter Michelle who, as a teenager, had suggested we attend that community church because it was so helpful to her.

"You're not the woman I married," Jerry continued.

"No," I answered with a stream of consciousness, "I'm not that adventurous young woman who was living, working and traveling in Europe on her own, who met and fell for the exciting older Foreign Service officer that you were. I am not the domesticated wife and mother who stayed home as a dedicated homemaker for ten years with our three precious offspring, while you started a new career stateside after living abroad for more than a decade. I had to change when I went back to work full time after Christopher started school. We both agreed that a second income was necessary to meet the mortgage. I'm changing again, knowing I must take responsibility for my own happiness. I'm through with being miserable."

As I learned more about the physical and psychological changes during menopause, I accepted it as a kind of second adolescence I could use to explain my erupting anger. My body was telling me something had to change: for starters, to give up being a victim. Having a career meant holding my own in the working world. It was taking an awful lot of energy to keep our dormant relationship going, not to mention my dead-end affairs which were the betrayal of my marriage and my husband and myself. However, those affairs were making me feel desired and desirable, a different, more confident person.

Was Joseph Campbell right when he said, "Give up the life you had planned in order to welcome the life waiting for you"?

Could I adjust to life outside the box of a marriage? Did I feel safer there because it was familiar even if unsatisfying? But while I was dreaming up my exit, I was grieving. Why did so much pain have to be part of the process? Did this midlife loss come with a guarantee of something better? Somewhere in the ether I read that our lives are soul directed. Was that true?

There were lots of tears in my ears while lying in that single bed. I felt that the scarlet letter A was embroidered on my chest. Must I take the dreaded next step, and be branded on my forehead with the dreaded letter D for divorcee?

I needed help. After Jerry left for work, I called in sick to the office, then dialed the family HMO with my ASAP request. Yes, an appointment with the psychologist was covered by insurance. After putting this melodramatic, emotionally charged woman on hold, the receptionist verified that Dr. Desmond would see me that afternoon. Receptionists recognize basket cases when they hear them.

Here I go, I thought. I am a psycho. But I was sane enough to be grateful knowing that help was forthcoming. Why hadn't I reached out before becoming so desperate?

◇ ◇ ◇

On that first of my three meetings with the psychologist, I revealed that early in our marriage, Jerry had warned me, "Don't get in a pissing contest with a skunk." (This foreboding remark about his temper and Type A interactions revealed why he was often fired from his jobs during the quarter century we were together.) I quickly learned when to stay quiet and not to argue. As one who avoided conflict, I gathered up chips without realizing what I was doing, not to mention the price of cashing them in.

Dr. Desmond elaborated on how stuffing down my feelings for so long and now secretly acting like a single woman was my passive-aggressive response.

"Your experience is not unique. Read the book *Women Who Love Too Much*. It will help you," she recommended.

"Oh, I couldn't do that," I assured her, "because I didn't love my husband enough! Surely if I had been more loving, he would have reciprocated."

After questioning my perception, "Are you sure about that?" she suggested the title *Men Who Hate Women and the Women Who Love Them: When you don't know why loving hurts so much* by Susan Forward, which I agreed to read. I added the descriptive noun "misogynist" to my vocabulary. I saw our relationship described on the back cover and answered YES to all the "pointing the finger" questions there (because it was all the man's fault, of course).

From that book, new in 1986, I recognized my co-dependence although it was still hard to believe that I wore the family-addicted label and was "domesticated to the depth of detriment to self." But wasn't raising offspring a priority as well as being age-appropriate? Was my marriage really all that bleak? Others tolerated being lonely even though married. Why couldn't I? Was this to be a story of my grasping for more? This Gemini always had two sides, and I lived as both of them: keeping to the to-do list as a mate, mother, homemaker and career woman, but having a sense of adventure and pleasure too.

"You've heard of Maslow's Hierarchy of Needs," Dr. Desmond added, "It is necessary to have one's physical, social and emotional needs met before evolving spiritually. You reached out to other men in an attempt to satisfy yourself emotionally and physically. It is healthy that you are now studying the Eastern paths. I am sure, given your interest in all things spiritual from an early age, that this study of yoga is the beginning of the deepest spiritual search of your life." That might also be age appropriate, I agreed.

◇ ◇ ◇

Dr. D. arranged for me to attend group therapy after our insurance-allotted three sessions were over.

"I don't belong here," I told myself as I went, inwardly kicking and screaming, to the first meeting. Feeling somewhat insane, yet definitely not as crazy as I perceived the others to be, I reluctantly sat in a circle with eleven women who were contemplating divorce. By the end of the third session, I was bad-mouthing my soon to be "was-band" with the best of them. I even started sharing hugs as I discovered I was wrong to feel superior. By our fourth meeting, these sharings gave me the courage to move, sooner rather than later, from a separate bedroom to out of the house. All agreed with me that I must escape what I felt to be emotional abuse. I appreciated their allowing me to be the victim. Making Jerry the "bad guy" was the only way this un-Catholic (once a Catholic, one is never non-Catholic) could justify even considering ending the marriage. Jerry became my "image of an enemy," the 100% bad guy I had to defeat in order to go through with the divorce. I had to head out in order to head in to find the renewed me: that or something better, dear Lord.

◇ ◇ ◇

The separation was complicated by the fact that Jerry, diagnosed two years before with Non-Hodgkin's Lymphoma, had undergone radiation and chemotherapy. This was serious, not like his previous occasions when his way of controlling me when I asserted myself, I believed, would be the onset of his immobilizing back problems. In the past, I would rise to the occasion and respond by experimenting with nutritional supplements (Adelle Davis style) and making good-for-the-soul chicken soup. Not any more. When he got cancer, as much as I hate to admit it, I was unsympathetic to the diagnosis.

"Wolf, wolf," he had cried so many times before about ailments that this time when the problem was much more serious, I just couldn't respond with compassion. While Jerry received his chemotherapy treatments, his older sister Jeannie waited for him in the hospital outpatient section while I was off with a lover. My heart was closed; he was my husband in name only.

I later learned that Jerry, just before he died three years after our divorce, had told our daughter Michelle that he knew that I was going to leave him and that he *got cancer* to try to prevent my departure. At the time that I planned to move out, Jerry had been in remission for a year. Although I felt jet-lagged over my guilty trips, I didn't change my free-style fantasies.

Think guilt, think church. After attending the Unitarian-Universalist church for seven years, I felt comfortable with the minister and the teachings, and went to see Reverend Rowley for advice.

He believed in service to humanity. He was impartial. He understood all sides of any philosophy, and his sermons would reveal the sacred and the shadow of each. Jesus may have been the ultimate lover of his brother as himself, but Jesus as God was a myth, he said. He would praise Christ, Buddha, Mohammed or Moses one Sunday, and intellectually discredit the religions arising from their teachings the next. (I sometimes feared someone would come through the door and attack him, because he sounded so radical.)

But, drawn to his brilliance and stature and the humanistic teachings of the UU church, I knew that I was no longer tied to the Pope. I didn't have to be a martyr or a saint. It was such a relief to give up the fear of eternal punishment and believe that the present was the only time there was.

I continued to make the most of the NOW as I lived out my awakened hedonistic tendencies. I heard what I wanted to hear on Sundays. Would I resonate with the answer to my latest question?

"Could I leave a man who had cancer?" I asked Reverend Rowley. "Do I have to wait another four more years of Jerry being in remission before I can go?"

The holy ordained one replied that if Jerry were dying, he would advise me not to go. Since my husband had been declared well for a year, he said, I should feel free to move on with my life. Then the Reverend made reference to Jerry's alcoholism, something that had never been labeled out loud before by anyone including me. Had I been an enabler?

"Thanks so much for your help," I said as I left, now ready to give up my part in this drama.

I reviewed what Margaret Mead professed: "We have all been married three times, even if it is to the same person." It was true for me: I was a bride in my first, a parenting partner in my second, and a failure in my empty nest third marriage.

◇ ◇ ◇

"I'm moving out tomorrow, I've rented a room," I said to Jerry, just as I had rehearsed it in my therapy group. Hardly had he lifted his head from the newspaper and put his glass of scotch down before I added, "Here's a check for one-half of the mortgage. I'll come back on my days off while you are at work to clear out stuff. I hope the house sells soon."

Before he could answer, I was out the door on my way to an Al Anon meeting.

"That's it. I've done it. I'm out of here regardless of the cost," I said to myself, feeling both honorable and bitter about paying month-to-month for space I wasn't occupying. We might have had a foreclosure on the property if I didn't contribute, and I was counting on half of the proceeds from the sale of the house, our one asset – nothing to fight about. My big high was the day I opened a personal checking account, never again to deposit my paycheck into that joint one we had always shared.

The next morning, my "I'm out of here" day, was September 28th, our 25th wedding anniversary. The only thing Silver about it was my changing hair color. The children knew not to plan a party. Jerry left for work before I was out of bed. On the fireplace marble mantelpiece he had left a note which read, "Thank you for 25 of the happiest years of my life."

Yeah sure, I thought, he is simply having a Jekyll moment to be followed soon by the opposite, which I won't be around to observe. I scrunched the paper, threw it away, walked out the door and went to work.

But I couldn't help but remember how this all began...

Flashback: Embryo of a Marriage

In the beginning, 26 years earlier, the year 1962, Jerry was on vacation from his Foreign Service office in Frankfurt, Germany, and I was en route to Israel having just quit my civilian position at a US Army Base on the Rhine. (I worked for the military just long enough to pay off my Boston University debt. My teaching English jobs in Scandinavia hardly paid for sustenance. Teaching at Berlitz in Germany, earning the equivalent of 75 cents an hour in those olden days, bought a half a chicken...).

I was on the Brindisi dock in Italy, waiting to board the same boat that Jerry and his brother-in-law were taking for the sail from the boot of Europe to the island of Greece. They were already on deck watching others head up the gangplank. As soon as I set foot on the Greek ferry carrying 75 passengers and one car, Jerry greeted me in German and I responded in kind, which was logical as we both looked European. Before long, we were having drinks on the deck and sharing pleasantries. By midnight, Bill, the brother-in-law, told Jerry that I was the woman he was going to marry. I decided it was time to end such talk and said good night after making arrangements to have breakfast with them the next morning when we docked at 8 a.m. in Piraeus.

Plans changed, however, when the ship's bells sounded at 3 a.m. with an announcement from the captain that we were arriving early. It was witch-pitch dark as we descended onto Greek soil.

Jerry sought me out. Knowing I didn't have plans until the bus left later that morning for Athens, he invited me to ride with them in that one car ferried over with us. As soon as his red Toyota Camry was unloaded from the ferry, the three of us got in and headed north on a narrow dirt road with little sign of activity anywhere.

Within the hour, we had a close call as we came inches away from crashing into a truck with no tail lights. The sheep on board bleated loud enough to drown out the swear words exchanged by both drivers. Deciding that continuing the course in the darkness before dawn while still hung over was not a good idea, we parked at the first available accommodations, and registered for separate rooms at an inn with hole-in-the-ground toilet facilities, a primitive first for me.

Arriving hours later at our second stop, an Athens hotel overlooking the Acropolis, I decided why not, and unpacked in Jerry's double to begin what became our first honeymoon.

After a week of taverna partying, visiting the wonders of ancient Athens, and enjoying the extras of love at first lust, Jerry and Bill left to return to Germany. I booked a flight to Israel, my next pre-arranged destination, for the next day. (What happened in those next 24 hours was a life changer – more on that will be revealed in another scene.)

Jerry didn't forget me while I was in Israel. He wrote me long love letters pleading with me to return to Germany and live with him. I took him up on the offer and showed up at his apartment in Frankfurt a couple of months later. I had hitchhiked most of the way from the Middle East.

Jerry's first glance at this road-weary backpacker must have made him wonder if I was the same woman he had courted in Greece. Fortunately, I "clean up good" and passed muster, after he took me shopping for a new wardrobe.

Short version of a kind of fairy tale match: I got pregnant, we got married, our first daughter was born in Frankfurt, Jerry quit his job, and we moved back to the United States with our first born 15 months later. (That move back stateside was four years to the day that I arrived in Europe to study in Denmark, to work in Germany, and to travel in the Middle East.)

Three

Lodger

OK, that's how my married life had begun, but what now? It was 1987 when my attention shifted to this new role in a rented room, after I separated from Jerry.

"This is my home," recently divorced landlady Sybil stressed immediately after my move to her extra bedroom, the single at the top of the stairs. This was my step from the swamp into more mud.

I perceived her as still struggling with having her husband leave her for his secretary after forty years of marriage. As a stay-at-home retired proper Bostonian intellectual who was meticulous about her property, Sybil was a perfect partner for me to continue the victim dance. I thought we would be friends, but she made it clear that I was just a lodger.

"This is your shelf in the fridge and you can use the cabinet on the far left for other groceries. Even though you often work in the evenings, don't plan on cooking after 6:30 p.m. You may do your laundry on Saturday mornings only. Don't disturb me when you come in or leave. Keep the volume down on your radio or CD. You can use my phone for the time being. Keep your calls short. No Long Distance calls without paying extra. Park at the far end of the driveway, not in the garage."

Why was I surprised? I just hadn't expected her to be so controlling. (Looking back, I most likely would have done the same.) I was incensed but had had practice in not showing my feelings. Didn't she realize I was a career woman with a life?

But I was no longer the mistress in my own home. I spent many a restless night going over and over the decision: what have I done? What have I given up? It was my idea to leave Jerry; why am I not happy to be free? Jerry was not here to blame. Who was responsible for my happiness? Changing living quarters was not the geographical cure that I'd anticipated. Changing the position of my feet on the globe didn't bring about a beautiful configuration out of the crisis of guilt and shame... and blame. Duhh.

Years later, a teacher reviewed the blame game in this way:

"First, I believe the other is at fault, the cause of the problem.
Second, I learn to take responsibility for half of the conflict.
Third, I accept responsibility for my life and everything in it.
Fourth, there is no blame. It is what it is. All is in perfect order."

Really, is it true that all is in perfect order? That's a tall order, similar to "loving what is." Even so, I did my best to stretch myself in this bit of life's curriculum. Kinda... Sorta... Maybe later...My search continued.

◇ ◇ ◇

While living at Sybil's, I began attending Twelve Step Al Anon meetings which were more upsetting than helpful. The women mirrored my bitterness, and the reflection was not pretty. All of our mates were assholes. Each of us was a victim. I did my partner bashing like the best of them. It was not healing, except for the part where I recognized and admitted "My life is out of control." I only attended a few meetings without getting anywhere close to completing the 12 Steps, which would have been helpful. Maybe I should have gone to Sex Addicts Anonymous instead.

◇ ◇ ◇

I wish I had been introduced to "The Work" by Byron Katie, the popular American queen of questioning, at that time. I needed her reminder that my most intimate relationship is with my own thoughts. She writes: "We are entering the dimension where we have control... the inside." As a modern version of the Hindu goddess Kali, this gentle, compassionate woman is called a fierce warrior against our fear-based stories. The four steps in her book *Loving What Is* (as well as on her website) are very effective for those who are dealing with their worst nightmares. She asks:

"Step one: Is it true?

Step two: Can you absolutely know it is true?

Step three: What happens when you believe that thought?

Step four: Who would you be without that thought?"

This superlative suggestion comes next: "Turn it around and give three examples of this 'turnaround' being as true or truer than the original belief." In doing her protocol by answering the questions, I would have to say:

1. It is a belief that my husband didn't love me,
2. No, I do not know whether or not that was absolutely true,
3. I went to outrageous lengths in my effort to feel loved, and
4. Without the thought that my husband didn't love me, there would be relief from the paralyzing pain of feeling like a failure.

The "turnaround" would be: "My husband did love me as much as I loved him, which was to the degree that either of us was able to love and accept each other or even ourselves at the time."

Three more examples of the turnaround: "We parented and raised three children together. We shared common backgrounds and a compatible enough lifestyle for 20 years. We grew together until we grew apart."

Thank you, Byron Katie, for The Work and the teaching that everyone is a mirror image of myself – my own thinking coming back to me. My projections were creating painful perceptions which I had to turn around.

My wise sister Gini, who watched sunsets in California for decades while I rose for sunrises on the East Coast, was extremely helpful at this time in my life. It was good to talk to her, a PhD in psychology and a divorcee who had learned lots from being a single mother with many monogamous partnerships (serial marriages as they were called in the 1960's). I had never even thought about such things from behind my white picket fence, far from West Coast ideas.

"Here, read this," she said, handing me a copy of *Illusions* by Richard Bach. "It will give you a different way of looking at appearances and reality."

Indeed, it was an eye-opener for me as I came upon an inspiring movie metaphor in this classic.

To quote the author, "Who's the cameraman, the projectionist, the theater manager, the ticket taker, the distributor, and who watches them all happen? Who is free to walk out in the middle, anytime, change the plot whenever; who is free to see the same film over and over again?"

Recognizing that the potential for freedom described there was available to me, I felt empowered. I was confident that I would never live with Jerry again.

◇ ◇ ◇

Back during our colonial home days, Jerry would often say, "Throw it away." But getting rid of stuff was an abhorrent thought to me. Now that I had moved out and was anxious to clear out almost everything connected with my previous life, I made frequent trips back to the homestead from my bed-sit to do just that. It was always at a time that I knew Jerry was away. Having always been a hoarder, this was a new role for me. I boxed up previously relished items: trinkets, crystals, linens (all things my husband considered to be clutter), and stashed them in the car. Wherever I went, I shared these goodies with whomever wanted them. It was such a relief to act out this new miraculous indifference to possessions. (Did I realize how hard it might have been for the children to no longer have a family home?)

◇ ◇ ◇

But Jerry began holding on. As I prepared the house for showings by decluttering the shelves, Jerry left a note for me.

"There's no need to do such clearing. The house hasn't sold yet. Don't touch my souvenirs."

I was letting go; he was not. A touch of compassion came over me as I noted our changing roles. I had only been able to get closer to filing for divorce by accenting all of the negatives of my husband, just as I had stayed faithful for 20 of our 25 years by concentrating on the positive aspects of our relationship. Sure, Jerry was both Hyde and Jekyll, but when he was good and funny and charming and brilliant, he was very good and very funny and very charming and very brilliant.

Besides our home (and the mortgage), hadn't we shared a commitment to our family life of kids and cats, an interest in exercise and political campaigning, and the UU church? Jerry adored our children and got along well with my parents. On four-day holidays, he would drive the 12 hours each way from New England to the Midwest (often through whiteouts on snow belt Route 20 before the Interstate was built) to take the five of us to visit them. The kids got to know their grandparents and play with their cousins, a bonding which still continues to this day.

Jerry checked the children's homework and put their "all-A" report cards up on the fridge. He also had the habit of sharing their successes, living as he did in reflected glory. He went to all their sports events and was often asked, as a good storyteller, to speak at many of their award banquets. Audiences loved it when he shared the most dramatic tales of his world travels with the Foreign Service.

Always up with the latest music and a good dancer (much better than me), he often sang along and rocked out with the children and their friends, to the delight of all. How I wished I could have afforded cha-cha lessons in those days.

He actually was often less "heavy" than I (did the booze help?) and far less tight with the purse. I worried about the overspending. He was a better typist, and I am grateful for how helpful he was in typing my master's thesis for me. (Those were the prehistoric computer days when I was also fortunate to have a secretary to polish my office reports.)

"Perhaps you can stop taking Jerry's inventory now and make your move," the wisest one said to me in our last divorce group therapy session. "Isn't it time to accept that there are no guarantees of a perfect partner coming to your rescue, and file for divorce? Why are you continuing to keep Jerry on the end of the rope, to pull back when you feel desperate?"

She was right. Somewhere in my psyche, I had been seeing Jerry like an item in the pawn shop, with the possibility of retrieval.

"You all have been so supportive," I told the other angry women, "I would never have moved out of the house without peer encouragement that I could do it. I know that I am trying the flat-fee lawyer's patience as I vacillate between filing and not filing. Thank you for allowing me to make Jerry the "bad guy". That's the only way I could rationalize moving on."

"Just do it! We believe in you. Sign the papers and have them delivered," my fellow sufferers insisted, assuring me that I was now big enough to stand on my own. I was buoyed up by their guidance as we gathered in a final circle before closing that chapter in our lives.

Soon after, Jerry asked to get together to talk. I accepted, taking the chips on my shoulder with me. We met in a bar as he requested. His friends happened to be there and sent over drinks. Jerry surprised me by saying he was now willing to go into marriage therapy. Honorable maybe, but unacceptable to me. I reminded him what had happened at a scheduled family therapy session a few years before. When challenged by the therapist with a leading question, he bolted and stormed out, expecting all of us to follow, which we did. (Now I would no longer trail along or put any more effort into the marriage. My heart was closed, fully armoured against him.)

I departed without taking a sip of the scotch, went straight away to the lawyer's office, then called and left a message on Jerry's voice mail. It seemed kinder to suggest he pick up the divorce papers from the courthouse to avoid being served at home by the Marshal.

He replied with a message for me at my office number, saying, "You're not planning on keeping my name, are you?"

Jerry then proceeded to hire his own lawyer and counter-sue me for divorce. I hadn't thought about how big a deal a man's name is to him, but countersuing? Why? We had no assets to fight over. I didn't believe he would sue me for adultery, convinced as I was that he didn't know.

I had no desire to keep his name as his ex, or to go back to using my maiden name as my father's daughter. So what should I call myself?

I decided to attach myself to my favorite saint (how dare I be so bold?) and make the "Instrument of Peace," simple St. Francis of Assisi, my partner for this third quarter of my life. Frances was my Godmother's name and my chosen confirmation name, so Laurel Ann Francis didn't sound foreign to me. Before the divorce was final, I legally made the change, against the advice of a girlfriend who thought the last name of Rockefeller would have been a more potent choice.

◇ ◇ ◇

After six months boarding with serious Sybil, I left and moved in with Louise, a friend who was living a different version of the single life after divorce. I began to appreciate the support of the "sisterhood." Coming of age in the 1950's, I was conditioned to compete with other women for the attention of men. Now I was being consoled, comforted and nurtured by women friends of all ages, both married and single, most of whom had recognized the demise of my marriage long before I did. It was a wonderful awakening. I had time for women, now that I had given up my relationship with the latest married man that I had been sleeping with. It ended like this:

"I can't be with someone who is married now that I no longer am. My getting a divorce makes it different," I told this charming professional man. His loving me had given me so much pleasure, making me feel worthy and beautiful. How he found time for me, I never understood.

"I'm not anxious to go," he said. "I am like the prisoner who, on finding the barred door unlocked, resists leaving the cell where he had worn a path in the floor with his pacing."

The poetic reference was so touching that I almost changed my mind. That relationship would have given me status (and a big mess) had it not been so secretive. Sneaky yes. I got over it and trust he did too.

Still working long hours and feeling unsettled in a rented space while waiting for the divorce to become final and the house to sell, I turned more and more inward in an attempt to find myself without men in my life. Jerry had written me out of his life; he was so angry he wouldn't speak to me, nor did I initiate any sharing with him.

I sought closure on my own by using a "Rite of Divorce" ceremony as a guide. This three-page script was by Rudolph W. Nemser, copyrighted 1966. His premise, to view divorce as being just as sacred as marriage, was helpful. As suggested in the Rite, I pictured Jerry with me, experiencing all our feelings of sadness as well as relief.

Divorce represented the death of our relationship as husband and wife. I went on to visualize a new relationship with Jerry, one in which we were still bonded, albeit in a different way. We still shared the love of our children and concern for their welfare. I sought to let go of the fear, pity, and anger that I felt towards him (as my former partner), and wished that he would forgive me. I prayed that both of us would forget how to hurt each other. I set an intention to work on myself regarding the divorce. Then I mailed Jerry a copy of the Rite, telling him that I hoped to heal, and how much I wished for him to also be healed. He never responded.

◇ ◇ ◇

On the day the divorce was final, my girlfriends took me out to dinner and surprised me with a second stop at a bar featuring a male stripper show, a special treat to celebrate my new status. Out of sync with my latest mindset, I feigned enthusiasm. I appreciated their good intentions but was anxious to slink back to Louise's digs for more self-absorption.

This friend seemed to know what I needed most. Louise lit a fire in the fireplace, poured me a glass of red wine, and left me alone. I took this opportunity to dramatically burn my marriage license (silly girl) and a year's worth of my journals. It shocked me to recognize the entries as boring, repetitive renditions of my misery while stuck in my pitiful pit. It was a relief to see that part of my past in flames. I celebrated my newfound resolve to let go for good (good in more ways than one).

Jerry remained in the victim stage, often telling anyone who would listen that I had broken my commitment while I pondered the biblical phrase: "What God hath joined together, let no man put asunder."

To many, this means no divorce. I chose to define not to "put asunder" in the broader sense of our all being One. Jerry and I would never be separate, just as I am not separate from anyone in the Mind of Spirit.

My beliefs changed as I changed. Convenient. Now to consistently love my neighbor as myself and live that way in love as "One" was my assignment with lots of homework. Good luck, Laurel. As I've read somewhere, "Midlife might be an OK time for a fuck-up, but too soon to be a lost cause."

What next? Sure, the career was going well. There had to be more. More of what, or how to get it, I didn't know, but the cookie crumbs were leading to a spiritual retreat.

From Darkness to Light

4:00 a.m., the 3rd of February, Good Lord year 1988, marked the first day of my four weeks of structured healing time. Far away in miles and methods from my career, I patted Laurel Ann Francis on the back for having arranged so much time away from the office (and my rented room), using a combination of vacation and comp time.

"Clang, clang, clang." I woke to the sound of the morning bell rung by the resident doing the routine hall rounds. So began each predawn of my semi-monastic life at Kripalu, a Hindu ashram/healing center in western Massachusetts. I slipped into my 100% cotton yoga wear, grabbed my tooth-brush tote, and followed my roommate down the hall to the dorm bathroom. By 4:25 a.m., still in silence, I was seated on my brand new blue zafu pillow in a basketball court size hall surrounded by yogis ready for Pranayama breath control practices used in preparation for meditation. (Without a doubt, I could use all the help.) It was total darkness except for the candles surrounding the presenter seated upright on a slightly elevated platform.

"Dirga Pranayama, sweet three part breath," he announced with a minimum of direction about the belly, rib cage and upper chest breathing. I was sure I was doing it perfectly because I hadn't passed out by the time we started the second practice.

"Nadi Shodhana, alternate nostril breathing: to calm the mind and nervous system," the voice from the front of the room directed, leading my favorite practice from previous experience. "Continue inhaling and exhaling from alternate nostrils for each round, remembering to breathe in from the same nostril from which you just exhaled. Use the ring finger to open and close the left nostril and the thumb for the right nostril.

1. "Close the right nostril with the right thumb and exhale gently through the left nostril. Now inhale from the left nostril for a count of eight.
2. Close the left nostril with the right ring finger and at the same time remove the thumb from the right nostril. Exhale through the right nostril to a count of four. Now inhale through the right nostril to a count of eight. End of one full round. Continue for nine rounds."

It seemed to work! I felt centered until we moved on to the next practice.

After many attempts, I still had difficulty with "Ujjaya," the ocean sounding breath coming from the back of the throat. I was embarrassed when teachers came around to listen to each of us individually and passed me by without a "good, well done" remark.

The pace of "Kapalbhati," the intermediate to advanced practice of short, powerful exhales and inhales, also took a lot of effort, but was a source of immediate gratification upon completion. After a pause where I felt pulsing throughout my body, my mind moved to empty and slid into silence. Truth be told, this well-intentioned but untrained mind did soon wander to wonder about the classical Eight Limbs of Yoga. I knew a bit about hatha yoga postures, pranayama and meditation. What were the other five?

◊ ◊ ◊

"Being an ashram," Guru Amrit Desai declared in a morning talk to a rapt audience, "we are a family of loving brothers and sisters." He thus reiterated the required celibacy policy for residents and guests alike at Kripalu. Called Gurudev by his hundreds of devoted followers, this long-dark-haired holy Indian man was attractive, as were his longtime disciples. They were all so spiritual and beautiful, even without makeup or shaving or much of a wardrobe.

I want what they have, I decided, embracing the stringent schedule and the strict vegetarian diet. We were offered dairy, thank goodness, from the

Indian "sacred cow," but never flesh. I gave up nightshades eventually, being told that they were the cause of my arthritis. I even fasted on brown rice for five days and survived. "Less mass, more lightness" read one of the posters.

"Welcome to this first massage class," said our movie star beauty of a teacher, her thick auburn hair wrapped in a bun on top of her head, at the mid-morning session of my chosen curriculum.

"As specified in the brochure, women only massage women; men only massage men during their course as well. First we will learn draping. We always start with the nude client face down. Keep the body draped from the waist down while massaging the back. Re-cover the back before uncovering the right leg. Re-cover the right leg before doing the back of the left. Make sure the woman has plenty of time to turn over under the sheet, before you work on her upper chest, but not the breasts. The right arm is next, then the left. Have the body completely covered before starting and finishing on the face and head. Everyone clear on this? Now let us begin. I have divided the class in half, and you will now practice draping on each other."

I got the picture and did as I was told. Never having had a professional massage, I took these draping directions as standard. True as they were in this setting, they were not gospel elsewhere.

The clients, my fellow classmates, were unwitting props as first steps in changing my perspective of body image and reality. I conveniently forgot the rule from the 12- step program about not taking other's inventories, as my critical mind was bookmarking every flaw of my classmates' bodies.

God, she's got huge hips, I judged. It's obvious that the so round, so firm, so fully packed woman "A" has had a boob job. That other woman looks to be as old as me, and most of us at this age aren't that firm, I thought. Or maybe it's because I nursed my three babies that I hang down more. Woman "B" had hers surgically reduced, I'm sure, because I saw the scars under her breasts.

Stubby "C" was not tall enough to carry all that weight. Long legged "D" was round shouldered like me. She also walked with her head forward-leaning and yearning for something other than the here and now. Perhaps only one of the females in that class had a model's figure, and even she had complaints about her nose. My opinionated eyes found lots of physical "flaws" in myself and others.

Eventually becoming aware of my growing register of imperfections of each and every body, I determined to get over these hateful judgments, this media conditioning, this Hollywood brainwashing.

"God, help me to be more accepting and loving." But there was more to it than that. Would I grasp in this lifetime that my body is not me; bodies are not the truth of what we are?

"I'm Rachel, a magnificent goddess," one of my classmates said when we introduced ourselves at a sharing session.

"Like what?" I must have said out loud as I looked at her twice, and all the others turned to look at me. I was embarrassed but still didn't understand the goddess bit. Rachel wasn't anything special. My first thought was "how vain can you get!"

As introductions continued, I began to comprehend the concept of self-love. It was OK; expected, even, to claim one's divinity in circles like this. I don't remember how I labeled myself.

Then I recalled the prayer, "Father, help me to believe the truth about myself, regardless of how beautiful it is."

Even more specifically, I later learned another oft-quoted Marianne Williamson message: "Our deepest fear is not that we are inadequate. Our deepest fear is that we are powerful beyond measure. We ask ourselves, 'Who am I to be brilliant, gorgeous, talented, fabulous?' Actually, who are you not to be? You are a child of God..."

It was obvious I was delinquent in the divinity curriculum and also pretty ignorant about homosexuality. I found it strange that with all the separation of the sexes, there seemed to be no rules against lesbians massaging their partners after hours. It made me uncomfortable, even after a wiser woman tried to educate me.

"Laurel, you can accept the color blind and those who are left-handed, can't you? Homosexuality is just another minority characteristic."

I had much to resolve around sexual issues, and I was not alone. Years later, Gurudev was asked to leave the ashram in Lennox, Massachusetts, for not practicing the restraint that he preached regarding relationships with the opposite sex. By the time I heard of it, I was a bit more aware of guru worship and its pitfalls for both the guru and the disciple.

A little over a decade after that, I attended a talk by this same Amrit Desai where, with his wife at his side, he spoke of his fall and the forgiveness he experienced as he atoned. Nevertheless, at the time I was at Kripalu, the spiritual community appeared idyllic. I suspected nothing. It was uplifting to meditate before sunrise and to believe in the wisdom of the guru. I relished the practice of yoga twice a day, attending massage classes, and singing and dancing to New Age music.

There was one problem. Complaining to Rahul, the practitioner most supportive to me at this experimental, experiential time of my life, I said, "I've been at Kripalu for four weeks and I'm not ready to leave. My breathing is still shallow. My body is still tight. I haven't had the rebirthing experience! I still don't understand what Sheila was laughing about last week when she couldn't stop. What's so funny? What am I missing?"

In response, my gentle Indian friend Rahul offered to help if I was willing to do another yoga session right there, right then, just as the others left.

Leaving the music on, he spread one of the mats out and said, "First get on all fours and do the cat and cow postures. Good, now move into the modified camel and fish positions. I'll help you. Good, on your back now in savasana, and concentrate on your breathing. Stick with the breathing. You know how to do abdominal breathing. Keep using your diaphragm. Concentrate and don't stop those full, deep, three part breaths."

As I was working hard, Rahul cradled my head with his gentle hands and performed some energetic craniosacral magic until, resting quietly in the restorative corpse pose, I seemed to go into a trance, unaware even of when he left. Was I alone or not? I began to feel the most unusual energy in my left hand.

I felt somebody holding my hand and moving it from my side to slightly above shoulder level and saying "Come with Me."

Was it God speaking? My right hand felt heavy until I consciously let go of some of my resentments towards my husband. Then I felt guided to bring my hands together over my heart, feeling joyful while hearing repetitions of a simple chant attributed to Parahansa Yogananda.

"Listen, listen, listen to my heart's song. I will never forget you. I will never forsake you..." The song ended, and I awoke alone in a darkened room.

"I'm so grateful and I feel like I've been healed in many areas, but I'm still not ready to go back to work," I told Rahul later, after thanking him for helping me.

"I didn't do it, you did," he said, encouraging me to get over my dependency issues. Turning to Spirit was much better than looking to a man to be my savior.

"We're all leaving now, yet I have one final thought for you," Rahul added. "Every time you despair, think of the love you felt here and say, 'My future is more wonderful than I can imagine.'"

I promised I would, and repeated the mantra as a favorite for many years. By trusting such an affirmation, I continued to be delightfully amazed by life. One sweet surprise was when my eldest daughter Dianna stopped by for a day during that month of retreat and said she hardly recognized me in my yogi role.

◇ ◇ ◇

"Christopher," I said to my son, who was back in our hometown from college for the weekend soon after I returned to work, "You introduced me to meditation while you were in high school because you were so excited about the Maharishi effect of Transcendental Meditation. I understand that you are under a lot of stress. Would you go if I arranged an introductory weekend for you at Kripalu? I found the meditations most helpful. It's not far from your college."

To my delight, my son agreed. When we spoke after his visit there, he admitted he fell in love, platonically of course, with one of the older women yogis there.

"Returning to the frat house," Christopher said, "my brothers bowed, called me Guru, chorested an 'ohm', and teased me about my new angel love and hippie mother."

I applauded his sense of humor as well as his willingness to give meditation another try.

◇ ◇ ◇

I was warmly welcomed back to my work reality with a new attitude. I continued to teach, recruit and manage volunteers, plan county events for youth, show up for college in-service training, and study on my own to improve my skills and fill the gaps in my education. A lifelong student I'll always be. I now was also dedicated to a different way of being.

"You look great, Laurel, so relaxed. Tell us about it," prompted my secretary, Marge, at coffee hour on my return from Kripalu. The five staff and secretaries at the table laughed at my attraction to the deep-breathing men and my version of the goddess story. I left out the more spiritual stuff.

At our next luncheon meeting, in those days before we all became so much more conscious of our food choices, my fellow educators questioned my menu difficulties when we went out to eat.

"What do you mean you don't eat tomatoes or potatoes or eggplant? You'll never again order another Reuben?"

Not only did I have different food preferences, but the priorities for my life were no longer the same. Kripalu had offered a buffet of possibilities, and I wanted to taste more of these new ways of being. My spiritual appetite was now bigger than my secular and sexual ones. I was as hungry for information that would feed my soul as a child was for Halloween treats.

I felt out of place at work. I seemed to be in a cul de sac with no way out. To compensate for doubts about my destiny, I put even more effort than usual into my career. I applied for the promotion I was in line for after seven years of employment. Then came another bright idea. In an effort to have it both ways: career success and spiritual advancement, I started doing research about taking a twelve-month sabbatical, also an option for educators with my tenure. It would be at my own expense, but I would receive half-pay for that period. But how could I justify taking a year off for myself, and combine that with professional development? I felt I had to escape the status quo and the constraints of the political and economic structure, but how?

I focused my plan around self-esteem issues and life skills for youth, which were big (and broad enough) mission-based topics of this period, for the leaders and members whom I served. I wrote a proposal to travel for a year and study "stress reduction techniques," including meditation (beginning with a retreat with Ram Dass, one of the most popular teachers at that time). I even threw in a bit of international service:

"I plan to travel to Costa Rica for three months, study Spanish, and volunteer as an instructor for a youth program there. This will be an introduction to the American way of life and language for a group of teenagers, before they begin their nine-month-long, family stays in the States."

Hallelujah! Both the college and my advisory council approved my sabbatical request. I imagined they considered my stress levels and agreed I needed the time to get my life back together post divorce. With that permission and the expectation of monthly half paychecks, plus fifty percent from the sale of our house yet to come, I prepared for my three-hundred sixty-five day escape.

I needed to finish clearing out the colonial. Getting all my stuff from an eight room house down to four boxes and three suitcases felt great. Later, dwarfing it all to the size of a backpack became my ultimate goal. Everything about the household felt burdensome, reminders of old patterns. I wanted none of it. It was no problem leaving the furniture, appliances and tools for Jerry to dispose of when our house (no longer a home) finally sold. I had already given most of the decorative items, silverware, and wedding gifts away after our children took what they wanted (and had space to store now that the homestead was no more).

"You will no longer be able to keep your treasures in storage at 21 Park Boulevard," I had to tell the kids as the clearing continued, with Jerry living there with his beloved souvenirs. He wouldn't let me touch the balalaika and belly dancers' drum, the brass bells and tray, the African masks and "Bamko" the warrior sculpture. (I held onto the Matryoshka doll, which I considered a comforting symbol of hospitality and motherhood.) My problem wasn't his mementoes, but where to put my remaining possessions (I felt more empathy for my children's storage dilemma).

"May I stash my career wardrobe and the few boxes containing some household goods for my next apartment under your stairs while I am gone?" I asked Richard, my latest lover, a widower with a prominent position. (Let's make him an investment broker.) He had a knack for making money and lived in a McMansion with space to store my stuff, instead of my having to rent a storage unit.

"Of course," he said, "as long as you let me come with you to the Ram Dass retreat you are attending. Let me take care of the registration and the flights. Because of you, I am curious about meditation."

Because he appeared to be as interested as I was in his spiritual development as well as his body, I readily agreed. Richard was most generous, and very motivated to start a new life after his unhappy marriage and his wife's difficult death. Although semi-retired, he went daily to the professional building with his name on it. I assumed it was to check on his partners for something to do.

He was happy to have me in his life. I, in turn, was getting used to being with a rich man, even if he was quite a bit older and an inch shorter. He was handsome with his well-cut, thick, wavy, salt and pepper hair, dapper (I shivered on embracing all that cashmere and silk), an excellent cook, and amazingly virile for a 70-year-old. I was satisfied, as well as impressed with the silk sheets.

We met while he was walking his Cavalier King Charles Spaniel at the time and place I was strolling the very morning after the divorce papers had been served. Six months of his spoiling me materially and physically kept me coming back for more. I hadn't turned down his invitation for a first-class trip to the Northwest, which had opened my eyes to how the upper crust lived. Why not travel in style for another week? I let him make the arrangements for both of us. Thus began my sabbatical, with a meditation retreat, the first stress reduction technique on my plan.

Full Year at Half Pay

ichard and I departed for St. John, Virgin Islands, to begin a seven
day Omega Institute retreat. Called "Conversations and Meditations,"
it was taught by Ram Dass of the Seva Foundation, an international
Love, Serve, Remember organization. Known in his previous career as Dr.
Richard Alpert, prominent Harvard psychologist and LSD pioneer, our
teacher didn't address that life-changing part of his story except to say,
"Psychedelics helped me to escape... albeit momentarily... from the prison of
my mind. They overrode the habit patterns of thought, and I was able to taste
innocence again." (Would I ever taste innocence again? Should I try LSD?)

I saw this master as the laughing Buddha, joyous and loving as he offered
a Western articulation of Eastern philosophy. He shared about his relationship with his teacher, Neem Karoli Baba. Maharaji, as he called his guru, who
had given him his Indian name Ram Dass, which means "Servant of God" in
Hindi, a role he took seriously.

Quoting from his book *Be Here Now*, charismatic Ram Dass seemed to
be talking directly to me as he said, "Early in the journey, you wonder how
long the journey will take and whether you can make it in this lifetime. Later
you will see that where you are going is *here* and you will arrive *now*, so you
stop asking." (It took me years and thousands of miles to understand that
particular "journey without distance from a place I never left.")

I was so engulfed with guilt from the past and fear of the future, I knew
I had come to the right teacher at the right time, especially when he added,
"Every time we surrender a role or a quality of life to something new, holding

on to the past causes suffering. Ultimately, even in the act of dying, the suffering is created by holding onto living. Part of the secret of non-clinging is to be fully in the moment." I resolved once again to let go of my past to avoid suffering, and to be totally present, even if I wasn't ready to die.

Whoever had the idea of packaging spirituality seminars and New Age workshops into a Caribbean retreat (Blissed Out in St. John) did a fabulous job of attracting fascinating people to congregate and learn. On the second night, without Richard who was hobnobbing elsewhere, I sat down to dinner at a small table overlooking the sea with an attractive couple who lived in Vermont. We began discussing the discourse of the day. As longtime students of the Eastern ways of being, R.C. and Annabelle clarified some of the over-my-head concepts of Oneness. They reminded me of how Ram Dass had said: "We are all affecting the world every moment, whether we mean to or not, because we're so deeply interconnected with one another."

"I'm glad that my man friend isn't here for this conversation," I admitted to my dinner mates, describing Richard as a meditation newbie. "Oh, I knew there must be a man accompanying a woman as attractive as you," the tall Southern gentleman R.C. said, beginning a flirtatious conversation which I found both flattering and uncomfortable. However, Annabelle, his beautiful, long-limbed partner from California, was right there, and she didn't appear to mind his attention to me, a reaction I didn't expect.

Annabelle continued to be kind and responsive to me, serving as a role model of life as love and compassion, traits she considered her life's work.

"You mean I should treat everyone I meet as if they are God in drag," I added, remembering that one-liner from the morning discourse, and thinking of my absent partner of the week, whom I assumed was having fun elsewhere.

Might I be up for a "menage a trois"? This was the question I pondered when, at the end of the evening, this couple from Vermont, unlike any I had ever met before, issued an invitation.

"Do sail with us next week, Laurel," Annabelle said, "when we depart from the island of Tortola British Virgin Islands and sail to Virgin Gorda. Our 49-foot cutter rigged sloop named 'Goldenrod' has plenty of room. You can have the forward cabin."

As unsure as I was of their intentions and my own projections, I silenced my fears and said yes, trusting my intuition. Hadn't I promised myself to allow new opportunities to unfold and to leave behind my past ways of limiting myself? I was open to flow with what came forth; was I half wishing for something sexy? As Ram Dass had said, "Everything in your life is a vehicle for transformation. Use it!"

◇ ◇ ◇

With the retreat ending, Richard was harboring the idea of joining me in California the next month for another course of study that I had planned.

"That is not to be," I told him before he left. "I love and appreciate you," I professed, "but I am not ready to enter a longer or more serious relationship." (I wasn't even tempted as he dangled the promise of a Jaguar in front of me – not having the wardrobe to go with such a status symbol.) I trusted that he understood my self-serving (my way or the highway) decision and reminded him that I would see him at the end of the year when I returned to my job back east.

"This is my personal spiritual sojourn," I emphasized, quoting Ram Dass once more, "I can do nothing for you but work on myself – you can do nothing for me but work on yourself." He didn't appreciate that philosophy being suggested at that time, but he was a proper gentleman and didn't beg. I was relieved to leave behind that version of prostitution and try out my sea legs. (So ends my interest in his spiritual development and his body.)

◇ ◇ ◇

Sailing the Caribbean from the mountainous island of Tortola to the beautiful bays of St. John with R.C. and Annabelle the following week turned out to be an idyllic and innocent journey. The winds opened my heart as they filled the sloop's jib and mainsail.

At anchor, when Annabelle was not busy reading the charts and RC was free from manning the sails, they arose at sunrise to do yoga on deck. RC then sat to write poetry or do sketches while Annabelle prepared breakfast. I enjoyed a short freshwater shower at the bow. There was plenty of time to share our fish stories even as the present adventure provided plenty of reminisces for later rendezvous.

Besides her spiritual side, Annabelle Westling was passionate about social and political issues. I was most intrigued by her birthing and editing a compilation of stories about counterculture life in the late 1960'and 1970's. Her book: *Handmade Lives, A Collective Memoir* (Firefall Press) by some 44 individuals, including herself and her children, was about their immersion in a Canyon, California commune. In this inside story of the flower children of that era, "We were experimenting with creating a new and just society," my new friend declared, "by embracing ideals of peace and love and organic gardening and simple living in community, with all its freedoms and challenges."

For me, those hippie era values were not on my radar when I did the "supposed to get married" thing, and lived behind a white picket fence on the stolid East Coast. I accepted my new friend's dialogues, first hand stories about the love generation with its dark and light sides, as an explanation of why R.C. and Annabelle were in a long committed relationship and not married, and why she was so non-possessive. More power to them, I thought.

Every evening at sunset, anchored at a mooring off a tropical Virgin Island, R.C. Williams would read aloud from his poetry book, *Low Sweet Notes* (Mellon Poetry Press). I can hear his melodic voice now, sharing the beginning of the poem:

The Cloud From Which You Fell

"You have to start small," said the drop of water to the light.
Come fall through me as if you were suffering.
See how we can make a rainbow together.
See how you must break apart to arch over the tussling corn...

His verse expressed the higher consciousness of this flamboyant ex-pilot from Tennessee. He was an architect specializing in second homes, and a watercolorist who was restaging his life as a minimalist, and sharing it with the woman of his dreams. The three of us became the best of friends as we swapped life stories and morsels of philosophy. (I have both their books in my library, visit them each summer in Vermont, and have sailed and walked some isolated islands with them in the archipelago that is Fiji... returning home with a backpack full of oversized clam shells.)

As we ended this first voyage together and they sailed off without me, I waved away tears and then hopped a plane back across the archipelago to Omega, St. John, for another course.

During this retreat, author Pat Rodegast was the presenter. This bright light of a woman, clothed in flowing robes, introduced us to the entity named Emanuel, "The Loving Spook," an angel she channeled. I had never been with a channel before, and it was fascinating to see the author go into a trance. She would answer questions with wisdom from the "other side" in a gravelly voice from beyond the tomb.

I appreciated Emanuel's tolerance when I asked his opinion on being divorced: "When love is gone, just walk away."

When I inquired about how to reconcile the demands of the working world with one's spiritual values, Emanuel's answer was, "Someday, my dear, you will not go back to the office." How prophetic was that!

But I wasn't thinking about the office when I met the next male in my life. This New Yorker, retired from business in horse racing (whatever that means) and tobacco sales, was named Herb, a rather flavorful handle befitting a well seasoned older man. I wasn't initially attracted to this loud, bald, big, prosperous-looking Jew, hardly what the world considered handsome, but grew to appreciate him as my first truly spiritual man friend. Being an insulin-dependent diabetic didn't appear to stop Herb from living to the max. This interested male sought me out during the Emanuel retreat and became another of my teachers, taking great effort to explain mindfulness and "unconditional awareness" to me during the week he courted me.

We became good friends, good enough for him to invite me to visit him in NYC, where he promised to share the city with me and to introduce me to his hospice work. Herb also asked me to attend another Omega retreat with him, this one focusing on couples' communication skills. It was to be held in Rhinebeck, NY, the following fall (synchronistically at the time of my return to the Northeast from California).

"A couples retreat?" I exclaimed, noting that I had known him for a week and would not be seeing him for months. "We're not even a couple."

His "we might be" was reason enough for my acceptance.

"Let's call it an investment," he said as we lingered over our goodbyes, pleased with arrangements to meet again.

Six

Big Sur, California

My second sabbatical destination was in Big Sur (loved the name) on the high cliffs of the central Pacific coast where I registered as a "work study" for eight weeks at the somewhat isolated 120 acres of the Esalen Institute. I pictured myself wearing crystals while learning more psychobabble. At 3,000 miles away from my East Coast career life with its New England values, this would serve as space and time to recreate myself as part of the "human potential movement" in California style. Did that mean I was going west to go wild?

Just being on the cliff's edge by the hot springs overlooking the ocean was breathtaking for this shallow breather. It was no problem adapting to working 32 hours a week in the kitchen-dining room and living in a dorm, which made me feel like a college girl again. I practically pranced down the Highway One mile from the South Coast Center dorm to the Institute twice a day so enlivened by the budding of spring, the coming and going of the monarch butterflies, and the singing of the sea below. My initial four-week study group scheduled for four evenings a week filled the hours from 8 p.m. – 10 p.m.

"We will begin our session with a personal weather report from each of you as an emotional check-in. Be the meteorologist of your mind and body as you describe your mood," requested our teacher.

That was easy. I felt like a clear baby-blue sky with wispy cloud thoughts floating by for this first introduction to the 17 other participants in the Gestalt Therapy program. I was looking forward to studying with Judith

Brown, PhD., who was one of the best therapists in the field. She was also a friend of a friend.

"I'm so glad you are here," she said when I spoke to her privately after our first class, "and I understand your decision to not encourage your ex-lover to join you any further. I realize you are looking to become a more authentic self without depending on men in your life. The existential, experiential form of psychotherapy we offer here emphasizes personal responsibility. You have come to the right place." Thus began my study and application of the teachings of the famous 1960's psychologist Fritz Perls as facilitated by one of his most dedicated students.

"There are two kinds of mystics in the world," Dr. Brown began, "optimystics and pessimystics. Pessimystics claim to be more in touch with reality; optimystics are happier and live longer. 'The sky is falling,' says the pessimist, while the optimist claims it just looks that way because we are ascending."

Any way you look at it, we all laughed. After that, each of us arrived at the group session on time because our teacher began by telling a series of jokes, off-color openings to motivate the punctual behavior she expected. I caught the humor, but found the group dynamics to be highly charged and quite unfamiliar.

"You're projecting. Don't treat me like your son; I am not your son," one of the young men yelled at me early on. I wasn't even sure what projection meant. Obviously I was still acting like the mother of three children in spite of feeling like I was in my twenties myself.

Finally, at a day-long session when we had a guest instructor, I got it. I was ready to give a chair "a piece of my mind." I volunteered for an "empty chair" Gestalt intervention by walking forward and sitting down with therapist-teacher John Soper on one side of me and an empty chair in front of me. I reached deep to touch my "here and now" feelings and flush out what I felt to be my major internal issue of the moment: should I have admitted my affairs to my now ex-husband?

"You know what to do," Dr. Soper reviewed, "Visualize the person with whom you are in conflict sitting in the empty chair, and communicate with that person, first speaking as yourself, and then switching chairs and speaking as you imagine the other to respond."

In order to challenge my own perceived cowering toward my ex, I began verbalizing a confession with a "visualized Jerry." After admitting my affairs to him, I moved to the other chair and voiced what I believed to be his response: "I suspected it. When I saw the lingerie in your bureau and the sexy clothes in your closet, I knew you weren't wearing them for me."

He got angrier; I voiced his fury. "Tell me who the men are. I will confront them at their workplaces and go to their homes and tell their wives of their betrayal!" he screamed. I imagined the verbal threats increasing. I broke down crying and couldn't go on with the pissing contest.

"Stay with it," Dr. Soper suggested as I blew my nose a few times and dried my eyes. "What is happening with you here and now?"

After a final tremor, I admitted that I reacted just as I would have if Jerry and I had had that conversation, to which he replied, "Here and now might be a good time to have a dialogue with yourself, Laurel." He placed another chair beside me and asked my wise self to sit in it. "Tell us what you are thinking."

I moved to the empty "wise one" chair beside me, swallowed some tears, probably screwed up my face, and pondered awhile before the "wiser me" concluded, "Just confessing my affairs doesn't feel like enough. Perhaps I expect to be given a penance, remembering the relief I felt after coming out of the confessional box in the Catholic Church as a child. You, John, as a therapist, are not doing what a priest would have done. When I said my 'Father, forgive me for I have sinned,' making the sign of the cross over my forehead, heart and shoulders, I would recite my 'sins' and seek absolution. After listening to my transgressions, the priest would assign something like three Our Fathers and five Hail Marys before saying 'Go in peace, your sins are forgiven you.'"

"However," I continued, " this confession of adultery surely would require at least ten recitations of the rosary and daily Mass for a month, if not more, as absolution for my affairs. Gestalt doesn't offer me penance or a Savior like the church did. I know this memory is a reflection of the deep internal tension and guilt I feel within myself. I know that I am making Jerry the bad guy, the Type A personality that I felt had failed me in our marriage. I also realize I project onto Jerry the anger and guilt I feel about my affairs and the frustration over how dishonest I dreamed I had to be to escape my self-made prison of a marriage. Will I ever get over the guilt?"

"You are correct. Gestalt is about self-responsibility," Dr. Soper summarized. "It offers you a chance to come to the power of the present and do a reversal. What could you do here and now for a more satisfying outcome instead of crying reactively?" He was inviting me to speak my present truth as a better way of responding.

I moved back to the chair across from Jerry's assigned seat, imagined him sitting there, and bravely began addressing him: "I refuse to give you the names of the men I was with. I accept responsibility for doing what I did. I accept the consequences of the end of our marriage and I am sorry that it had to end this way. I will not, however, satisfy your urge to violate the rights of others by attacking them with your judgments of who they are and what they did."

Moving back to sitting in the "wise self" chair, I constructed a new version of the old situation and began affirming myself with a slew of I-messages: "I can't *uncrack* the egg, nor do I want to do so. It was wise of me to remain silent about my affairs since I would have been unable at that time to deal with Jerry's rage. My secret also spared hurting his ego had the truth been verbalized. Both of us wanted the 'don't ask, don't tell' version of our lives. I accept that he chose to be in denial as much as I sought a change in my identity and my destiny. I had made a choice to turn to other men for the recognition of who I was as my own person. I destroyed my life as a wife as I experienced my fantasies. I am awake now to a new dream, and I am thankful to the men who shared in my growth process. As radical as it was, I would not alter the way I behaved at that 'change of life stage,' knowing how important my affairs were in allowing me to become my own person. Here the soap opera ends with the divorce."

"Well done, Laurel," Soper concluded, "As you realized, you make your husband the bad guy so that the good little girl could go through with the divorce you wanted so much. Now it appears you are taking responsibility for half of the outcome, correct?" After thanking him, I walked away feeling 50% lighter. But I felt I still had work to do. And next on the horizon...

◊ ◊ ◊

"Your therapy session with the new wonder on campus sounds terrific. I'll make an appointment with him," I told a well-balanced friend who knew I was always looking for the savior-therapist who would finally fix me. From

Eric's curriculum vitae, I learned he was a graduate of a narrative medicine program which looked impressive. When I met him, however, I was immediately turned both on and off by the beautiful head on his broad shoulders and his youth.

"How could someone as young as you deal with my mature problems?" I asked. He responded with an offer of a free introduction to his method, which I didn't refuse.

"Let's start, Laurel, with what you are feeling at the moment."

"I want to be free. I want to fly!"

"How can I help you to get what you want? I am here to help you fly. Decide where you want to launch."

"I'll go to the top of the cliff overlooking the sea and fly from there."

"Close your eyes and put yourself there and I will accompany you on your mission."

Perhaps because of the magic of Esalen, not to mention my wisdom and age, I felt empowered to imagine myself on a cliff's edge and prepared to surrender to the wind beneath my wings. "I'll just wait for the next gentle breeze to give me a start."

"All right, fly when you are ready."

The next thing I remember, I was flat on my face on the floor. I didn't feel wise any more. Eric's beautiful face looked horrified. Neither of us had lived up to the expectations of the other. Was he anticipating that I would start flapping my arms? Did I really expect to grow wings on the way down? In my crash landing, I missed the radiator by a fraction of an inch, thus avoiding all that blood and the emptying of my thoughts all over the rug. Eric and I didn't schedule a follow-up.

◇ ◇ ◇

At the beginning of my second four week work-study program at Esalen, everyone seemed hypnotized by an aura of light surrounding the young man just out of India who was to present "Creative Expression" with our group. Adam was fresh from the Himalayas where he had spent forty days meditating in a cave. I joined the others in projecting enlightenment onto him. All went well for about a week until I found his exercises more hurtful than helpful. The honeymoon was over for me on the sixth evening. Our facilitator introduced a relationship ritual like the old "pick the people for your team," a painful reminder of being one of the last ones chosen for a playground game. The classes began to be even more competitive than constructive. After one last lesson plan, our instructor's ideas ran out and the class anarchists stepped in to "help" before putting themselves in charge.

I hung around until a particularly painful two-hour session: it was an experiment in exploring anger and expressing it as a form of release, an opportunity to gain ultimate freedom with the directive: "Let it all hang out!"

I'm not going to like this game, I decided, as a woman who had had enough experience with such real or unexpressed outbursts. It became obvious I was failing the exercise as I couldn't get into the thrashing and lashing out. My repressed rage wasn't ready to reveal itself in the stomping and screaming goings-on. Where were the pillows, plastic bats and padded primal scream therapy rooms of the 1970's that might have made it more fun?

The group took it as a challenge to get me to "express," pushing me from my pouting to the point of punching by circling around me with clenched hands and jaws and tense shoulders. The bullying and insulting: "You're dumb, ugly, a fish out of water, you have stringy hair" went on ad nauseum. You get the gist. But the mouthing off didn't work to get me to vent. All I could do was feel shame and sadness. I started to cry, unwilling to get angry and go mad. I had had my share of not being good enough, disappointments, traumas, and fears. Triggers reminding me of them brought up more gloom than anger. I later learned studies show that catharsis doesn't work, and venting of anger is "a form of public littering."

The ridicule ruined that day and that group for me, and I took flight rather than fight. Believing I wasn't suppressing anything, I never returned to that madhouse and spent more time in the hot tub. I should have stuck around long enough for the processing. How would the group have responded if I had defended myself by admitting that I'd repressed my rage for years? When the pent up emotions had festered much too long, I reverted to passive-aggressive behaviors. I could have told them that when I realized what I was doing, anger became the energy and impetus for me to peel myself away from my partner, a more positive step than behaving as the bitch I had become in the marriage. That's my story and I'm sticking to it.

One afternoon in this diplomatic district where I resided, I strolled by an open office with a sign that read Plastic Surgery. I was curious and interested, stopped and took a step back; impulse then took over. Costa Rica was reputed to have highly skilled plastic surgeons at most reasonable prices. And Rosalynn Carter, the President's wife, had just had her eyes done. I opened the door and took the first step. Why not me?

Crying my way out of marriage had left me with bags under my eyes. What could be done?

"No problem," the plastic surgeon assured me. I believed him, and without any contemplation, scheduled a Saturday morning appointment to have the magic tucks performed around my eyes.

When I returned to my host's home, told Roxanne in my broken Spanish of my plans and showed her the papers, she appeared shocked. I came to understand it was not what I was going to do – "everybody" did it when they came to Costa Rica – but she wanted to check out the plastic surgeon. This concerned woman called her friend who worked at the American Consulate, and asked for her opinion before giving me a chance to chat. Louise was an expat who had lived and worked in San Jose for a decade.

"I strongly recommend a French doctor," she said. "I know a number of people who have gone to him. Rest assured, he is the best plastic surgeon around, and his prices are less than half what we pay in the States."

When I agreed to take her advice, Roxanne managed all the details in Spanish, cancelling the appointment I had made, and arranging my initial consultation with the famous doctor the following afternoon.

The handsome French doctor with long fingers on his beautiful hands didn't speak English, and used an interpreter to explain what he was doing as he scrutinized my face.

"Not just eyes," I understood him to say with his wonderful accent before lapsing into French and recommending a complete face lift. That bad? Such an outlandish idea, but I succumbed to the suggestion because it cost $1500, which didn't seem like much. (Half of the money from the sale of our home had just been deposited in my savings account. I took it as a sign to begin a new life with a new face.)

An appointment for the surgery was scheduled for the weekend. I must first have pre-op tests to assure that I was healthy enough to undergo the procedure. I had never researched plastic surgery, so had no idea how serious an operation a complete face lift can be. I naively followed in the footsteps of hundreds of other middle-aged women unhappy with their looks.

I went to the clinic at 6:00 a.m. on Saturday and woke up five hours later with a splitting ache in a head completely wrapped in gauze. This white turban framed a face I was delighted to see in any reflection. The lines from all my frowning were no more. I was given a pain killer and told the bandages would be removed on Monday.

My host family whisked me to their country home for the weekend. They said it was a fresh air recovery respite, but it seemed more like an opportunity to show off the face of their American guest.

"Usted es hermosa! Se vea bonita." Excited conversations went on by my bedside as the village's peasant women came by to stare at me and offer their opinions on my cosmetic surgery. It was a bit like a circus, but since it all sounded positive, all I could do was smile and say "muchas gracias." Some cupped their fingers on their cheekbones to demonstrate how they would look if they had a facelift, wishing they could have the same procedure. We all giggled as the examination continued.

"Duele, Señora?" Does it hurt, ma'am?

A couple of days later, I started Spanish classes wearing sunglasses to mask the bruising, and headscarves until my hair grew back. My classmates didn't comment, but I had trouble concentrating and felt vulnerable. Being the oldest in the class of eight and the least quick in catching on, I didn't learn much Spanish. I was weepy and would have had regrets except that when I glanced in the mirror, the Narcissus in me didn't want to stop looking at the ten-years-younger me reflected in the pool.

When seeing the surgeon post-op, he voiced his satisfaction, saying I wouldn't need another facelift for ten years. I knew that wasn't going to happen (although I could have used one or two since then).

"I do have one question, Doctor. Why did I have the strangest pain in my heels for a long time after the operation?"

The interpreter translated the doctor's serious response. "You are so tall,

much taller than my usual patients. Your heels rested on the edge of the oper-
ating table. That probably caused the sensation." Mystery solved, although I
was somewhat critical of his handling of that detail.

That was minor, considering the skill it took to perform the procedure,
details I later came to appreciate after reading the first chapter of *Stiff: The
Curious Lives of Human Cadavers* by Mary Roach. Plastic surgeons learn
facial anatomy and practice facelifts on fresh, unembalmed, severed heads of
donated cadavers.

I pause here to express gratitude to the deceased who, willingly or unwillingly, ended up as parts for the advancement of medicine. If I could have, I
would have attended the memorial service medical students hold to honor
the donors after their cremation. (I am still too attached to my body to sign
up to donate it at death for such purposes, even if cremation comes free in the
deal.) Plastic surgery patients like me are fortunate to have surgeons experienced at doing the cutting and pasting on that important part of their skeleton. As the *Stiff* author stated, "A good head is a terrible thing to waste."

Moving on to the volunteer opportunity I had arranged in Costa Rica, I
welled up as I said goodbye to my kindest of kind host family and ventured
forth once again. It was a 16-kilometer trip from San Jose to a camp / conference center. The secretary and I shared a room with a bath on the mountainside of coffee orchards and grazing fields. I spent most days studying Spanish
on my own and dreaming up ideas for my evening and weekend role.

It was more play than work to help some of the 142 teenagers with their
assignments from their formal classes with weekday paid teachers of English
as a Second Language, and to encourage them to turn their "Spain English"
into American. They did well practicing slinging slang and singing American
songs. I expected they would learn the swear words on their own, if they
didn't know them already.

The teens and I had fun times as they role-played participating in all the
holidays on our stateside calendars. They liked the Halloween costume custom best: coming made up as clowns, using twigs to turn themselves into
birds, even borrowing cooking utensils to be presented as a kitchen. (Me too:

I put many of my outfits on backwards and inside out, took a bent-over posture, pushed a cart of boxes as possessions, and called myself a "bag lady.")

"Come dance," one of my Costa Rican students encouraged at the usual Sunday afternoon Salsa party, an important part of their camp life. There was to be no hesitation as Jose pulled me into the circle, ready to involve his teacher in one of their favorite pastimes. That tested my stamina. The energy of the scene was contagious. however, and I even started looking forward to sharing the floor with them (for a while).

Enthusiastic, bright, and cooperative, the students were a worthy product of their mandatory state funded comprehensive education. It was the first time most of them would travel any distance from their close-to-the-equator Costa Rican home. They were interested in anything having to do with my country far north of the border, especially "gangsters" after watching too many flicks. They were curious about the American military; their country hadn't had an army since it was constitutionally abolished in 1948, long before they were born.

I didn't confront them with my surprise at seeing the prevalence of heavily armed guards in San Jose around the properties of the rich and famous, or how I'd been mugged when walking with my host mother along the Caribbean beach close to her family's second home.

These students lived in a beautiful civilized country. Invited to accompany them on scheduled field trips, I walked the misty Monteverde Cloud Forest. All of us were dead quiet in this rain jungle after being warned not to disturb the wildlife or wake up the poisonous snakes. Costa Ricans appreciated nature and ecotourism was becoming a big part of their way of life. I wish I had seen the long-tailed quetzal, the red breasted tropical bird that many glimpsed in the forest that day. I settled for buying a fabric facsimile in the tourist market later.

There was one other disappointment with our outings. I should have been grateful to have had a free lunch during our visit to the Del Monte Tropical Fruit Company plantation. It tasted good, but I was looking forward to a fresh banana or pineapple dessert instead of a cookie. There was not a ripe fruit to be seen or shared. All was for export, picked and packed while green.

Bananas of medium size were shipped to America. I learned, then remembered, how consistent in size purchased produce is in USA supermarkets.

Phase Three, my third month in Costa Rica, began back in San Jose, where I volunteered at the 1989 "Seeking the True Meaning of Peace International Conference." The Buddha came back into my life as the 14th Dalai Lama of Tibet, the keynote speaker. It was my first introduction to contemporary Buddhist activism, and after listening to this unpretentious personification of love, I so wanted to develop the good heart His Holiness spoke of, and to practice "internal disarmament" too.

He said, "If at the beginning and end of our lives we depend on others' kindness, why then in the middle should we not be kind to others?" I was in a "kind to myself" stage and felt a little guilt about not doing enough to help others. Never enough, however I looked at it.

The following year, the Dalai Lama was awarded the Nobel Peace Prize. I choose not to remember if I was pushy in order to get close enough to touch this guru, teacher, and mentor on the sleeve as he walked by my aisle. I didn't go so far as to throw myself at his feet in an attempt to touch the hem of his garment even though I felt like this man had messiah powers.

I stretched to grasp the high-minded notes of the next three lectures. Dr Robert Muller, longtime Assistant Secretary General of the UN, called the "philosopher of the United Nations," motivated the audience by speaking about his vision of the cosmological future, a more universal paradigm in which we don't just look at our own little isolated back yard, but see the world as if looking at the globe for the first time from a spaceship. (He also told a story of how he asked a Burmese man why women, after centuries of following their men, now walk ahead. The answer: "There were many unexploded land mines since the war.")

Earth scholar Father Thomas Berry, self-described as a "geologian" and author of *The Great Work*, inspired us with his reflections of earth as a sacred community: "The destiny of humans cannot be separated from the destiny of earth."

When the renowned futurist Hazel Henderson went to the podium, I was impressed by all that this woman near my age had accomplished in her life's work as an evolutionary economist. These messages of a new cosmology of inclusiveness and equality in sharing of resources were so encouraging, I wanted to believe that sustainable development was already a reality, not just a vision.

"We can't 'grow on' like this," somebody quipped. Now, looking back, it seems the rose has yet to blossom on the compost heap. What can I do with my one short precious life to contribute more than I consume?

More Southern California

B y now, I was nine months into my sabbatical, following the plan as I jumped into everything as an adventure (sometimes even remembering my unscripted spiritual quest). My next journey was back to California for a month-long women's retreat at the Ojai Foundation. There I learned to further appreciate the feminine of all ages, in all her different costumes. The emphasis for those 30 days was on meditation, mediation, organic gardening, and Native American healing modalities. (Would I get a chance to smoke the tobacco peace pipe?)

To stay there, I paid about $1,000 for the four weeks involving daily chores (no problem), and structured weekend studies (great), as well as a women's primitive camping trip (we were warned it would include fasting and isolation on a deserted beach). It was simple living in a rustic facility on 40 acres of land, a place where I got to again appreciate silence. I usually favored water environments, so living in the Upper Ojai Valley of Southern California emphasized my earth, fire, and sky elements, as well as deepening my appreciation of water.

The power behind the center, nicknamed Wizard's Camp, was the brilliant anthropologist Joan Halifax. She taught me another concept of motherhood, among other things. Although she had no children of her own, she was a true earth mother; one of the most well-rounded women that I have ever met. I held a prejudice that a woman was not fulfilled until she had given birth to a child. It became clear to me that Joan's children were her creative projects: her books and teachings based on her personal studies with master shamans and academics from around the world. And that was before I knew much about reincarnation and the belief that we have probably played all the family roles in previous lives anyway. Imagining being a man was a stretch.

When ethnobotanist Terence McKenna came to Ojai to lead a separate retreat on the virtues of hallucinogens, I began to question another of my beliefs after dialoguing with some of the participants. Where once it was crystal clear to me that I shouldn't do drugs, I now saw the dilemma between the very real fact of drug abuse and the beneficial psycho-spiritual effects of mind expanding plant substances. I was determined to dissolve my limiting conditioning and overcome materialism in order to develop spiritually. I wondered if I could, by simply ingesting mushrooms, experience altered states of consciousness and reach a psychedelic-spiritual perception of myself as imperishable "Self," as many others had done. Could that be the path of redemption for this fallen woman?

◇ ◇ ◇

However, it wasn't yet time for me to attempt to "touch the Divine" through the use of hallucinogens; I remained on the hard road of spiritual discipline, as I defined it.

Nevertheless, I was curious about the men who were attending the McKenna retreat, most notably the tall, slim, fiftyish, Polish-looking one with slightly graying, thick, wavy hair, a crown that I was tempted to run my fingers through. I sat with him at lunch and at supper, and even later, at evening tea.

I judged Joe, an artist, to be a high-minded hippie as he spoke of his teacher's "garden of psychedelic delights." What fascinated me most was the fact that this holy grailer had hung out with the Maharishi in India when the Beatles were there and had the honor of painting the background for the guru's portraits. (Nothing wrong with a little fame by association.)

Joe shared custody of his children after getting divorced. He spoke of being his wife's only assistant at the birth of his second son in the middle of Guatemala. (I realized how resentful I still was that I had been rushed off to the maternity ward soon after starting labor with our three.) He was an expert at growing pot and mushrooms. He showed me photos of his faux finishes (more on that later) and paintings of mythological women and animals.

His medium was acrylic paint with lots of gold flourishes, as was popular at that time. (I fantasized about being in one of those paintings.)

A few days later, October 8th (coincidentally, the same date as my son and ex's birthdays), was Joe's birthday. One kiss to honor the day led to another, then another. When he said he was leaving to go to the coast after the weekend, I accepted his invitation to go along, as I had a week free before my next commitment. More probably, I left the retreat before it was over – so much for my spiritual discipline.

We left Ojai the following Monday in Joe's ancient VW van. We stopped at beautiful overlooks, sushi shops and art galleries – a five day courtship of two "sincere spiritual seekers" drifting off to see the world. I labeled him "a real find." We planned to stay in touch when I left him to begin a two-week silent retreat. Time to get back to my whirlwind mission recalibrated to a snail's pace.

◊ ◊ ◊

After all that male attention and visceral excitement, it took a little while to settle in as I began the 14-day Vipassana women's retreat. It was held at Dhamma Dena Center, located in the southern California desert near Joshua Tree. That location meant lots of open space and a big sky. This was my introduction to Insight Meditation, and my first attempt at such a long commitment to silence. Sharing trailer accommodations plus locally grown vegetarian meals cost next to nothing, with a donation (dana) for the teachings being expected at the end. I did flash a fear about my budget. But, considering 14 days, times eight hours daily, of teacher guidance as equivalent to a semester college course, I decided it was best to recognize that being guided to enlightenment was priceless and show my appreciation.

Ruth Denison was an excellent teacher for this novice. She incorporated isometric bodywork into the sessions, directing us with simple movements such as "raise your right shoulder" or "stretch out your little fingers", which were helpful to me in staying alert, especially during the evening "sits."

It was hard work being with myself. All the solitude of a silent retreat made me aware of how much talking I normally do, often about unimportant things. It was quite a challenge to not verbalize out loud for a couple of weeks (even though there was lots of "talking" going on in my head). I became aware of my criticisms not spoken and gossip not spread by asking myself: Is it true? Is it kind? Is it necessary? (Usually it was not; hardly a surprise.)

I recognized the gift of not having to make clever conversation or keep running commentaries. In silence, even eating became more conscious as I observed myself, me feeding me from a balcony perspective: the chewing, tasting and swallowing processes.

Yet by the sixth day of nothing to do but sit, and nowhere to go but a few hundred yards out into the desert, I was having a lot of trouble with being there.

Nobody told me this would be easy, I reminded myself. Whose idea was this, to try to get enlightened?

On the seventh day, fortunately for my so-called sanity, Ruth took us to a nearby hot spring for a different movement meditation. She was aware that some of us were not holding up well with the discipline. We were allowed to speak while luxuriating in the holy waters, and after the first few words, which were almost hard to say, I fell back into the illusion of the senses and had a happy day, delusional or not.

On the twelfth retreat day, during one of my better semi-deep meditations, I was tapped on the shoulder and informed that I had an emergency phone call. Heart pounding, I rushed to the phone.

It was not a tragic call, but Joe saying he couldn't live another day without me. Holy as I was trying to be, I couldn't resist the call of chemistry, and agreed to let him pick me up the next morning. Ruth accepted a flimsy excuse I made for departing two days early, said I did well for a first-timer, and presented me with a copy of the book *Peace Pilgrim*, which turned out to be quite an inspiration on this new path of mine. I so wanted everybody to give up the image of an enemy just as this author had done.

Joe drove up to the end of the driveway at 8 a.m. the next day, parking that love nest of a VW van too close to be unnoticed. It was exciting to go to be with a lover after such a retreat. I felt centered and open and quiet; Joe was full of himself and the outside world, with lots of appealing plans and energy and lust that was catchy. I was delighted to be back on the planet of distractions in sunny southern California with this man who knew his way around and was so anxious to share it with me.

After a few days on our own, Joe had to return to work as well as take his turn caring for his children. Not ready to let go of this lover, I accepted his invitation to go along with him, to get to know him better.

And what a right (certainly not wrong) livelihood he had as an artist. His specialty was faux painting, turning huge concrete columns supporting the roofs of mansions in Beverly Hills into marble columns. I loved watching his magical transformations, not to mention being on the inside of newly constructed palaces, one of which had a garage large enough to park the owner's 14 vintage cars. This was indeed a different reality.

After all the foreplay and orgasms and the adventure of being just the two of us, it wasn't nearly as much fun when Joe was with his children. The honeymoon was over soon after we arrived at the Escondido home of his ex-wife who took off to claim her respite with her lover. Joe was back in charge of the lives of his 11- and 13-year-olds, a daughter and a son (the older 16-year-old son was on his own).

They were not being raised as I had raised my children, so I had judgments. They were most polite, but I found their needs to be in conflict with mine. I resented their claiming their father's attention and expectation of his preparing three squares a day. I wanted Joe in bed with me, all for myself.

So, this was the price of being with the best hung man in the world. I had turned into the "hungry ghost." In the Buddhist tradition, this is represented as a vase with a short, fat body, tiny neck, and pinhole mouth opening at the top, never able to get enough sustenance to satisfy itself. I felt like a nymphomaniac, and I wanted nothing to do with raising three more children. I didn't like my attitude and the lust was painful.

"Dear God, please take this desire away," I prayed. When that didn't happen, feeling both regret and relief, I decided to leave. It was definitely time for another stress reduction technique. I reminded myself that this was my sabbatical mission, and headed north in my search for God in this world of form.

Nine

Hot Pools / Cool Colors

My latest efforts while waiting for God to give me the flash (or maybe simply a burning bush) might have gotten tedious, even for me, if I hadn't thrown in some nudity. Now at the end of my sabbatical, I headed to Harbin Hot Springs, a non-profit retreat and workshop center set in a lovely rural area north of Sacramento. It was the first time I'd ever been to a "clothing optional" community, and I perceived it to be spiritual because it was run by the Heart Consciousness Church.

The hot pools were wonderful – it felt so good to be naked in them. I wasn't at all uncomfortable being baby bare, except perhaps on our free weekends between classes, when the voyeurs would come from the cities and hang out doing their thing. (I avoided getting near the edges where they sat on the side with their legs spread open.)

"I'd like to sign up for the Trager course," I told the semi-dressed staffer at the welcoming desk.

"You'll love the teacher Annemarie," she said, and I did. It didn't matter that this ten-day learning modality (like many of my trainings) had no practical vocational value; becoming a massage therapist was not in my life plan. I was along for the loosening up with the gentle rocking and lengthening movements when we students took turns on each other, giving and receiving treatments which were designed to "release the body of chronic states of tension and become more flexible with less pain." Three cheers for such an outcome!

It helped, as did the Shiatsu course I took after that. As in acupressure,

I, as a practicing student, was taught to apply pressure to points on the body connected to so-called meridians. Sometimes, as hard as I tried, I didn't meet those expectations and apologized to fellow students, many of whom struggled with the same issue. Time to soak my head...

◇ ◇ ◇

One early Monday morning before classes, I scheduled an hour-long Watsu treatment with Harold Dull, the originator of the method as taught at Harbin. He was well over six feet and extremely slim, not looking nearly as strong as he turned out to be. He had to be fit, working on bodies ranging from non-floating muscular to oversized huge to those of us in-betweens.

What a 60 minutes that was. Being continually and gracefully glided, folded, and stretched through the 90 degree fahrenheit hot springs water was like floating in amniotic fluid. Harold's gentle caresses were so nurturing and the acupressure point work so healing that it felt like a rebirthing experience. Having trusted and let go enough to receive such love, I emerged from the pool feeling more alive, with an increased range of motion in body and Spirit.

Longing to hold on to the blessing, I also signed up for the Watsu 101 course. Annemarie, who had practiced the technique for many years, was once again to be my instructor. I didn't find it easy to do the Watsu moves that Harold had done so effortlessly. It was quite a challenge holding one arm under the client's head to keep my victim's face out of the water, working the correct (lots of luck!) pressure points with my other hand, all while moving our two bodies in a flowing motion.

To this day, however, I enjoy playing at water therapy, even though I seldom get to practice in hot springs. Is any of the above transferable knowledge? It definitely was California cool, or should I say hot. I'm not even sure I mentioned Harbin on my sabbatical report. Was it because I was embarrassed about the nudity?

Performing any kind of body work required me to be "present." Not practicing long enough for the moves to become habitual, giving a treatment nevertheless focused my attention on subtle nuances. I often got "high" on those holy instances.

◇ ◇ ◇

Soon after, feeling complete with Harbin and ready to put my clothes back on, I moved southward to Esalen once again. That was where I had felt the most free, and where I'd found a different way of being "in the zone."

Ecstatic about being back in Big Sur, I called Joe and gave him credit.

"It's your inspiration," I told him. "You seem to have so much fun as an artist that I, too, want to try my hand at painting before going back to work. I'm not a work-study this time. I've signed up for 'The Painting Process Rediscovered,' a spontaneous expression class which sounds both perfectly Zen and free-flowing. Michele Cassou, the teacher, is French with an oh-la-la bio. Wish me luck."

Painting in a bright Esalen studio on a cliff overlooking the ocean was all that was scheduled for the five class days. Michelle taught us without presenting techniques. The first moments were the hardest because we were told to "simply stand in front of the paper on your easel and let whatever flows flow." (Visualize painters' block.)

That blank paper would have been scary if I hadn't been tempted like a preschool child by the assortment of brushes and eight bright bottles of beautiful poster paints in individual containers in the tray. The idea was to create without judgment, allowing the creative right side of the brain to move the paintbrush.

Here I got to experience a teaching from my pedagogy courses: the teacher needs only to structure the environment for learning to take place. This is not to say that it was without challenges to my ego. I had to learn to stop comparing myself with others and to trust my own creativity. Certainly the woman in the corner who kept painting the word "me" inside of hearts all over her paper, didn't care what anybody else thought of it.

One day when I felt ready to declare a particularly special painting of mine finished and sign it, Michelle asked, "Is there anything else that needs to go into this painting?"

"Actually, yes," I admitted, "a white horse just off center would be nice, but I don't know how to paint one."

Giving me confidence, the teacher directed, "Just put the white paint on a brush and put the brush on the paper."

You can imagine my surprise when a reasonable facsimile of a horse emerged from beneath my hand. I was delighted, except for a few smudges around the feet of the beast, which I turned into winged feet with four small black paint brush strokes. Satisfied, I signed my Van Gogh to the lower right corner, convinced that I would continue to paint even after the class ended.

Ten

The Last Tango / Tangle

I could hardly believe that I was ready to go back to my career, which felt more familiar. It was now fall, the appointed hour for me to leave behind the lightness and brightness of the Pacific coast and return to my once naughty Northeast. I had one more adventure before returning to the office. It was on the East Coast, and a grand finale of sorts, even if it hadn't been on my year's plan. It had to do with Herb's "investment" – remember my first spiritual man friend that I met at Omega, St. John, early on my sabbatical? Herb had registered us for a course at Omega Institute in Rhinebeck, NY, which sounded intriguing.

I was excited to fly to NYC to visit Herb and get to know him better during the week before beginning the experiential workshop called "Sharing The Path: A Couples' Retreat" with him. It was also a chance for an inside look at a Manhattan lifestyle from his home, a 6th Avenue flat above a store, which had a Pan (Greek god of nature) fountain by the street window to whiten the traffic noise. We walked his rescue dog each morning in that cacophony of sound. Herb left the flat keys with the storekeeper and carried $20 in his pocket; mugger's money, he called it. That was new to me. The broad daylight didn't feel threatening, but what did I know about big city living? My naivety was never challenged and I didn't mind being spared.

I was looking forward to having another wealthy Jewish friend spend money on me. As generous as he was, however, it was a matter of principle for Herb not to have me as a kept woman, and he insisted politely that I make a contribution towards whatever we did. I was to take care of my needs in regard to initiating sex if I wanted it, to share in any decisions regarding plans, and to contribute to tips. Fair enough; a reasonable contract.

"Read this book, *Who Dies?* by my friend Stephen Levine, who also wrote *A Year To Live,*" suggested Herb, a hospice volunteer for many years. "It'll give you a better idea what my life, any life, and death is about. Care to come with me on a hospice visit?"

In Room 632, New York General Hospital, a massive medical facility, I was touched by how very lovingly this big tough guy oiled and massaged the feet of Rob, a dying AIDS patient. How wisely he comforted the frail creature on the bed with his words and made him laugh with his jokes.

"We've become good friends over these past weeks," Herb said, speaking of his hospice patient, "I'll miss him."

Herb also had a beautiful voice which I appreciated when hearing him chant at the Jewish temple service we attended one evening after we went out to dinner. The next night he hailed a cab (just like in the movies), and we headed uptown to a 5th Avenue ballroom. He was an excellent dancer, as I discovered as we waltzed. I just had to relax enough to enjoy it.

On the train from NYC to upstate Rhinebeck, NY, for the four-day retreat meant to clarify both autonomy and intimacy in a couple's relationship, Herb spoke of the living enlightened master in Lucknow, India, whom he visited every winter.

"I'm a disciple of Poonjaji who, following the teachings of Ramana Maharshi, is the clearest voice I know for clarifying consciousness. Perhaps you will go there in the future to have darshan with him," Herb suggested, willing to share what he knew about spiritual journeying. I was all ears, determined to glean as much as I could about the path of awakening from this wise man who appeared to have good directions (even if it meant going to India?).

The Omega Couples Communication Retreat was being taught by long-term friends of Herb's who exemplified the ultimate in a mutually appreciative relationship as well as being sugar candy on the eyes. (I was a bit jealous of their having it all.)

Hank and Ronda greeted Herb personally before making us all

comfortable with their particular approach to communication in advance of getting the couples to introduce themselves. We 12 doubles were as varied as any two-piece outfits, and not all matches were male and female.

Directions for the active listening sessions involved switching from one partner to another for brief exchanges to state one's needs, clarify beliefs, and listen defenselessly to each other's views.

We chose who was to be A and B and were instructed to move chairs into two rows facing each other. The Bs, the non-moving row, would be the questioners and the listeners in the first round. As an A in the mostly female row, I studied the bespectacled man across from me and he smiled.

My first response to the question "What first attracted you to this partner?" was easy. As I moved on, though, I became confused because none of the questions seemed relevant to my relationship with Herb, whom I had known for only two weeks, and really didn't know at all, except that he was "spiritual" and good to me both in and out of bed. I started thinking of answers as if I were talking about my partnership with my ex.

But even then I was stumped. Jerry and I never spoke about ourselves as a couple, only about our children, the bills, and his job. That's an oversimplification, but you get the drift. I deserved a D in communication. To my dismay, I realized that I still had a lot of resentment towards Jerry and felt like a failure as I struggled to respond to the assigned questions.

For example:

Q: What are you afraid to say to your partner?
   (*A: almost anything*)

Q: What would you most like to change about your partner?
   (*A: almost everything*)

Q: How do you initiate a heart-to-heart talk with your mate?
   (*A: I don't; he doesn't*)

Q: What could you do to be happier in your relationship?
   (*A: Live separate lives?*)

Q: On what issues does it feel like you are walking on eggshells?
(A: alcohol, money, his jobs, but not sex because that was never discussed)

Q: Is there anything you need to apologize for?
(A. Where should I begin?)

It appeared I didn't practice "healthy confrontation" in my relationship with my husband, although I must have done so in dealing with work peers and political efforts when necessary.

Given the difficulty I was having, it is understandable that Herb was having trouble with me too. I definitely deserved the "F" he most likely gave me for wasting his time and money.

In the next to last session, I said something (I have no idea what) that must have pushed the last of his buttons. He just looked at me, shook his head, got to his feet, said "I give up; you're hopeless" and walked out of the room.

So much for the investment in our relationship. If he had harbored any idea of living with me in New England, he was over it.

◇ ◇ ◇

The teachers were as shocked as I was and sent someone after him. Herb responded by letting them know that he was meditating and not planning to return for the closing session which was about to begin.

It was a couples' dance, and there I was, without a partner. The idea was for each twosome to dance while the rest of us held hands to form a sacred space around them.

The music started and couples took turns in the center.

"Come dance with us," more than one couple offered. I had no difficulty declining. I felt secure enough to dance by myself after the 11 couples had had their turn. I glided through a flowing song as a single. (How could that be so natural and easy, immediately after the rejection?)

I was congratulated by the teachers for my composed self-reliance. I certainly wasn't hopeless; of that I was confident, after remembering a quote from another Stephen Levine book called *A Gradual Awakening* which Herb had read to me on the trip over.

The passage encouraged us to "recognize that everything matters equally. Watch with clear attention that isn't colored by judgement or choice: an openness to receive things as they are. When there is clear attention, when there is just watching, there's not wanting."

Had Herb forgotten that as he bolted? I was watching. Was he wanting? Perhaps Herb was the teacher who felt his student was not ready. I was OK with that, but still had doubts. What did I know?

In spite of my composure, it was awkward going back to the room I shared with Herb, so I headed to the sauna to flush out what had happened. It was crowded but I relaxed as the shared conversations made me laugh. I was confused but hardly pining.

Herb wasn't in the room when I dressed for dinner. He was nowhere in sight as I headed up the stairs to the dining room alone.

The second surprise of the day came at that moment.

"Good evening, Laurel," said a tall, blond gentleman leaning against the railing. "Do you remember me? We studied in Scandinavia together?"

Halting in my steps to revive those memories, I replied, "That was thirty years ago! Oh, you do look familiar. Remind me of that time, your name."

"I'm Matthew who studied in Sweden when you were in Denmark. Remember how we got close that Christmas when the Scandinavian Seminar reunited for the holidays in Oslo? I'm here for the Sufi retreat. I recognized your laugh this afternoon in the steam room."

"Only my laugh?" I jested, noting we were all in the nude as we sweated. Thus began another fling, this time with an ex-lover: me, a recent divorcee, ditched by her current partner, and Matthew, a commercial artist-architect who had just gotten married after being a bachelor for decades. His status should have been a stop sign, but since we had already been lovers, I justified our having a good time under a quickly manufactured grandfather clause.

Such duality: a major rejection and a spontaneous reunion all within a few hours. My ego was spared any reflection time by this instant gratification, a coupling that was over as quickly as it began. Just as well. Though I judged it a miracle that took place on blessed ground, I couldn't count on it to advance my sainthood.

Herb and I were both uncomfortable as we departed Omega and sat in separate aisles on the return train. Back in NYC, I made a quick exit to the airport for a flight to New Hampshire. It wasn't the best of finales to my sabbatical symphony.

Post Sabbatical

In the weeks back East that I allowed myself before returning to work, I stayed with Louise again. Christopher drove up from college to help me shop for a new-to-me Toyota, delighted that he could keep my Corolla after using it for a year. Daughter Dianna and I took time to play in Boston together but being with Michelle in London was not in the cards yet. For new lodgings, I chose not to return to live in the capital city, where my ex-life might haunt me. Instead, I signed a year's lease on an upstairs flat in a small country town, a few blocks from my office.

Next stop was at Richard's to collect possessions I had stored at his home. This ex-lover had had no problem letting me and my stuff go. He had taken up with a new woman friend soon after we parted in St. John. I was happy for them and content being single.

◇ ◇ ◇

Ugh, if my winter clothes didn't smell like mothballs it would have been perfect. I was almost surprised to be so enthusiastically welcomed back by my colleagues and the volunteers I recruited and managed as coordinator of a county program for youth. But why not? Besides the usual cooking, fashion, drama, sewing, career and craft clubs which the leaders traditionally guided with hopes of getting blue ribbons from judges whom I recruited for the county fair, I planned some fun field trips.

Environmental education was a big deal, and though the other coordinator could name all the plants and identify skat, I was successful in leading an early winter outdoor overnight camping trip which turned out to be more than I'd counted on, as a freak snowfall almost overcame the less than professional lean-to we built to sleep under.

The teens and parents who were drivers for the career exploration club also agreed that a "Night Watchers" field trip was doable. Who were all those people who went to their jobs long after sunset? We were invited to see a short film for free before visiting the projector room in the movie house balcony, and visited a jail where the kids got a chance to be locked up and talk to each other through the prisoner/visitor window. Stopping by the fire station was most popular. The teens slid down the pole, tried on the gear, slipped into the boots, turned on the flashing lights, took up positions on the fire truck, and consumed energy bars from the firefighters' kitchen.

Even the Animal Rescue Center let us peek at the sleeping animals in their cages before touring the dispensary. I was as happy as everyone else when we ended up at a bakery at 4 a.m. to gawk at the busy baker until he offered us donuts to keep us awake long enough to get back to carpools and go home to bed. (How do those night workers adjust to such a schedule was one of the questions the teens asked each of them.)

Yes, I was ready to dig into work again, looking and feeling young, energized and unstressed. For the first time in my life, I had plenty of money (all relative, of course), as I had been granted a raise along with a promotion. More gratitude.

Feeling free as a single woman, with the children having graduated from college and on their own, I did not experience the empty nest syndrome. In my new life and comfy quarters, I remained committed to saving my soul while temporarily on the side road that I considered my career to be. Dense of me not to realize it is all grist for the mill.

Life seemed to provide a nodding head to my suggestions, great ideas for reports, a recommendation for specific roles, and even someone to provide a tissue when I needed to cry. Although I planned to be back at my workplace for only a year, I enthusiastically took part in writing an ambitious five-year plan for my youth program. I could now do my job, let others do theirs, and concentrate on the things that brought me joy in life's tasks while keeping my spiritual goals in mind, if not on the front burner. Even when things didn't work out exactly as expected, it was a win-win period because I took it more lightly.

In my apartment, I created an art studio in one of the spare rooms, covering all the walls with cork boards so that I could have many different paintings in process at the same time. Following Joe's long-distance advice and his hands-on help when he came East to visit (even once bringing the children for a summer camp experience), I purchased the best paint brushes and acrylics available and proceeded to play at being an artist, staying up late on many nights to paint. Feeling especially confident, I even accepted an offer to do a presentation on peace at a UU church service and spoke at the podium, using my 3' by 5' painting with the traditional dove and flower symbols as a visual.

"My future is more wonderful than I can imagine," remained my mantra, and it was a self-fulfilling prophecy. I was grateful to the wise man who recommended it early on my path.

"That's all you need to remember," he had assured me, and following his advice, I was experiencing that truth. Alone in my studio with a paintbrush in hand and canvas before me, I agreed that my life was most wonderful. What a gift to have had such positive learning in my sabbatical year and to finally be more open to the flow all those happy people talked about. Time passed quickly.

Almost too quickly. In November 1990, which I had planned would be the next to last month of the committed year's return to my career, I felt conflicted about leaving my job. I was getting reattached. I was also concerned about what people would think if I admitted I was contemplating quitting to run off with an artist (even if I left out the part about living in his van). Frankly, I was scared to leap off into an unstructured existence. No longer having health insurance seemed too risky, although I never gave a thought to finding another job or saving money for retirement. I must have decided that when I was enlightened, I wouldn't need to worry about such things. (Hadn't yet heard that one chopped wood and carried water both before and after enlightenment.) I was sold on a life of "voluntary simplicity" as my salvation.

My East coast / West coast romance with Joe offered intriguing interludes, but I had doubts about a full-time commitment. I still wanted to fly, and landed on the idea of joining the Peace Corps. It sounded so altruistic, so full of foreign intrigue, while providing health insurance and enough structure to be a safety net for my next launching. So, what if the application process seemed geared to younger people?

If President Jimmy Carter's mother joined at 90 years of age, I could certainly qualify while in my fifties. However, the forms only asked for one's employment history from the previous ten years, and I had a longer career life than that. I had no opportunity to impress the selection committee with my European studies, teaching ESL overseas, or skill in working in foreign countries. Didn't raising a family also count for something?

Being required to have an AIDS test as part of the physical was traumatic. Though I had not engaged in the so-called high-risk behaviors of sharing needles or visiting prostitutes (are there male ones?), I had had my allotment of serial lovers and unprotected sex.

"One never knows" shrieked a guilty voice in my head as I painfully waited two weeks for the all clear results before I sighed with relief and put that dread behind me.

I was happy to be accepted into the Peace Corps. But when I was assigned to a Caribbean island post as a forestry expert (who me?) rather than stationed in Nepal as an English teacher, per my request, I let it be known that I was not satisfied.

"We're not a travel agency," retorted the administrator, so I dropped out before I dropped in and forgave myself for that fantasy. Time to make up Plan B.

True to my yearning inspired by Joseph Campbell's famous saying, "Follow your bliss and don't be afraid, as doors will open where you didn't know they were going to be," I resigned in early January 1991. At my exit interview, the department head at the college asked the usual questions.

I answered philosophically: "There has to be more than this." (I didn't verbalize my Jean-Paul Sartre quote held over from childhood: "One cannot become a saint when one is working 16 hours a day.")

I was given a big warm going away party, passed my career wardrobe on to a colleague, destroyed my redundant business cards, moved out at the end of my lease, and headed west. With my bike strapped to the roof of my Toyota

Tercel station wagon full of all my earthly possessions, I was on my way back across the country. Free at last...of career constraints, perhaps, but not free in my soul.

Twelve

Mea Culpa

Sheepishly, I spent my first "homeless" night at the retreat center in western Massachusetts, knowing I could find a bed in an empty dorm and come and go without being noticed. Very early the next morning, I unstrapped my bike from atop my car and parked it in a designated area for my favorite resident to have and enjoy, just as we had prearranged. Somehow I felt that justified my sneaky behavior. I then headed off on the long drive to New Mexico and a peaceful Zen Center, where I waited for Joe to join me.

It was in February that I dialed the 781 number for my weekly check-in with my eldest daughter Dianna who lived in Boston, and couldn't reach her, only her answering machine. Hearing the message, "I have been called away on an emergency," I immediately contacted her fiancé.

He told me my ex-husband had died while in the hospital in North Carolina where he had moved to work. It was just two and a half years after we had separated. Why wasn't I told, I wondered.

I rang my son who told me categorically not to attend the funeral: "This is Papa's day and he wouldn't want you there."

I reacted emphatically. "I was married to Jerry for more years than you have been alive and I want to be there." We ended the conversation, both of us in a distraught state.

Without going to coffee or chocolate first this time, I turned to God to deal with my stress and went to the nearby Catholic church seeking peace from the religion in which both Jerry and I were raised. I was met at the door by a priest who responded to my emotional state of mind. He offered a funeral service, having not offered Mass that day.

I knelt in front of the altar in that little chapel in the San Cristobal Mountains while Father Xavier offered the litany for Jerry's soul. He gave a sweet eulogy with the information I provided, and offered me Holy Communion. I was so moved by the loving ceremony, so important in my youth, that my grieving and guilt turned to peaceful acceptance of what I took to be God's Will, "all in perfect order," as the New-Agers say. I should have let that be the closure with Jerry's death, but I didn't.

I made arrangements and flew back east for the funeral, feeling more like the beautiful grieving widow than a divorcee, naively ready to be a part of the drama of such an occasion.

It was not as I expected and it hurt a lot (me, me, it's always about me). My three children appeared conflicted when surrounded by Jerry's five siblings and their partners. They acted as if I wasn't there, and I shouldn't have been! Only Jerry's elder brother Herb, always a Good Samaritan with a wonderful sense of humor, actually spoke to me. Fortunately, I was escorted and supported by Judy, a beloved friend of ours for over 20 years. For everyone else, I was persona non grata.

I was remorseful finding it confirmed that Jerry, on his deathbed, had requested that I not be at his funeral. That shouldn't have surprised me. Upon doing the soul searching, I realized how much ego was involved in my actions and the extent of my clinging on at this period when I was so new to letting go. Jerry, however, had really let go. The doctor had told our children that their father had died of no known cause, as his cancer was in remission. He was fully expected to live with only a slight disability due to other complications. Perhaps, the doctor speculated, he died of a broken heart. I didn't want to go there and surmised it was because he didn't want to live with a handicap or be a burden (a thought I found honorable). However, not everyone dies just because they want to...

The most poignant part of the ceremony, to me, was at the gravesite where Jerry's longtime friend Justin from their Foreign Service days spoke so honestly and lovingly of his buddy's gifts, without neglecting to roast him for his maverick nature. I would have liked to have told this good man how much I appreciated his eulogy, but I didn't, knowing they would not be welcome words from me. I had learned a lesson the hard way. In the others' eyes, having hurt their father, brother and friend by divorcing him, I had no right to join them in Jerry's final earthly goodbye ceremony. They were correct; I was wrong. This was "another egg I couldn't uncrack." I had more work to do.

Occasionally, over the early years after his death, I was drawn to communicate with Jerry in my mind on matters related to our children. Being as he had "an immortality of influence" on our offspring, I asked him, as their father, to support them when they were troubled and I didn't seem to be much help. (Had I also asked for forgiveness?)

I choose to believe that he celebrated the birth of our five granddaughters. Now that our three are mature adults with children of their own, I see them as doing fine and I simply applaud their lives. Dianne and Michelle accepted my apology about the funeral. I believe they have worked out the issues about their upbringing and the divorce. It was not until my son Christopher got married that he experienced some healing on these issues with me. Only as he grappled with the magnitude of marriage, his own and that of others, was he able to better understand the relationship of his parents. For that, I am most grateful.

Heaven on Earth

Feeling penitent, it was a relief to leave New England.

I flew back to New Mexico where an affectionate Joe was wait-ing to welcome an equally eager me. We enjoyed another honeymoon until it was time for the father to care for his children once again. I knew enough not to be with my lover during this shared custody period, so off I went.

Returning that late autumn to northern California, my Buddhist friends took me to meditate at the San Francisco Zen Center, followed by the Sunday service at the affiliated Green Gulch Farm. I became enamored with the Zen abbot and the monks with shaved heads and peaceful countenances, beatific and beautiful in their black robes. I wanted the trusting aura part, and sought an opportunity to serve in a similar environment. The thought of being immersed in Zen appealed to me even more than being with Joe. (I was back to my sabbatical style explorations without the half-pay!)

The Tassajara Zen Mountain Center, 16 miles away from the nearest paved road, offered the getaway and Zen experience I was longing for. "Join us for a focus on work and community living during the transition on either side of the summer guest season," read the brochure.

Indeed, I would. I signed up and headed inland from the Big Sur Highway 1 coast into the Ventana Wilderness to spend the month of April cleaning cabins at the retreat center. There was no money exchange, but food and a bed in a cabin were provided for six-and-a-half hours of daily work, with the option to attend morning and evening meditations and join informal discussions about the Zen tradition. The time spent relaxing in the hot springs was an additional surprise. This Zen Mountain Center was also renowned for its vegetarian cuisine, which I once enjoyed at their Greens Restaurant and Tassajara Bakery in San Francisco. Here at pre-season, the chefs were preparing for the guests and our crew was served daily samples of the outstanding menu. I also learned (and have forgotten) how to eat with an oryoki set, the formal eating bowl the monks used, a practice done all in silence.

The Tassajara Center's mission, "to access, embody, and express the wisdom and compassion of the Buddha," was practiced, and gradually I grew quieter. (It was all so familiar and yet different with a beginner's mind.)

It would have been hard not to, given the beauty of the meditation practice called zazen in the Japanese Soto tradition. Each morning and evening, I responded to the ritual of the sound of the mallet being struck on the han (wooden block) outside the zendo in a quiet, isolated area. It was hit in measured beats that quickened as the time to meditate approached. Seconds before the mallet was silent, I stepped with the left foot first over the threshold, bowed, and took a seat on a platform facing a wall.

This disciplined sitting was taught with strict attention to upright posture, breath awareness, and silencing the mind. Again and again I attempted to do my best. I welcomed Suzuki Roshi's words: "In the beginner's mind there are many possibilities; in the expert's mind there are few." I noted my many emotions before ideally letting them drift by like clouds in the sky. (Yeah, right.)

Sitting "to see what is, and to accept what is, here in the eternal now" was taught to widen one's field of awareness, which led to equanimity. "Sitting" was for inquiry rather than to achieve a goal. (But equanimity was one of my goals!)

I sat with my head erect in the best yogic posture I could manage, and faced the wall with my eyes half open and half closed, my tongue on my upper palate, while counting my breaths. After what seemed like an endless "eternal now" 25 minutes, it was time to walk around the room for five minutes. The ritual was beautiful even if strenuous. I prevailed because I loved the sounds of zazen: the temple bell, the clang of the gongs, and the echo of the clappers to mark the periods of sitting and walking.

I remained determined to get enlightened while pondering if there was an easier way. In my searching with renewed focus, being with Joe became less important. I wrote him a "Dear John" letter: "I do hope you understand."

He certainly did. I was anticipating a little less understanding, a little more resistance to the separation idea. It was obvious that while I was fixated on the Buddha, Joe was not suffering from longing for me. True to non-attachment, he wished me well and simply requested that we keep in correspondence. So be it, and so it was.

It was back to the happy hunting grounds for another attempt to catch that elusive enlightened carrot at the end of the stick. Summer offered both a grounding and uplifting experience in New Mexico.

How could I resist this mission statement? "The purpose of the Lama Foundation is to be a sustainable spiritual community and educational center dedicated to the awakening of consciousness, spiritual practice and respect for all traditions, service and stewardship of the land." Another home away from home, once again rustic, simple, loving.

"Since Lama's beginning, daily meditation, a strict no drugs/no alcohol policy, consensus decision-making and a spirit of inquiry into one's own spiritual practice have been the formative tools for individual and community development." Perfect.

It was close to heaven with expansive views at 8,500 feet above sea level within the beautiful and rugged Carson National Forest in the Sangre de Cristo Mountains, not far from Taos. Because the oneness of all paths was emphasized, I got to take part in a diversity of practices while celebrating community.

I checked in as a "work-study," paying $15 a day for tent space and food while committing to work (called seva or selfless service) four hours a day in the vegetarian kitchen or the prayer-flag-making shop. It was a primitive setting by city standards, yet I loved sleeping in a tent, which I got to position on the high deck of the old ceramic factory building that was no longer in use. It was a magnificent spot to watch the brilliant sunsets after work. I used the back seat of a van as a couch on my porch that overlooked the majestic gorge and the Rio Grande River with its natural hot pools.

Soaking there was one of my free pastimes; going to see foreign films in Taos was another. I also rejoiced in being introduced to natural building processes, mainly straw bale houses, and actively rehabilitating soil though permaculture. Never would have thought that I would enjoy bringing depleted earth back to life by first covering it with cardboard, a resource I didn't suspect would be valuable in farming. I even fell in love with worms while doing lots of shoveling. As I relaxed into the labors, the work became play. Who wouldn't have been refreshed by the natural spring water we drank, and enlivened by the meals we shared from the organic gardens we planted and harvested?

We gathered every morning for meditation in the "kuti," a sacred underground dome, a chamber where reverence was palpable. Stillness took over my world upon entry.

Many of the other core practices, the ancient heart traditions of Shabbat and Zikr, were new to me. Perhaps just like the hippies in the 1960's, I was most turned on by the Dances of Universal Peace scheduled for Sunday afternoon. These originated when a mystic named Murshid Samuel Lewis started circles of singing and dancing in his San Francisco Bay Area garage for the young bearded and braless ones who gathered around him. This incredible Sufi master, Zen teacher, peace activist, horticulturist and scientist might have been rejected by polite society, but not by the flower children who ate at his table and embraced his teachings.

Murshid Sufi Sam taught peace through the arts by incorporating the shared truths of all the religious traditions in dance and song. One of my favorites was a chant we sang over and over to each new partner as we circled around the hall:

"Let my heart reflect Thy Light, Lord
As the moon reflects the light of the sun
In Love. Always in Love.
Hu Allah. Hu Allah. Hu Allah Hu."

The word "Hu" in the chorus translates as the name of God as well as the Word of God, so as we sang "Hu Allah," we were joining in God. It was my first exposure to Islam and the mystical Sufis. The dancing was uplifting and hypnotic, and I was quite impressed by the devotion of the whirling dervishes who joined us from time to time. Being in the collective trance and gazing into each other's eyes offered quite a contrast with the more introspective Buddhist practices also offered at Lama.

It was the practice of Buddhism that inspired my middle daughter to fly from London to Lama for a Vipassana retreat combined with a reunion with me. I was delighted with Michelle's willingness to visit and the wisdom to register with the well known and well-worth knowing Insight Meditation teacher, beloved Jack Kornfield.

Four years previously, Michelle had moved to London after graduating from Boston College to begin studies to qualify as a chartered surveyor. Now working at such a high-powered career, she realized she needed to take time off to learn how to do nothing but sit and breathe, and to put some of those 60,000 thoughts a day on something besides work.

Michelle and I spent three days touring New Mexico and Utah before returning to Lama where I helped her pitch her tent on a knoll not far from where I slept, and wished her well before she went into silence for the ten-day practice. Because I had gotten used to the rugged setting, I didn't realize how frightened my big city girl was of the new moon darkness and the quiet of the high desert.

After finishing work each of those ten days, I joined the rest of the staff sitting in with the retreaters for the evening discourses led by this soft-spoken awareness teacher. I was impressed with what my daughter was studying and practicing. Jack Kornfield warned the Westerners not to bring their ambitions and striving into their meditation, because it might cause them to use the practice to judge themselves and increase their dissatisfaction. Yes, they were to make a dedicated effort to develop concentration and quiet their minds, but only with an open heart and loving kindness to themselves. He spoke of the voidness that unites everything; how all beings and things live interdependently. Therefore we must have concern and compassion for all others as well as ourselves. He went on about "form being emptiness and emptiness being form," which I found completely beyond my comprehension.

Many years later, after I had more exposure to Advaita (non-duality), I told Michelle that I probably would have saved myself years of my somewhat frenzied journeying if I had taken the entire retreat with her that summer. My daughter returned to London and her profession as a wiser woman.

Summer progressed, as pilgrims from the world over arrived at Lama for short visits or long retreats. After I finished my food prep duties before meals, I chose to sit and converse with the not-in-silence guests who enrolled in classes. I was most impressed with how many of the women visitors (as well as staff) had gone to India on their own. I began to anticipate doing the same. All summer long, I talked "India" to glean tips from the "been there done thats." Three months later, I had a two-inch stack of notes with names of gurus, various ashrams and monasteries, and suggestions on places to visit in the Motherland. Most of the travelers were in their twenties.

"I can do it if you did it," I told Cynthia who was my age. Summer was coming to a close as I pondered the when and the how.

◁ Act Two ▷

One-way Ticket to India

Fourteen

Off with a Backpack

Having decided to travel to India on my own, I needed more direction. Fortunately Moti, with whom I had worked all summer, offered suggestions regarding my itinerary. This globetrotter had spent many years traveling to The Motherland from his home in Berlin. I had great confidence in what he laid out for me after he sorted my pile of notes about ashrams and gurus into northern and southern locations. He also educated me as to which gurus were called by several different names – more than one was beloved as Papaji. His advice was helpful and clear:

"I suggest that you begin in northern India and attend the Divine Mother Festival of Lights which is held every October in the Himalayas," he advised, outlining a "man of few words" four-step itinerary:

1. "Fly to New Delhi at the end of September.
2. In New Delhi, take the night bus to Haldwani.
3. In Haldwani, go to Patel Chowk and meet Shri Muniraji, mentioning my name.
4. Shri Muniraji will direct you to the Babaji Ashram where the seekers gather before going to the Divine Mother Festival of Lights.
5. Period."

Was that all there was to getting started in India? Could I do it? I could do it. I had less than a month to get organized: to acquire my one-way ticket, visa and vaccinations, buy a backpack, and sell my car. I drove back East, this time to Cleveland and my brother David's home where I unloaded what remained of my life's possessions from the Toyota's back seat and stored them under his cellar steps. None of us expected it would be five years before that area saw the light of day again. (Thanks so much for your tolerance, David and Karen.)

Knowing I would be living more simply in India, to state the obvious, while traveling without my beloved Toyota which had held provisions for all occasions, it was necessary to pack only what I could carry on those buses and trains I would be using to gypsy around Asia. That meant living out of a single backpack and small daypack, plus the gifted fanny pack for my passport, shot record, airline tickets, one credit card, access to savings, and some cash.

Convinced that travelling light would be much more fun and more spiritual, not to mention mandatory for a budget traveler, I went shopping at a nearby REI for the gear. I was overwhelmed by the selection of backpacks. My first choice was a bright backpack in spiritual purple which turned out to be too conspicuous looking and much too heavy to carry when packed. I returned it, stopped by a New2You store, and found an experienced slender navy blue one with straps that folded in, making it look more like a suitcase.

I packed and repacked until somewhat satisfied with having fit in one black cotton dress, a long T-shirt to sleep in, a sweater and a shawl, flip-flops, and a poncho which also was to serve as a mattress cover for budget hotels. Some vitamins, anti-malaria pills, aspirin (before I knew about Arnica), suntan and skin lotion, shampoo, toothbrush and paste, dental floss, hand towel and washcloth, a bar of soap, writing paper, pen and address book were each tucked into the compartments. My travel outfit was a two-piece rayon geometric print. It didn't quite go with my Teva sandals which are standard apparel for India's potholed streets and monsoon season. I thought it wise to be more practical than put-together.

I left behind my Loving Care hair coloring lotion. After eight years of retaining my auburn color, I was done with that vanity. I took only an eyeliner pencil as makeup, since women in India accent their eyes. Within easy reach in the front pocket, I packed *The Lonely Planet Guide to India*, the bible of the day for budget travelers, which would serve as an answer to my prayers in many of the strange places I found myself.

◊ ◊ ◊

Ready, set, go. My brother David, after promising to sell my car for me, delivered me at the Cleveland airport with a going away present from his wife Karen: a miniature sewing kit I hadn't even realized I would need. I was too excited to be nervous, look back, or even doubt my decision as I made stopovers first in Boston, then in London for quick, brief but loving visits with my daughters Dianna and Michelle. Though glad to be with me and share my excitement, they seemed not at all concerned with my launch on an unusual journey. I delighted in finding them involved in their new careers and doing well. Without worrying about them, I was free to focus on my mission. Clutching my one way ticket to India at the departure gate at London's Heathrow Air Port, i boarded the boeing 747, and mentally created a rendition of *Leaving on a Jet Plane* to *Fly Like an Eagle* going *Somewhere Over the Rainbow* like *Lucy in the Sky*, in an attempt to calm myself about a future more wonderful than I could imagine.

No. 1: "Fly to New Delhi at the end of September."

Getting off United Airlines flight #486 in New Delhi on September 26th, 1991 was the first step successfully completed; but I couldn't savor it as the reality of the sweltering heat made me feel heavy with perspiration and fear. My fellow 500 disembarking passengers swelled into thousands waiting to go through customs. It was even more nightmarish after getting my backpack from Baggage Claim as I moved into the chasm where arriving and departing travelers merged and juggled to find their direction in and out of this old-world terminal. There were bodies to be pushed against, bodies to step over, and then two bodies I recognized!

With *The Lonely Planet Guide* in hand, I moved toward the handsome Dutchman and his supple Duchess with whom I had chatted briefly at the London airport before departure.

"Best get some rupees before you head off," suggested the hunk.

"Will do," I replied, checking the security of my fanny pack.

"You know where you are spending the night?" his braless partner inquired, looking at the book in my hand.

"Come with us," they said in unison to my unsure response. "We're heading off to an inexpensive hotel where we always stay when we fly in. We'll catch a bus to Shakti Road, much less hectic than trying to bargain with taxi drivers."

Accepting their guidance, I found the shortest Currency Exchange line and traded a hundred-dollar Travelers Check for a pile of brightly colored, different sized, dirty bills and a few odd-shaped coins. Following my saviors out into the muggy night air, I stayed close behind as they sought out the correct bus to board among the dozens revving their engines ready to depart. I was most grateful for this random act of kindness as they encouraged me to board first, after pointing out the required coins for the fare.

Even with the door closed, the sensations of the surroundings rattled me as much as did the ancient vehicle in which we traveled. I heard the honking of the impatient drivers in the traffic jam. I saw people sleeping in the meridian. I felt the sticky bodies of fellow passengers. I imagined I could taste the curry I smelled on my seat partner's breath.

"Here's where we get off," whispered my lifesaving guides, pointing this drowsy one in the direction of the door. Out on the avenue, my backpack felt rock solid heavy as I lifted it and my legs over a male body sleeping on the curb. Maybe he was dead; could that be? We crossed the four lanes and turned left into a much narrower street, its entrance marked by a flickering streetlight. Relatively quiet and devil dark, this alley doubled as another bedroom of the impoverished. As my eyes adjusted to the darkness, I looked at the tunnel of side-by-side doors and shuttered windows.

"I would not have found this place by myself," I admitted.

Halfway down the alley, out of the pitch and in the quiet, we heard the sound of hooves before we sighted the herd of five spooked cows on a rampage, heading towards us. We fell flat back against the walls witnessing something not described in any Indian travel guide I'd read.

"Whew," the Dutchman said, "That was a one and only, thank Krishna."

Peeling ourselves and our backpacks off the shutters, we stepped back into the lane and perused the barrage of signs for #29, the Shri Shri Hotel, our destination.

"Right, here it is, and locked as usual at this hour," the Dutchman said as he knocked on the window to rouse one of the Indians sleeping on the floor of the ten-foot-wide lobby. The others didn't stir as we stepped over them to get to some standing space. After registering for side-by-side rooms, we climbed four flights of the dimly lit, windowless stairway to our floor, where I said a hurried goodbye and thank you, admitting that I really had to pee.

I unbolted the outside slider and entered a small single, heading for the promised bathroom to find a hole-in-the-floor toilet just like I had used in the Greek countryside, but hardly expected on the fourth floor of a big city hotel. There was no toilet paper, as forewarned, but rather a plastic cup and water from the tap sticking out of the left-side wall about a foot off the floor.

After a shower from another pipe coming out of the wall at eye level, I felt better, but very thirsty. I filled my water bottle with tap water from the small sink by the bed and added an iodine tablet, having to look up in my bible how long to wait before it was purified enough to drink.

It eventually dawned on me to bolt the door on the inside. I was somewhat worried, wondering whether someone could bolt the door from the outside also and lock me in this cell forever.

This is what I signed up for, I told myself: guru shopping in India on $10 a day, so I'll live (or die) with it. Perhaps the window as an escape? I checked out the glassless opening: it wasn't big enough to crawl through, even if it hadn't had bars. At least that was assurance that I would not have any guest entering through that portal.

Before crawling into bed, I put my plastic poncho over the mattress, but under the sheet, as suggested by previous 'been here / done this' budget travelers who had experienced bed-bugs. I turned on the ceiling fan which, though noisy, didn't do much to muffle the street sounds and chanting below. No problem, I was tired enough to sleep soundly and gratefully.

I assumed my neighbors had departed before I awoke, so I had to summon up my courage and take charge of myself. I packed up, descended the four flights, and checked out.

"Where is the nearest place to eat?" I asked the desk clerk.

"Just three doors to the left. Very good food, yes, yes." The hard part was next because the lane, so quiet the night before (except for the sacred cows), was shoulder to shoulder with a wide palette of local color. I felt quite conspicuous in my white jet lagged body dressed in backpacker basic, totally out of place in this neighborhood scene.

I forged ahead, ignoring six beggars, four bicycle rickshaw drivers, and some overly persuasive vendors, while silently repeating my mantra, "I am divinely guided and protected." It didn't seem like my future was more wonderful than I could imagine at this moment, no matter how many times I parroted it.

I dashed into the so-called restaurant, which was more like a hallway with a row of tables along one wall. Not understanding the menu, I ordered plate after plate of white buttered toast and more and more sugary chai in order to comfort myself and stall before making the next move on Moti's list.

No. 2. "In New Delhi, take the night bus to Haldwani."

OK, I knew what to do, but how best to do it was another issue. Full of sugar energy if not enthusiasm, I paid my bill, handing over a colorful but dirty note and getting a handful of coins in return. Picking up my backpack, I walked out of the restaurant and jumped into the first bicycle rickshaw I saw.

"Take me to the bus station." How brain-lagged I was! There must be 500 bus stations in New Delhi, and I soon discovered that the first three drop-offs by three different drivers were not where I needed to be. My panic and frustration levels accelerated with each mistake. Eventually, after a lot of questions and more than a few prayers, my wits returned and I got into a motorized, diesel fueled three-wheeler with a blackened-toothed driver who signaled me to get in after spitting out the betel nut he was chewing.

"Haldwani bus, yes, yes," he said with a shake of his head. I relaxed and even began to enjoy the adventure, especially the crossing of the Yamuna River. The four-lane rush of the cars, buses, trucks (garish with Godly garnish), an overabundance of rickshaws and even an elephant passing by tickled me so much that I happily gave rupees to all of those soulful, dark-eyed ones who stuck their open palms into my face each time we were stalled in traffic.

Even after living two years in India, I never did fully come to peace about how to deal with the beggars: sad mothers with sick babies; skinny, tenacious kids learning the pathetic trade at an early age; old men with vacant eyes. Sometimes I gave biscuits, more often rupees; or presented them with plastic bangles or holy pictures. Other times I turned away or just smiled or frowned. Once at a bus station, after I had given coins to the poor, I was robbed of the change purse which was pinned inside my larger shoulder bag. As I was concentrating on boarding a bus (always a bit of a jostle to find a seat), a pickpocket reached inside my bag and ripped off that pouch for the poor while I was totally unaware.

I kept repeating to myself, "Number Two: In New Delhi, take the night bus to Haldwani," until my chariot came to a full stop.

"Thank you so much," I said sincerely, paying and giving a tip to the rickshaw driver who had in fact transported me to the correct bus station for my trip north. Putting my pack on my back, I tentatively left the shelter of that little tin can on three wheels and entered another sea of sentient beings at the Red Fort bus station. More outstretched hands, more large black-circled eyes, more cows greeted me. The unloved dogs, tails between their weak legs under their caved-in backs, slithered away. I felt a bit downtrodden myself, weariness and wariness overcoming me once more.

I entered the relative coolness of the cavernous bus station, sought and found the toilets, and paid the rupee (about five cents) required to use the facilities. I like to think I put another coin in the tip jar for the attendant who spent so many hours there cleaning the stalls, but I may not have done so.

Relieved, I collapsed on a hard, straight backed bench and composed myself by opening my bible, *The Lonely Planet Guide*, before moving on to purchasing my bus ticket. I opened the "Advice for Travelers" section and read: "A single woman traveling alone on a bus in India is advised to reserve a seat in the front of the bus where the women sit, preferably not over a wheel. Best to avoid buses that offer video entertainment because it is usually scratchy and loud and plays all night long."

Mentally noting the advice, I easily found the correct ticket window for the northern routes, which was labeled in both English and Hindi. (Thanks to the historic British occupation of India, the English language was the common one for trade and commerce.) Before I paid the fare, however, I sought reassurances regarding my requirements. "Acha," the Indian version of OK, repeated the cashier again and again, complete with the affirming head shaking which is common, in response to my requests in keeping with the guidebook suggestions. "Be at Gate #57 at 10 p.m. for boarding."

It seems logical that I would have used the eight-and-a-half hours before departure for sightseeing, which was my plan. Taking a good look at the impressive Red Fort structure across the boulevard, and contemplating the energy it would take to accomplish the feat of getting there and touring the attraction, I decided against it. Even though I could store my backpack for the day, I didn't have the stamina to get my bag of body bones over there. I soothed my "should-do-but-did-not" feelings by eating lots of bananas and exotic-looking candies. I also bought nuts and more fruit for the trip.

Later, after cat-napping, I moved towards a bench where some other folks my color were waiting. A young Irishman with a nice accent started a traveler's conversation with me. He had a good sense of humor, but I don't think he was kidding when he told me about his last trip to the Himalayas.

"It was a dark night on a narrow close to the edge mountain road," he said, "I sat behind the driver and saw him hit a pedestrian, which sent the body flying through the air over the top of the bus. He didn't stop. That's an example of how cheap life is in India." That was not at all reassuring to me as a visitor (or to my soul). Some of the other stories shared were not so troubling, thank the goddess.

Just before 10 p.m., I went to Gate #57 to board my bus to Haldwani. Sure enough, my name was on the list. I had a reserved seat but it was not with the other women.

"There must be a mistake," I insisted, but the attendant just shook his head as I was hustled onto the bus to the assigned seat 22B in the back of the bus over a wheel, next to a man, with too good a view of the video (Bollywood at its best).

Determined to fulfill my mission in spite of these odds, I had to accept what was. Then I double checked with the driver as to what time we'd be arriving at Haldwani and how I would know the stop.

"The bus will be arriving at 7:30 a.m. and it will be a rest stop, no problem," he replied. That was not true, as it turned out. I do not think the Indians believe that they are lying. I imagine they just feel it is natural and right to tell someone what they want to hear. Who cares about the details?

I was the lone Westerner on the bus. Unlike some of my future bus companions, the man next to me was a gentleman. The only time he touched me was with a shoulder shake at 5:30 the next morning (two hours earlier than told), when he roused me from a deep sleep to tell me we were passing through Haldwani and it was time for me to get off. I shot up and stumbled down the aisle and out the open door. The kind stranger (bless him) put my knapsack down beside me on the highway on the outskirts of the town. Door closed, the bus sped off, and I was left coughing in the dust and diesel exhaust.

No. 3: "In Haldwani, go to Patel Chowk and meet Shri Muniraji."

I had my assignment. It was still India ink dark and no one was around. I started walking east into what seemed to be a sunrise, and entered an area of shuttered shop fronts. I sat down on some steps. Right across the street was a knee-level outdoor water tap and a man dressed only in a loincloth taking a version of a morning shower. This involved squatting and pouring water over his head, beard and body while loudly clearing his throat. After drying off somewhat with a rectangle of cloth which he then tied and tucked in around his waist, he then moved on a few feet, stood before a shrine of sorts, and said a few prayers. Viewing his devotions, I felt that seeing a holy man in prayer was an auspicious sign, a blessing on my day. I knew he must be a real sadhu on a spiritual journey because he was dressed in white.

Now it was minutes past 7:00 a.m. and I had to move from the steps of one shop to the steps of another as shutters were raised and doors were opened. I asked the friendliest-looking shopkeeper about the location of Patel Chowk, which turned out to be the name of a nearby intersection. He pointed left to the next lane.

"Shri Muniraji? Yes, yes, he is there," he said, and I headed off as directed. It wasn't long before I stood in front of my destination which was a book-keeping establishment.

"He's not here yet," the person opening the shutters informed me, "but you are welcome to take a seat." I proceeded to stretch out on three hard, straight-back wooden chairs and sleep, my head covered with my shawl.

I awoke startled as I heard greetings and saw everyone bowing and kissing the feet of a tall man, obviously holy, as he came through the door. I quickly sat up as Shri Muniraji took a seat behind a desk. He waited for me to approach before he asked, "Who are you and why are you here?"

Recalling No. 4: "Shri Muniraji will direct you to the Babaji Ashram where people gather before going to the festival," I replied, "I am Laurel Ann Francis, on my first spiritual journey to India. Moti from Berlin, who visited with you last year, suggested I attend the Divine Mother Festival of Lights as the first stop on my pilgrimage. Here is a letter of introduction from Moti. Would Shri Muniraji please advise me as to how best to proceed from here?"

The exalted one glanced at the post then asked me questions, to ascertain my spiritual aspirations perhaps? Apparently satisfied with my answers, he offered me the opportunity to go along with some devotees on a bus that was leaving that afternoon for the Himalayan hill station of Haidakhan, U.P. I thanked him and then admitted I was hungry. He called for a rickshaw and gave the driver five rupees and directions. I got in and was taken to a small coffee shop. I bought some deep-fried, heavily sugared confections and some tea for myself and a quarter pound of cashews for my holy benefactor. I was aware enough to know never to go empty handed to visit holy people or sacred places.

But I didn't know how to get back to Muniraji's shop. Outside the cafe there were many rickshaw drivers, and I couldn't distinguish if the one that had brought me was waiting. The trip that cost five rupees to get there cost me ten to get back.

Muniraji accepted my simple gift offer on my return to the shop. He introduced me to two other pilgrims and an Indian medical doctor whom I was to accompany on the bus trip to the original Haidakhan Ashram. During the six-hour drive through the beautiful northern India countryside, I got acquainted with Dr. Raghu, my seatmate who told me he was in charge of the hospital that the guru had established there to care for the poor in the area. He offered to show me around, as I expressed appreciation for his mission.

After miles of turning up dirt and rounding countless bends, it was late in the day when the bus stopped at our destination on the top of a hill. Our party of four disembarked and was met by a couple of young men from the ashram who were there to porter our baggage the last half mile of our trip. Jet-lagged as I was, I was glad they did. It took all the energy I had left just to stumble along the downhill path behind the group. When we reached the ashram, a series of neat buildings on a cliff overlooking the river, my doctor host invited me into the kitchen where he offered me supper. He scooped some spicy white rice from a pot on the stove onto two fresh leaves sewn together, which served as a plate. I sat on a mat on the floor beside him to eat my first of many rice-based meals, although seldom as spicy. There were no utensils, so I ate with my fingers after balling up the rice as he had done. Being right-handed, I didn't consciously have to remember never to eat with my left hand in this land where that appendature was reserved for Charmin-less toileting.

I started feeling more secure by the minute. Given my room assignment, I greeted a fellow Westerner who helped me settle in after a minimum of intro-duction. It was all I could handle before falling into a deep sleep.

Fifteen

At Babaji's Ashram

"Laurel, wake up, it's time to bathe," whispered a voice as softly and sweetly as I would expect from a holy woman in this blessed space.

"What time is it?" I mumbled back, squinting my eyes in an attempt to see in total darkness.

"4 a.m. Here, put this on and grab your clothes," my roommate said, handing me a soft cotton something which I was to wear strapless. I stepped into the long, wide tube of a skirt, tightened the cord under my armpits, and headed out after her for the beginning of my first full day at the Haidakhan Babaji Ashram.

"Watch your step, actually 108 of them," Jasmine informed me as we started down the stone stairs to the loudly rushing river below. Only on the way back up did I even try to imagine the names of God that I thought the steps represented, before learning there are so many more definitions in Wikipedia.

Possibly each step depicted afflictions/vices instead: six sense impressions through eyes, nose, ears, tongue, body, thought x three reactions (positive, negative, indifferent) x two "attachment to or detachment from pleasure" of above x three manifestations of vices in past, present, future time (6x3x2x3 equals 108). Reciting the names of God seemed more doable since I could visualize God in everything I saw when I chose to do so. To be mindful of my potential 108 vices felt above my paygrade at this conjuncture.

The air, soft and balmy, was in sharp contrast to the cold Gautama Ganges River into which we stepped at this women's bathing pool section, the men's being further downstream. Little did I realize at the time how close I was to the headwaters of this famous Holy Mother River. I shuddered as the half slip clung to my goose bumps. The hour and the exertion, along with this added chill, meant I needed lots more intention to "overcome the inertia of my physicality" during this first purification practice of the day.

"Physicality" seems to be the problem in many spiritual circles. Perhaps the expression "Cleanliness is next to Godliness" had its origin here in India, I imagined, remembering the aura and handsome physique of the loin-clothed local man I had observed the day before during his morning bathing ritual beside an outdoor tap. I thought it easier to be submerged here up to my neck, soaping up and rinsing off under and around the half slip in the privacy of darkness, than having to pour water over myself one cup at a time. What I didn't know then was that I would get to practice that dipper technique many times more than the submerging one on this spiritual journey in India. It wasn't easy, that first time, to pat dry and step out of the soaking wet half-slip before modestly dressing in western clothes.

Back at the Haidakhan Babaji Ashram on the hill, we went to the temple for Puja. The bell ringing, drumming, chanting, fire and incense ceremony took me back to my Catholic childhood where we fasted before receiving Holy Communion at Sunday mass. Would I faint here too? I felt lightheaded, and would have appreciated having some of the raw milk and ghee (clarified butter) that were being poured over the icon in the center of the altar.

This three-foot tall, slender, rounded marble phallus (Weber's "representation of the penis as an embodiment of generative power") with a fresh floral garland draped over it was my first glimpse of the adored *Shiva's Lingam*. Set inside a *yoni* (Weber's "stylized vulva"; external organs of the female), representing the Hindu female deity Shakti's primordial cosmic energy, the Lingam is the main icon found in every Hindu temple.

A bit strange, I thought, comparing the holy penis and vagina symbols to the crucified Christ image that was the center of attention in the Roman church, which might be equally shocking to the uninitiated. Jesus was never decorated with flowers while on the cross, however, while here blossoms were placed everywhere.

The conch shell was blown, vibrating through me. Dogs reacted by howling, an eerie response. More welcome was the gift giving and receiving, mostly hard candies, fruit, or sugar cubes. I ate the sweets, which raised my blood sugar level, and gave small coins to a line of beggars squatting in what appeared to be an assigned space for them.

The next pre-dawn morning, I was given a flashlight as I joined the other international and Indian guests for a climb to one of many topside Mt. Kailash temples. We circled an ancient rock-walled shrine three times for wish fulfillment. Thinking it best to wish for something holy, "I desire to be desireless, I desire to be desireless, I desire to be desireless" became my mantra.

The 4:30 a.m. sky was still star-studded as we descended. I saw what appeared as three moon rises over the foothills of the Himalayas that early morning. Each bend in the path, we caught another view. The reason it felt so blessed, I was told, was because this amazing location is the original Haidakhan Babaji Ashram where the "Immortal One" materialized, lived most of his life, and was buried in 1984.

I felt more purified and acclimated three days later while traveling with a group of Indian devotees on the annual pilgrimage to the Divine Mother Festival of Lights scheduled at Babaji's second ashram. We boarded a decorated bus and drove many hours to higher altitudes in the Himalayas, stopping only at a roadside stand for food and a toilet break without the toilets. I wished I had been wearing a long skirt instead of slacks to the designated spot in a field to do what needed to be done. Nobody seemed to notice, I convinced myself, never looking back to see if I had mooned anyone.

We arrived at our holy destination many miles later in a state which borders Tibet, the closest I ever got to that holy land. Our local bus pulled into the parking spot next to a Greyhound-like coach where a group of well- dressed Western women, were busily collecting two pieces of luggage each. I collected my backpack and followed my Indian bus mates, who directed me as to where to register and to pay the $2 a day fee for the ten-day event. The natives then retreated to their housing, and I was shown into the dorm that I was to share with the international entourage of Sondra Roy, the popular "Liberation Breathing" workshop leader, who was a disciple of Guru Haidakhan Babaji. She packaged a trip here every year from the States, combining her rebirthing breath techniques with the devotions scheduled at the festival.

We moved in together. After exchanging a few quick hi's, I waited to find an available out-of-the-way spot as my roommates, the other non-Indian ladies, were busy unpacking and claiming the floor space where they spread out their thick mats on top of the provided mattresses. They were paying an American rate for this adventure, so I didn't begrudge them their first choice. I surmised I was assigned this dorm because I was also from the West. The locals were most likely more comfortable without my foreign presence.

It all felt quite alien. This ashram was a spiritual community centered on the teaching of the enlightened "Babaji" who is believed to be immortal, although not physically present. Babaji had implied that he was identical to Mahavatar Babaji, described in Yogananda's *Autobiography of a Yogi*. (This is disputed by the "Self-Realization Fellowship" founded by Paramahansa Yogananda.)

Shri Muniraji, my original host, was the chosen disciple who carried on the lineage. He sat on a guru bench below a picture of the master and meditated there during all the devotions of this winter season's Divine Mother Festival of Lights. Also called Navratri or Dvali, this ancient time of ritual brought together priests, musicians and worshipers (or journeyers like me), who followed a schedule of ceremonies designed to awaken Divine Consciousness. We were there to worship the Mother Goddess in all her forms.

At morning Aarti (devotional singing), we did "Japa" which is repetitive chanting of the names of God. The mantra "Om Namah Shivaya," which means, "I bow to Lord Shiva," was mesmerizing. It is believed that by concentrating on the name of the Lord (like "His Holy and Righteous Name" in the gospel songs), the mind becomes purified of all negative and useless thoughts. To find increased space, energy, and freedom within sure sounded like worthwhile goals to me. However, given my intense search for liberation, who had put me or was keeping me in bondage?

Ceremonial "chandan" followed the chanting. I queued in front of the holy man who thumb-printed each of us in the area between the eyebrows with a red-colored sandalwood paste. Set as a "third eye," because the two physical eyes are not enough to see what is most important, this "bindi" is meant to "cool the mind" and mark the presence of divine energy and light entering the forehead. It was a ritual that reminded me of the once-a-year Ash

Wednesday tradition ("Dust thou art and unto dust thou shalt return") at the beginning of the Catholic Lenten season.

For many in India, it was done daily. If not in ceremony, the bindi is applied artistically with a sticker or a bead. Is there a place where spirituality ends and fashion begins? Or is it all God?

There were fire ceremonies called Yagna every evening and morning as well. Fire is worshipped by the Hindus as a form of God. ("Where is God? God is everywhere," I remembered from my catechism.) Devotees brought fruits, incense, seeds and ghee to the hallowed men who offered their gifts to the fire while reciting mantras. This ritual was used to transform material objects into a subtle force for the further achievement of harmony and balance. It was also a good time to petition for the fulfillment of personal desires. I began to desire a sari which was considered to be appropriate attire for the ceremonies. The belief was that by dressing in these traditional garments, the wearer's attitude and behavior would change and assist them in their devotion. I'd known for a long time that my attitude needed changing.

I skipped the afternoon rest time and followed my roommates on a shopping trip instead. The vendors surrounding the ashram were more than ready to supply any need we had, pursuing us and persuading us to buy by promising "good price." Immersed in the overwhelming piles of color and texture, I struggled with the selection and the pricing before choosing a sari, basically three to six yards of material which is wrapped around the body. I purchased three saris from the cotton stack: one in light blue, one a lavender color, and a third, bright pink polished cotton trimmed in gold for special occasions.

My choices were cheaper and conservative compared to those of my roommates. Was this to be a lesson in non-comparison? I judged it all as conspicuous consumption by those with a high prosperity consciousness. The bazaar later moved into the dorm as the 25 women unfolded meters of soft silks and starchy glittered fabrics. It was quite a fashion show as they modeled their decorated, brilliantly colored saris which were worn over short, tight-fitting, matching blouses above, and half-slips tied at the waist below. My roommates were delighted to teach me the how-to of female Indian dress while overlooking my improvised top, since the ones sold in the stalls didn't fit my less thin bust and arms. Here my blouses had to be made to order.

I found it all quite exotic, wearing a sari to the devotions. Rousing bell ringing and the blowing of the conch shell, chanting, fire ceremonies, tabla drumming and temple dancing, are all forms of worship of the Divine Presence. I certainly felt closer to God when costumed in a sari, but not close enough, I discovered, when the devotees did a full prostration before the guru at the close of the evening session. No way was I going to lay face down in adoration of any man, no matter how holy he was!

Day two came and went, as did day three. On the evening of day four, I paid more attention to the fact that the prostrating devotees received candy and beads upon arising from the position. I wanted candy and beads while reminding myself that I had come to India "to experience another way of being." Letting go of a little ego while giving in to more desire, I joined the queue. When it was my turn, I got on my knees, bowed, stretched out flat on the floor in front of the elevated Shri Muniraji, rose again as gracefully as I could, and extended my hand for Prasad and a mala.

After coming down from the Prasad sugar high, I pondered again what all this guru business was about. I wasn't the first Westerner who had to be taught that the guru, having attained enlightenment while in human form, is a sign of our own potential and thus deserves our worship. Since the guru had realized God while still in the body, it meant that we too could aspire to do so, and indeed were predestined to eventually awaken to the truth of who we are.

And what was this truth of who I am? Would I have to do decades of twisted or balanced postures and years of chanting and fasting to be purified enough to go beyond the ordinary? Could I meditate my way out of the conditioned self to non-dual non-self, whatever that meant? Wouldn't I rather find the holy person who would simply slap me on the back to awaken my kundalini? Can't I please find THE teacher who will wake me up from the disillusionment and discontent that I felt about the way things were: the politics and policies in America (not to mention the divorce), which had put me on this wild chase in search of God?

◇ ◇ ◇

I got sick on the evening of the fifth day of the festival and spent the next five days in bed or on the toilet. Only my quest for enlightenment was on hold as everything about my body seemed to be letting go of something it could not stomach. Hadn't I prayed to be stripped of my bourgeois veneers? Was my illness because of the spicy food or a reaction to the inoculations I received before my flight? Most likely it was caused by the anti-malarial pills I was taking. It certainly was a cleansing.

"Sickness is a defense against the truth," one of my roomies quoted, attempting to cajole me into changing my mind and going back to the ceremonies. Rebecca, a student of *A Course In Miracles*, which I had never heard of, only wanted to help, as she read me what was written in Lesson 136 in the *ACIM Workbook*.

"Sickness is a defense... a decision of the mind... an insane device for self-deception... to hide reality... to keep the truth from being whole... a secret magic wand you wave when truth appears to distort what you would believe. It seems to be external to your own intent, a happening beyond your state of mind, an outcome with a real effect on you, instead of one effected by yourself. It proves the body is not separate from you, and so you must be separate from the truth. You suffer pain because the body does, and in that pain are you made one with it. Thus, your 'true' identity is preserved, and the strange haunting thought that you might be something beyond this little pile of dust silenced and stilled." She ended the quote and I thanked her, agreeing my sickness may be a defense, but it felt more like diarrhea as I got up to go only as far as the toilet. It took me years more before I understood the passage and realized its relevance.

Sixteen

On the Road with Bonnie

The illness left me weak, without an appetite and pounds lighter, but I was strong enough to rise again on the last day of the festival, ready to move on. Could it be true that I had been ill because I wasn't able to deal with all this truth to which I was being exposed? Whatever, I thought, as I made an announcement in the women's dorm the night before we left, stating that I was beginning a tour of India and that I would like a traveling companion. "Anyone interested in coming with me?"

"Ah wheel," shouted a voice in a strong Texas accent, "I'd love to come. I don't want to go home. I want to see more of India too!"

Looking at this bleached blonde, buxom 23-year-old cowgirl, I momentarily wondered what I had gotten myself into. But with a feeling of relief, I was grateful that at least somebody wanted to travel with me on this sub-continent adventure. So what if she didn't look that spiritual? Perhaps my own holiness wasn't that obvious either.

After a long chat about the constraints of my budget and an overview of *The Lonely Planet Guide to India* as a travel bible, Bonnie agreed that living on $10 a day was doable. It would work for her because it would stretch her allowance from Daddy over more miles.

No longer sequestered in an ashram community, we were glad to travel in each other's company as we set out as two excited newcomers to explore this strange land that continued to bombard our senses. From the windows of the local buses we rode through the countryside, we witnessed little girls catching fresh dung from the sacred cows who walked freely everywhere. Dried cow-dung cakes were just one source of fuel.

In the evenings, as we walked in the cities, we had to cover our noses to protect our lungs while passing small circles of squatting men socializing around fires of burning tires. Strong smells of burning fuel, cumin and curry spices, or whiffs of incense permeated the air from local factories, open shops, or tiny shrines. The human hive on city streets was a hum of foreign languages and hawking vendors. Skinny dogs with heads and tails hung low scurried away in fear. Beggars of all ages expressed a gamut of emotions as they yanked at our clothes. Children with coal-circled eyes and blank expressions held out their hands as their mothers sat on the steps with listless infants on their laps. It was rare to escape being surrounded by sound: one transistor radio drowning out another while playing Bollywood favorites, people chanting, traders pleading, bangles and anklets tinkling, traffic horns and angry shouts, and the beating of drums. Color, color everywhere.

We touristed New Delhi and the markets of Jaipur in Rajasthan, and visited the Taj Mahal. (I rattle those sites off so nonchalantly – was I still ill and unavailable? Definitely overwhelmed.) Sometimes we took tour buses, where there was a hospitality book passengers were expected to sign. As the ledger came into my hands, I once playfully scribed my name as "Beverly Hill" (which was the name of one of my former students), and my residence as Hollywood, California. I shouldn't have been surprised that our bus-mates called Bonnie "Beverly" for the rest of that tour – it was much more her image than mine.

◇ ◇ ◇

As my digestive system healed, my appetite returned and I added most vegetarian options one by one to my white toast diet. There were plenty of choices, as long as they weren't too spicy. Mashed potatoes, samosa patties, lots of dhal, yogurt, hard boiled eggs, and roasted peanuts or corn. Everything was boiled, fried, or roasted, never raw, with the exception of bananas and peeled cucumbers. Giving up meat and poultry was no sacrifice after seeing fly-covered carcasses in open air markets and lots of blood on butchers' knives. (That's one way to become conscious of cruelty to animals and to choose not to be part of it.) I was happy to discover how to eat Indian food the "thali" way, where the sweet, salty, bitter, astringent, and spicy offerings are served in separate half-cups set on a metal plate. I'm getting hungry for Indian food just thinking of such meals. I never managed to remember the Indian names of particular favorites, and often asked for a yogurt dessert or drink or side dish of raita to cool the heat of the more spicy foods.

The Indians loved their ledgers, no matter what the business, in the days before computers became standard. Bookkeeping often required three signatures on multiple copies of each transaction. We would go to numerous clerks in sundry departments on different floors just to get the business done, the account opened, the Travelers' Check cashed or money transferred, tickets purchased or reservations made. There were rows of desks in colorless offices, barred windows, bored bureaucrats, files and more files, doors to open, stairs to climb.

The only type of business that happened fast was exchanging money on the black market, which always had a better rate than the banks. With a knowledgeable fellow tourist leading the way, we would surreptitiously make our way down an alley and into a back room where two men were waiting, one standing and one sitting behind the desk. I handed over my dollars, knowing that they would give me grief if the greenbacks were not clean and crisp. The Indian currency bills given in exchange, though bountiful, were dirty and ripped, dog-eared, taped, and marked up, obviously not laundered or counterfeit. Isn't it ironic that I had no qualms about using illegally acquired monies to fund my spiritual search for good?

Bonnie and I decided to travel as cheaply as possible to Nepal. We were excited to climb on the top of a northbound bus with the other backpackers, swap stories, and sing along with the black-bearded guitarist. It was an awesome adventure as we traveled through the mountains on winding roads with more spectacular views around each curve... until the sun went down.

The temperature dropped precipitously. No matter how much we hunkered down and huddled together, we suffered, teeth chattering so much we couldn't even voice our complaints. We practically birthed like glacial ice off the bus at the next rest stop. Even though the locals were already crowded in every available inch below, they somehow made space for us. It was more than cozy, but for the first time in Asia, I didn't mind being cheek to jowl with the natives. (We Americans are used to our wide-open spaces.) I always flew in and out of Kathmandu, however, after that lesson.

Once in Nepal, we made a full moon reservation at the Tourist Jungle Lodge in the Royal Chitwan National Park. I would write home about our adventures by candle and moonlight, the scariest entry being about rafting down the Tisula River with its share of white water and us without helmets. I thought that was risky until we got into an equally dangerous tippy dugout for alligator and bird watching.

"Stay on the trail behind the guide with a weapon in case we come across startled species," we were told when on a jungle walk.

The most anticipated treat of our packaged tour was our scheduled Asian elephant ride through the jungle, exciting from the very first moment that we mounted the seven foot tall, two-ton-plus beast. We sat bareback directly behind our own strong-thighed guide who had both of his legs straddling the neck of this second largest of land mammals (African elephants also have larger ears). I didn't complain as my thighs touched the elephant boy's as he applied pressure to guide the elephant in the right direction. I felt rather like I was riding a wave because of the rising and falling movements of the hips and shoulders of this huge four-legged beast who made a path through the jungle by breaking branches and pulling up trees. Sometime before the end of the four miles per hour gait of our amazing chariots, our adventures climaxed as eight of us circled a white, one-horned rhino. This rare hunk, the third largest mammal, looked so docile that I wondered if he had been drugged into good behavior. Maybe the one-horned one was just depressed because it was one of the last of its species and didn't have a mate.

I'd love to go back to Asia just to be with these beauties of nature again.

◇　◇　◇

Bonnie and I stayed for two weeks in the Kathmandu area relishing its templescape and pagoda architecture. Escaping from too many Westerners who were happily shopping, we joined locals to turn the prayer wheels as we made the ritual circumnavigation of the Boudhanath Stupa, the largest and holiest of Buddhist stupas outside Tibet. Its gilded domed roof was painted with those bewitching Buddha eyes and draped with prayer flags which were kept busy by the breeze, actively sending prayers to the heavens. Just standing and viewing this elaborate temple representing the Buddha was thought to be enough to provide enlightenment. Lucky us.

We trekked to Pokhara, after renting hiking boots for Rh15 (35 cents) a day, and rested on the rooftop of a guest house overlooking the peak of Machhapuchhre, the fishtail mountain. Continuing on to other mountain lodges to get a better look at the Annapurna range, I relished a bucket-shower each evening with hot water heated by our hosts for our comfort over a wood fire. Only later did I become aware of how much a part of the problem of deforestation I was by taking advantage of such a luxury there.

Poonjaji, in Lucknow

ll that sightseeing eventually wore us down. Bonnie and I made the decision to return to seeking the "Kingdom" once again. We set off on a quest to find the Shangri-La where an entire group of people were said to become enlightened together by sitting at the feet of a living master.

At the top on my list was Poonjaji, the teacher recommended by my NYC friend Herb. This guru lived in Lucknow, a major metropolitan city and the capital of the state of Uttar Pradesh. It was described as being a garden city, but did not give us that impression as we attempted to find the home of the master.

Shri H.W.L. Poonja lived with his closest disciples at 20/144A Indira Nagar, a modest house, and held satsang (open discussions) in a hall and dining area three blocks away. Mission accomplished, we sought our own nearby housing. Without difficulty, I found a room in a home in this residential area where the locals welcomed the income they received from renting rooms to spiritual seekers. Bonnie checked into a more proper guest house.

The next morning, outside the satsang hall, we were signed in and informed that as newcomers, we were entitled to have front row seats for our first three days. We entered the hall after making our way through the overflowing crowd of internationals waiting outside to find as many more devotees inside the already crowded hall. Soon after settling on the available cushions, we rose again with the others as the renowned beloved "Lion of Lucknow" entered. Poonjaji, a bald-headed, husky looking man, was wearing an off-white cotton kurta set.

"Namaste" was his greeting, which we returned, our hands in prayer position as we bowed and believed "The Divinity in me recognizes the Divinity in you." He sat in a yogic posture on an elevated carpeted platform draped with cloth and decorated with flowers. How fortunate I felt to have a seat so close to him and to catch his vibe. Was this similar to sitting at the feet of the Buddha? I found myself comparing Poonjaji's countenance with that of the peaceful saint Ramana Maharshi, his South Indian guru, whose portrait, graced with fresh garlands around the frame, was hanging behind this living master. I trembled a bit with a realization that this was a rare up-close and personal introduction to the powerful Advita lineage.

It turned out to be the most auspicious day. Satsang began with Poonjaji reciting: "Om. Let there be peace and love among all beings of the Universe. Let there be peace, let there be peace. Om Shanti, Shanti, Shanti."

The enlightened one spoke slowly in accented English, "There is no teacher, no teaching, and no student. Just sitting and being and self-inquiry are the teaching." I was too impressed by his presence to forsake seeing him as a teacher. I wanted to be his student and be here now for his darshan.

What I wanted most to learn from Poonjaji, and the hardest to internalize, given my strong identification with my form, was his focus on "not-self." Is it true that there is nobody here to be either a victim or a perpetrator?

When anybody would ask a question about a perceived problem, they usually had a story and requested a solution. Before having a chance to even finish their tale, Poonjaji would stop them by asking, "Who was hurt? Who suffers? Who has ever put you in bondage?" This was the lineage lesson, another way of asking "Who am I?"

Papaji, as he was called by his devotees, or Poonjaji, as he is formally named, led us in a guided meditation reiterating the words of his non-dual guru, Ramana Maharshi, stressing our Oneness: "There is no place where 'I' end and 'you' begin."

Looking into his loving and sincere eyes as he said these words, I must have received the transmission I had heard others speak of, because at that moment I felt blissed out of my mind. My eyes closed as his words guided us "back, not forward but back, back, back to our true selves."

◇ ◇ ◇

Something magical happened. The world disappeared, as well as any feeling of separation from others. It was, for me, like the feeling one has when "falling in love" – in this case more like "rising in love."

I remained suspended in an altered space while words drifted by as he answered questions and read letters from his followers. Sometime later, in the timeless cloud I was in, I found myself standing and moving forward in response to Papaji's request that I approach and sit by him.

He asked me about my experience, and I babbled something about how 'I' was no more. There was only the connection between each of us in the room, the connection between the room and the community, and the country, and the world. I felt an expansion in my heart that may not have been nirvana, but it was my first personal taste of the interconnectedness of all things. It was most gratifying, having touched that space, to receive what is called Shaktipat, an act of grace in the presence of the guru.

I like the photo someone took of an ecstatic me sitting next to a smiling Papaji at that moment. Back at my seat, as the session ended, I felt lifted to my feet. Many bowed to me as I floated out of the room.

Unexpectedly, at the exit, a tall, handsome German man embraced me and passionately French-kissed me. I wondered if this was a fringe benefit of enlightenment. Later I recognized how appealing we all find those who are experiencing blissful energy states as we try to capture a bit of the "Force" in whatever way we can. I even heard that sucking on the toe of the guru, for example, was reported to be a good method to enter into bliss. Is it any wonder, then, that the guru keeps himself protected by a close-knit entourage surrounding him?

I was fortunate that a gentleman from my guest home, a young and radiantly pure Canadian who had just left a monastery in Thailand, offered to take this "me / not me" to lunch and to escort me back to our residence. I was in too rarified a state to be concerned with such worldly activities.

Hours later he warned, "Laurel, this isn't going to last." He had seen this rather common phenomenon associated with Papaji before, the result of a transmission, which didn't feel at all common to me. I just looked at him in loving disbelief. My heavenly bliss, however, lasted only eighteen hours.

When I awoke the next morning, I was disappointed with being back in ordinary time, but not discouraged.

◇ ◇ ◇

On the evening before the third day, our last with front row seats, I felt moved to write a letter to the Master. The next morning he picked up my written request and after reading the first line, "Dear Papaji, I humbly ask that you perform my marriage ceremony," he inquired, "Who wrote this?"

I raised my hand.

"Oh, I have performed weddings before," he stated before reading more of what I had written: "I want silence to be the music and your presence to be a blessing in this marriage of my ego self to my Divine Self."

I felt quite holy writing that letter. Papaji seemed impressed with my petition. Removing his glasses as he always did after reading, he said that only once before had he performed a ceremony such as I described: one between the ego and the Divine.

He called me forward and had me sit by him. I was elated as a little voice inside me said, "I've made it; I've made it." I was certain that after the meeting I'd be welcomed into the inner sanctum, his private chamber.

Poonjaji went on reading letters and answering questions. He didn't perform the ceremony I requested; didn't even look at me again, even as I sat so near to him. He left the room after the satsang without signaling me to follow.

Dejected, I came down to earth with all the air out of my fantasy, deflated and shriveled. It was a tough way to learn that whenever the ego thinks you've got it, you find out that you don't. One of the hardest traits for a spiritual seeker to overcome is spiritual pride. I realized I wasn't being the "I" of the "I Am That I Am" with no personal ego attachment.

Satsang by satsang, discussion by discussion, by questioning and just being, however, I was feeling more and more grounded in the loving non-dual teachings. I was joyful even as I vacillated between self and nonself as days waxed into weeks. I so appreciated the Advaita teachings, the non-dual path leading to enlightenment that says we all have it right NOW. Still, if "what I was looking for is what I am looking from," why didn't I get it and retain the got-it?

If only I could embody his satsang on "Leela," then I would wake up... It's as if "the truth of who I am" is dreaming. Just like when sleeping, this daily dream is so real, I forget I make up this movie and play actor, director and producer too. I get carried away in the drama of it all and sometimes suffer as I react, believing in it as reality. It's often hard to wake up from a nightmare. On the other hand, I want to keep dreaming about my "happily ever after." Pain from aversion and attachment is the result. The lesson is to reframe this dream as a movie on the screen of Consciousness. I don't see bullet holes in the screen after a cowboy flick. Nor is it wet after a river flows or burnt after a campfire. Consciousness, the hologram, the Truth of who I am, is not affected. Simple? Yes and no.

◇ ◇ ◇

We all laughed and smiled with Papaji as we shared in this happy master's stories as lessons, and hung out with the other truth-seekers. One of those in the inner entourage was Herb, my ex-lover from New York City who originally told me about this guru. It was only when I got restless and decided to move on to what I hoped would be my next awakening that Herb made his presence known and moved back into my movie.

"You can't leave now! You're getting it! Don't go," he insisted, seemingly shocked. I shouldn't have been surprised to see him there because he was a longtime disciple of Papaji, but I was curious as to why I hadn't bumped into him earlier. I was also taken aback by such comments from the man who had declared me hopeless just months before, when we were a twosome at the Omega couples communications retreat. At that time, he was so convinced of my inability to be even a little "aware" that he ended the relationship with the "you're hopeless" remark.

"I am pleased to see you here in Lucknow," Herb now said. "I have been observing your progress. You're so close. You are doing so well. You just need more time here to truly grasp the Ineffable."

Herb ought to know, I thought. "Alright, I appreciate your encouragement, but I will ask Papaji what I should do," I said, knowing that it was reasonable that after an awakening experience, the student should stay with the teacher. Nevertheless, this restless one was looking forward to moving on to another ashram which I'd heard was quite a different experience but equally enlightening.

The next day in a semi-private interview after darshan, Papaji gave me his blessing and said "Go, go, you're ready. God is everywhere. Only you need to disappear; it is not possible for God to appear and you to appear." Then he all so humanly asked for his train schedules and pointed out that Poona was not far from Bombay, and offered suggestions regarding which train to take from Lucknow to get there. Gurus are good at all sorts of things. It didn't seem to bother him that I was continuing my guru shopping. Papaji had no problem with encouraging each of us to follow our hearts, even when he knew we were off to be with a different teacher. Little did I realize then that I was leaving one of the greatest living saints of the age.

The guru's response and the lure of the next wonder were stronger than Herb's advice. I left to follow my new German friends to the next ashram on my list. Calling themselves sannyasins, they were disciples of Osho, whose commune (no longer called an ashram) was described as a huge complex offering many spiritual growth opportunities. I was curious.

Bonnie decided to go also. We packed and followed our leaders southwest to Osho Commune International, which was nicknamed "Club Meditation – The Last Resort." I was so naive that I didn't realize until after I arrived that Osho was the new name taken by the controversial Bhagwan Shree Rajneesh, the guru of the ninety-three Rolls Royces. He had changed his name upon his return to India many years before, after being deported from Oregon because of conflicts between the commune and the host community, to say the least. Many followed and joined him in establishing this new Poona center.

Osho Commune International

"Set your intention," the wise ones say. Now that the decision was made to go to the Osho Commune, I needed to ask myself what I wanted to learn from this new experience. I already had a four-part harmony going with (1) my previous introductions to Kripalu yoga, (2) the "Be Here Now" course with Ram Dass, (3) the Divine Mother's rituals as a path to God, and (4) Papaji's non-duality. I had not, however, made meditation a daily practice, despite having had weeks of retreats. Meditation, therefore, was a priority.

However, this girl also wanted to have fun. Maybe meditation in movement, as introduced at Club Med and in Osho's book, *Meditation, the First and Last Freedom*, would suffice as exercises in both higher consciousness and highs. I was ready to dance as well as to dive deeper, as Papaji encouraged in his book titled *Wake Up And Roar*.

Poona, here we come! Here we are, ready or not. From the train station, Bonnie and I took a rickshaw to the leafy Koregaon Park area and the German Bakery which was a landmark destination. We felt we needed a caffeine fix before proceeding to the commune. The closer we got, the more maroon-robed BPs ("Beautiful People") we saw, the young and the not so young, speaking many different languages. We were about to become two more of the thousands of seekers from all over the world who came to immerse their unique selves in the energy of the Buddhafield inspired by the master.

Osho had died two years previously, but he had an enormous immortality of influence. His most out-of-the-ordinary campus, the Osho Multiversity, was dedicated to personal transformation: "A school for life designed to help dissolve the old prejudices that have brought misery to mankind." (Hadn't I heard that intention before?) Soon to come, as suggested in the brochure, was an interesting juxtaposition of the mixed energies of Gautama the Buddha and Zorba the Greek, "feet on the ground and fingertips touching the sky." It sounded like I could get back in my body and ascend too. YES.

Bonnie and I finished a rich Bavarian pastry (my choice, a Black Forest Cherry Cake for old times' sake) at the famous bakery and walked the half block to the main attraction. This village unto itself was bordered by high walls and lush vegetation which prevented even a glimpse within. The reception center was just inside to the left of the huge steel-gated entrance. We received a warm welcome, listened to an orientation talk, watched a glossy film glorifying Osho the mystic, and were given papers to fill out.

"AIDS test required," read the intake form. What's this? Why would we need an AIDS test? At other spiritual centers I had visited, celibacy was the norm. Here the exam was a pre-screening for "what comes naturally," which was obviously not discouraged. Being of the era when the dreaded disease was a death sentence, the test was a precaution. Sexuality and spirituality were considered compatible here. One's physicality was not to be overcome as was stressed (and caused me stress) in other ashrams. But this was not an ashram, but a commune. I was anxious to read Osho's *Sex Matters: From Sex to Superconsciousness*. It was welcome news to know that here was a place where I could be open about my unresolved sexual issues.

Was I or wasn't I worried about the AIDS test? I remembered being terrified when having to wait two weeks for the results of the test that was required two years earlier when I applied for the Peace Corps. After assuring ourselves that we had not engaged in any recent risky behavior, Bonnie and I decided to use two days before results were available, to behave accordingly and prepare to stay.

◊ ◊ ◊

First, where to live? Not being offered the luxury suites in the complex, which were reserved as residences for long-term *sannyasins* (disciples) who weren't bothered by the astronomical prices, we perused the list of suggested offerings in the neighborhood. Bonnie moved in with fellow Festival friends, and I was pleased to rent a room a few blocks away from the black pearly gates. It was on the second floor, had a squat toilet and a simple shower, no furniture. I liked its balcony overlooking the quiet street below and the hallway entrance which allowed me to enter and exit without disturbing the Indian family owners, whom I seldom saw. The rent was forty-five rupees a day, equivalent to $3, which was less than a third of my $10 daily spending limit. I bought a mat to sleep on and the coils to burn beside my bed each night to ward off mosquitoes. Only Shiva knows what long-term effect those burning coils had on my lungs. I only knew I needed protection from the night critters, as I was no longer ingesting the anti-malaria pills which had made me so ill. My saris served as bedding and a curtain. No kitchen necessary, as I planned to eat on campus or at local cafes.

Bonnie and I got together to shop for the required loose-fitting garb worn by both sexes to create a unifying atmosphere: two maroon robes, plus a shawl, in addition to a white robe and shawl for the evening programs. Comparing prices, it was easy to establish that buying them outside the complex was a thrifty idea. Scarcity, however, was a dirty word here, as Osho's insistence on both inner and outer abundance was the complete opposite of the traditional glorification of poverty and renunciation associated with most ashrams (I kept needing to remind myself that this was not an ashram but a commune).

Declared negative for AIDS and receiving the Schedule, we two novices took another look at the "Suggestions for Newcomers," put our rupees and passports in the Kuber Safe Deposit, and went over to another section of the compound, where we each rented a locker for day use.

Those German organizers thought of everything. We took time to celebrate our status at the Bodhidharma Tea Garden before checking out the Global Connections Communication Center and writing to family about this stage in the journey.

I was awake and dressed the next morning by 5:45 a.m. and arrived on time for 6 a.m. Dynamic Meditation, the energetic sunrise practice in Gautama the Buddha Auditorium. Called Buddha Hall for short, the space was used for programs on the hour daily. I was comfortable in my new robe, barefoot and braless, shoulders covered by my shawl until I got warmed up with the New Age recorded music. That didn't take long. The first 15 deep-breathing minutes of meditation were energizing as well as cathartic; they delivered the promised "opportunity to let go of all my accumulated emotions which have been repressed." The bouncing in the second section supposedly activated my life energy, offering a state of witnessing, which was followed by celebration through dance, then final relaxation. (Promises, promises with results that I longed for again and again.)

After such Dynamic Meditation, it was terrific having someone else cook vegetables for my breakfast at the Zorba the Greek Community Kitchen. I then had time to explore more of the campus before my next anticipated meditation. I filled my water bottle from one of the numerous free filtered water fountains available, each of which had a sign: "Wash out your personal water bottle with hydrogen peroxide frequently."

Branching out to the far end of the compound, I explored the winding paths of the formal Japanese garden with a serene Zen-like ambiance. It had a pristine stream, actually converted drain water, running through it. Statues of the Buddha attracted me. One was even on an island in a wider portion of the stream.

I was curious about possible greener grass on the other side of the gated garden so checked it out. Looking over a bridge on North Main Road outside the commune, I found the unfiltered waters dirty and littered. It made me realize to what lengths the founders had gone to make this acreage a paradise in the center of a city with different priorities. Its beauty was maintained partly by dedicated long-termers who did "work meditation" in exchange for dorm living on campus.

A couple of weeks later, I volunteered for the daily early morning hour long job of sweeping the swimming pool area in exchange for free pool access, as long as I wore the required maroon colored bathing suit. (Fortunately, the one I self-dyed held most of its color while I was there.) I had yet to experience using the art studio or the padded cell area. Not once did I visit the beauty shop, but the smooth-heeled ones certainly did (God, I couldn't help comparing).

I returned to Buddha Hall on the hour to participate in either active or passive meditations, depending on the day. Each had exotic names, styles, and benefits: Devavani, Nadabrahma, Nataraj, Kundalini. Most had three to five stages, the first of which was always active: fast, chaotic breathing or a period of humming or buzzing, chakra toning, even shaking or shivering body moves. This was usually followed by 15 minutes of free movement to music. After all that release of energy, all variations designed to "offer a window to other dimensions of the inner world" (oh where, oh where can the other dimensions be?), the last 15 minutes were to be spent resting on the floor in shavasana, the corpse position. Even if I fell asleep, I counted on it being integration time.

Daily admission at that time was the rupee equivalent of $1.00 and included access to these hourly offerings. My favorites were at noon, when we got to experience African dance led by live drummers, or Sufi dancing, which were more of a Zikr nature (inward-focused rapturous repetition of Arabic names of God) than the Lama Foundation's Dances of Universal Peace (simple celebratory circle dances from around the world with lots of partnering and often teary eye contact).

After full days, using the hot water showers and having access to a locker, I was able to change into my white robe for the evening "White Robe Brotherhood" without going back to my room. The atmosphere was serene and hushed each sundown as hundreds of us filed into the cavernous white-tented Buddha Hall for this focal program. Even the teachers who wore black robes in the daytime changed to mandatory white attire.

◊ ◊ ◊

"What's taking so long?" Bonnie asked on our first evening as we wove our way toward the doorway of Buddha Hall with hundreds of others.

"It's the sniffers," a regular responded, "They make sure that nobody entering is using scented cosmetics or deodorants. It's basically a carryover from the days when Osho was alive and unable to tolerate such scents."

A newbie behind Bonnie sniffed up close to her cheek and said sheepishly, "Oh, I'd like that job."

Once inside, we each sat down on BYO (bring your own) cushions or small carpets on the freshly-washed black marbled floor of this tremendous cavern. Nobody spoke as the musicians mesmerized us with melodies that blended well with the clicks and rubbing sounds of the swaying black bamboo stalks which surrounded the hall.

Darkness fell, and the guitarist, drummer and flutist left the platform and joined us sitting on the floor. A huge screen dropped into place and triumphant music signaled an "Osho, Osho, Osho" chant. A video began with the image of the guru flashing before us. Osho, appearing larger than life, made a grand entrance attired in a long, regal, rich fabric robe with Star Trek-like designer shoulders. A high collar framed his full-bearded face, his head covered with a Cossack-style cap which added to the illusion of height. After this elevated one took his seat center stage in a throne-like chair, there was recorded Indian music alternating with silence. We all sat in silence with closed eyes for about ten minutes. Three loud drum beats signaled the beginning of a video of Osho's discourse.

Osho, a former professor of philosophy, was a charismatic speaker who offered spellbinding rhetoric on the great Masters.

"There are many ways to get to the top of the mountain, and there is value and truth in all teachings," Osho would say (as is always said in Truth traditions), proving to be unattached to any specific philosophy. I listened transfixed as he spoke of his subjects, first in a glorifying, then in a demeaning manner. I was shocked when he presented Jesus as Christ most lovingly one night, only to irreverently dismiss him as myth the next. Neither the Buddha nor Lao-Tzu escaped both his eloquent praise and disrespectful scorn. Were these lessons in non-attachment? They were somewhat similar to Reverend Rowley's Universalist Unitarian sermons from the past.

I find it hard to summarize such paradoxes and contradictions: Osho's seeming refusal to take anything seriously while introducing cosmic consciousness. I was alert while he spoke uncommon wisdom about the dance of everything as sacred. Could all my human experiences, apparent separateness, and life of duality be embraced in the unity of opposites? Would these teachings push me beyond my mind as promised? (Oh where, oh where is that promised land?)

Just to make sure we didn't drift off during the two-hour program as we sat on the beautiful Italian marble floor, Osho salted and peppered his speeches with off-colored jokes so hilarious and so numerous that I imagined he had a staff of ghost gag writers. When we weren't laughing, we were in total silence as we listened. I never even heard anyone cough or clear their throat or sneeze for the entire session.

Sometimes he varied the lectures with a two-part meditation called "gibberish," which was far from silent in the beginning.

"Cleanse your minds of all kinds of dust; speak aloud any language you do not know, throwing all the craziness out," he would direct. This was all the encouragement we white-robed ones needed to shout, scream, babble nonsense, and wave our arms about in a mad frenzy. I loved it! This continued until Osho would shout out "STOP!" as a signal to begin a long period of silent meditation, a powerful practice time to ponder the ideas presented. Drumbeat would be the call to come back to listen to the voice of wisdom once again.

Most of his extemporaneous talks were available in print under hundreds of his book titles. Depending on the cost and length of the course, one or more of these transformational tools were given to participants at the offered classes. All Osho work is copyrighted, so I will simply offer a few titles here as an idea of the substance:

> *The Great Great Pilgrimage from Here to Here,*
> *Nirvana, The Last Nightmare* (in which he reminded me again that every human being is a Buddha),
> *Walk Without Feet, Fly Without Wings, Think Without Mind,* and
> *The Mustard Seed: The Revolutionary Teachings of Jesus.*

Since I always travelled light, I couldn't carry the books acquired with each class, so I perused them. I yellow-highlighted quotes which I hoped to remember, then realized I must later reference them elsewhere because they were so abundant. It was easier to simply salvage some of the jokes printed there. After cutting and pasting together a compilation of these humorous lines (unKosher as it was), I kept them for times when in need of cheering up (when spiritual readings didn't work, of course). Too bad that notebook was lost in a hurricane.

As if darshan with Osho wasn't enough for one evening, free form dancing followed the video exit of the guru.

On other evenings there were presentations by different guests. I would attempt to get a front row seat for spiritual dances performed by the Sufi Dervishes. Nine dancers wore conical felt hats (representing a tombstone and death of the ego) and long, full-circle, multicolored skirts which flared and rose as they whirled with open arms, their right arm directed to the sky, ready to receive God's beneficence, and their left hand turned to the earth. Their spinning in repetitive circles, meant to free the soul from worldly affairs and elevate it closer to God, continued for an hour or so to live Turkish reed and percussion instrumental music. Later, viewers had the opportunity to join in. Eventually, mesmerized by the music, I practiced and eventually could whirl for what I claimed was twenty minutes. Can't say that I achieved anything but dizziness from this practice, but maybe scrambling my brain cells was what I needed most.

There were other, equally captivating dance performances. "What immensity exists within the limitations of the human body? Who inhabits this body of flesh and bones? Is there someone home?" These are the questions that the three-dozen, silk-costumed Gurdjieff dancers seemed to ask with their sacred flowing current of changing forms: quick, slow, round, staccato. I marveled at their technique and the synchronization necessary to perform their spiritual practice. I watched in wonder while feeling I wasn't disciplined enough to learn such intricate dances.

The Osho Commune programs also served as my introduction to classical Hindu music and temple dance (not the Bollywood style). I was enchanted the night that Ravi Shankar, star sitar virtuoso of the 20th century, performed at Buddha Hall along with a tabla player. His music was like nothing I had ever heard before. I listened carefully as he attempted to explain "raga," which is more than a scale of notes upon which his melodies are constructed, 90% of which were improvised. Not being a musician, I didn't grasp the theory, but it was not necessary for my awe and appreciation. (I was even ready to applaud the warm-up, not realizing this was what it was). My heart still pulses with joy when I hear the haunting sounds of the sitar and the tabla. Where had I been all my life, not to have been exposed to that music, or to the fiery

Indian temple dancers who performed on a few other evenings? Better late than never.

All of the above happened under the white-tented dome of Buddha Hall on campus. In an open field near a river, miles away from the city under a half-mooned sky, quite a different experience was offered.

One evening, I went with a group to one of those techno dances, my first. Surrounding the dance floor of hard-packed earth, palm trees were painted with neon paint which glowed bright white when the rotating blacklight flashed on them. A disc jockey on a high platform, dressed all in black and flashing a white-toothed smile, manned the turntables and played the loudest, darkest music I have ever tried to close my ears to. I moved away from the speakers to where coffee and brownies were offered for sale, but decided not to indulge. The treats were placed in the center of some blankets spread out on the ground for the comfort of reclining customers. As I walked between the blankets, I was approached by vendors, some very young. They offered to sell me drugs, alcohol, sex: "anything you want," they emphasized. Finding it disconcerting, I went onto the dance floor once again and tried to fit in, but to no avail. (Perhaps I, like Alice, was the exception to getting whatever you wanted at her restaurant – for that night, anyway.)

Others from the commune seemed more used to the pace and practice. I found the energy of techno music to be depressing, and looked around for a way to return to Poona. The taxi drivers were already getting high. It was only by offering an extra fee that I was able to find a relatively sober one to make the trip back. Most were counting on hanging out all night to party beside their cabs until dawn, when most of the party goers departed.

The only reason I went to a second techno party a moon/month later was because an older and wiser sannyasin named Swami Satya offered to take me out on his motorcycle for the next morning's portion of the party. All things change in the light. I sat on the back of his Harley as we left Poona at 5 a.m. and arrived in time to catch the sunrise and watch the dancers holding each other up to slower techno music, sometimes falling into the nearby lake. We danced in each other's company, but didn't eat the brownies for breakfast. It turned out to be fun. When contemplating these dance experiences, I reflect on the image of the dancing Shiva and realize that, whether whirling or rocking, it's all Shiva.

Joining the Dance

I gazed like a kid on Christmas morning at the free-spirited atmosphere of the Osho Commune in which I had placed myself. I educated myself first by people-watching, checking out the citizens of many countries: mostly Westerners, especially Germans and Asians, primarily Japanese. There were Brazilians and Aussies, but relatively few Indians (because of the cost perhaps?). The sexual energy was visceral – but any drug scene was invisible to me. Since my hallucigen of choice was heterosexuality, hopefully moderated by spirituality, I didn't need chemicals. I not-so-fast-forwarded into the fun of the plethora of opportunities.

In this so-called "sex sanctuary," picking up someone was quite straightforward. Osho preached freedom and that was interpreted as sex without strings. It came with a kind of unwritten rule: one should not become attached to the sexual partner of the moment. Even couples who came together seldom stayed a twosome while there.

This particular idea of nonattachment was based on an interpretation of a tantric spiritual principle of "transformation of desire." It states that it is not the experience of pleasure that is the problem, but the grasping and attachment which puts one's personal gratification before the needs of others. Holding on was easy; letting go was something else and it took practice. This environment was treated as an opportunity for the ready and willing to live out their fantasies without guilt. The guru's idea was that in order to move beyond lust and hang-ups, one had to finish their acting out in the sexual arena. Desires were to be accepted and surpassed, rather than denied and repressed. Once the inner flowering had taken place, desires such as sex would be left behind, according to Osho.

I was aware of the sexually explicit sculptures in the temples in India, and the belief that "All of life is God's magic." Could I put all that art into perspective by realizing that the copulation exhibited so graphically represented the total unity of the enlightened spirit? Perhaps if I thought as intensely about Spirit as I did about my sacral chakra and sex, I could become a Buddha in this body.

Chakra energy has many levels for exploration. The system has been part of Buddhist and Hindu metaphysics for thousands of years. I was taught that the seven chakras (sometimes even nine, twelve, or more) are seen as spirals of energy which, although not part of the physical body, relate to it. These spinning wheels (root, sacral, solar plexus, heart, throat, third eye, and crown chakras) are often pictured as lotus blossoms and known as areas of connection between body and spirit. The idea is to "open" them through yogic practices and "spin" one's way to enlightenment. Kundalini Yoga in the Hindu system cleanses, purifies, and awakens the chakras. The sacred life energy, which lies coiled at the base of the spine like a serpent, can then rise up through the chakras from the root to the crown at the top of the head and thereby liberate the spirit.

Being as I was still in the sacral chakra stage, and most interested in exploring sex and spirituality, heaven forwarded a lesson plan in the form of a husky man my height with thick black hair and a ready smile. I was having breakfast by the pool when my version of a Greek god joined me at my table. He introduced himself as Demetrius and said that he had just arrived from Athens.

"I felt compelled to come here, to get out of the office for a few months," he said, adding that he was also new to this alternative lifestyle. At first, I was both attracted to him and cautious because he was Greek.

We spent the afternoon walking and sharing our stories. Later we had supper together after the White Robe Brotherhood. Everything heated up as we began our "I only have eyes for you" relationship. A few days later we became lovers, as I grew to appreciate him for the understanding and patient and loving man he was. I call it a holy relationship since it was healing for me.

The coupling was a redemption for a traumatic and life-changing experience (see below) I had had years before in quite a different situation. By loving one Greek man, I was able to forgive another.

Flashback: Rape and Reinvention

Here's the true-life confession. During the period when I was living and working in Europe after college, I stopped over in Greece while en route to Israel. I joined a group of tourists (including my future husband, Jerry, although I didn't consider him in that role at the time) partying every night for a week, in the taverna section near the Acropolis. On the evening after Jerry departed to return to his US Consulate job in Frankfurt, Germany, I made a poor decision. I accepted a ride back from the taverna area to my hotel with one of the Greek men we had chummed with earlier. When he offered to drive to the coast first, I was delighted, as I always love being by the sea.

How unwise of me. He became sexually aggressive as soon as we parked. I managed to talk my way out of forced intercourse, after somehow convincing him I was a virgin.

"I'm just 18," I lied. "I live with my family in Frankfurt where my Dad is stationed in the military."

However, he considered oral sex to be all right for virgins. Terrified, having never been sexually threatened before, I cooperated. Ugh. The trauma of that experience led me to reevaluate my lifestyle. First however, I called one of Jerry's friends at the Consulat to ask for advice. Frankly, she cut me off with: "Don't bother going to the police. They will blow you off, or worse, see you as more of an 'opportunity' than a victim. It happens all the time." With a "gotta go," she hung up.

I felt that my three-year bubble of safety as a single woman traveling alone in Europe was over. Distraught, I flew off the next morning for Israel, where I had a friend expecting me in Jerusalem, as well as plans to live in a kibbutz. This trip to the Middle East and the month's time at the kibbutz and in Jerusalem turned out to be shorter than I anticipated. Jerry (the Foreign Service American I had spent time with in Greece), started a love letter correspondence with me at that vulnerable time. His assertions of love and his offer to have me live with him in Frankfurt were appealing. My reading into them was the thought of having someone to protect me. After that traumatic rape scene in Greece, his encouragement was all I needed to return to Germany to be with him.

Admittedly, that is not exactly true: there was one other episode. More factual is something that happened between love letters. It was the moment I was getting it on with a movie-faced friend of my hostess during the week I spent in Jerusalem after my trauma in Greece (which one would believe should have modified my behavior).

In the middle of making love with this very gentle California teacher, he stopped, looked me straight in the eye, and asked, "What's a sweet woman like you doing having sex with a stranger like me? You should go home to America and get married."

Somehow, I took this as gospel, and it all came to be within a year. Here is the Reader's Digest version of my moving from me to we, from Miss to Mrs.

I hitchhiked back to Germany and moved into the Foreign Service apartments with Jerry and got pregnant. We soon married legally in Basel, Switzerland, to avoid paying the German taxes, and spent that money on our wedding night at the Grand Hotel Les Trois Rois. Three days later, we had a Catholic nuptial mass followed by a wild reception with all his Foreign Service friends in Frankfurt. Three months pregnant, I was nauseous the whole time. Our beautiful first daughter was born six months later at the military hospital near the Embassy, after a long, long, laborious labor. Jerry resigned from his ten-year Foreign Service career and his foreign intrigue lifestyle, and we sailed home first class on the RMS Queen Mary transatlantic ocean liner. I felt fame by association when past President Dwight Eisenhower and his wife Mamie greeted us while walking the deck, pushing our newborn in a fancy German pram. It was October 1st, 1963, when we docked in New York, exactly four years to the day (October 1st, 1959) after I had arrived in Europe as a student. Thus began our new family life in a small New England town, and the end of Jerry's being able to afford his preferred First Class comforts, although he never gave up his taste for them.

Playing the Role / Sannyasin

To get back to the story of being single once again, let us return to my Osho Commune days, 1991...

When Demetrius asked me to move in with him, I was not interested in cohabitating, and reminded him of my willingness to learn non-attachment. This commune was not the outside world, and I wanted to play the game in a new way, sex without strings. Nevertheless, in the weeks afterwards, when I would see him across the room being hugged by gorgeous Swedes, I would be jealous. I had no reason to be. We were committed to each other on some level, and would meet up at just the right moment to keep me sane, by providing that to which I was becoming accustomed. After two months of all that fun, Demetrius got a call from his ill mother: he had to return to Athens.

Synchronistically, on the day he left, my artist friend Joe arrived from California. I was surprised to see him there, because he had often expressed a negative attitude towards Rajneesh (now known as Osho and less controversial). He believed that many women had been hurt by the libertine atmosphere of his notorious Oregon commune.

Joe had come to save me! I assured him that I had no need to be saved, but making love again felt right. It was the first and only time in my life that I had sex with two different men on the same day. Joe and I picked up where we had left off. We had sex without strings; neither worried about the other. He got involved in the art scene, and I continued my exploration.

◇ ◇ ◇

Feeling as liberated as I did and as motivated as I was, I spent four months at the Osho Commune. Besides the morning meditations and the dances at noon, dozens of classes were offered. They ranged from two days to a month in length, covering many healing modalities and therapies derived from ancient and modern traditions, the gamut of New Age disciplines. It was easy to relate to the teachers, most of whom were Westerners who practiced as therapists in their home countries for most of the year. They returned to Poona in the wintertime, both to instruct and to collaborate/party with other leaders in the Human Potential Movement. Even though they were a colorful clan, they were garbed in black robes with white ties to honor their disciplines. In the classrooms, they stressed Osho-style freedom as prescribed in one of his textbooks called *The Diamond Sutra*: "where ordinary things, taboos, and inhibitions are put aside" in order to concentrate on how to become a Buddha.

I decided to take three courses, the first being an Introduction to Neuro-Linguistic Programming course taught by a bountiful, blazing redhead from Holland. Four weeks is not a long time to learn NLP, but thirty of us, an equal number of men and women (not unusual in multiversity classes), had fun trying. I chose to believe that hypnosis for behavior modification was the way that I could "step into a future of desired outcomes." Surely, understanding the fundamental dynamics between the mind, language, and programming involved in producing the human experience, and using a psycho-scientific methodology termed "modeling," my dreams would come true.

"If any human can do something, so can you," Ma Deva Ishta said, reiterating what I had heard before about reaching enlightenment because many holy humans had done so.

First, it was explained that "the map is not the territory," a major principle of NLP. It is not reality that limits or empowers me, but rather my personal map/perception of reality. That doesn't make my representation of reality wrong. My map is not the territory, as my valid interpretation of truth (my belief) is not the one Truth. Since each of us has all the resources we need within ourselves, we each act from the best choice available to us at that time, hence the importance of creating more choices.

I sat up and took notice as Ma Ishta further taught that all one's actions come from a positive intention in accordance with a person's psychology.

(I should have asked what effect my early belief in original sin had on my psyche.)

Choice and changes and charge, that's what we got as our teacher put us, as a class, under hypnosis twice a day. I welcomed the opportunity to review my beliefs, rewrite my past, and map out the future. Since NLP attracted those who wished to be better salespeople as well as those wanting simply to win friends and influence people (or know the Truth), we were taught how to be in charge. The person with the most flexibility of action was the more empowered person.

"It's most important to pay attention to the response one gets, the feedback from any communication, 90% of which is nonverbal," she said, "All responses are feedback: no mistakes, only outcomes."

OK, what then? We set about to learn a system of how "the complex me and the complex you" interacted and mutually influenced each other as we sought optimal states of balance and homeostasis. We learned to establish and maintain rapport with each other as client and practitioner. That involved much attention to the verbal and nonverbal behaviors which we attempted to match and mirror: fascinating new skills for me.

All my senses were involved as I accessed the movement of the eyes and the body language of a Brazilian man named Miguel, with whom I usually partnered. We got well acquainted with each other's beliefs, problems, and positive intentions as we rehearsed the skills and practiced inducing trance on each other. Hopefully, we helped each other to overcome limiting beliefs and integrate desired behaviors into our real-life situations.

I felt confident putting someone else under trance, especially Miguel, who expressed more than a classmate interest in me. Tempted and as attracted as I was to him, both in and out of trance, we didn't end up in bed. If Joe and I hadn't had such a comfortable relationship at that time, I might have taken up with that beautiful South American. Was my sex chakra finally in balance? Was Joe the extent of my desired outcome? I felt no need to rock what I considered to be my balanced psyche at that time.

◊ ◊ ◊

I had other modalities to explore, beginning with a course in art experimentation with a Japanese artist named Meera. She was the most liberated woman I had ever met, which was unexpected due to my quite different pre-conceived image of Japanese women. This two-week class didn't offer the techniques of painting, but got our creative juices flowing in unusual situations and ways. Whether indoors or outdoors, we usually painted while listening to live or recorded music. We forty male and female students became quite comfortable painting nudes while nude ourselves, all taking turns sketching each other. Meera and a male guest often modeled some creative yogic poses.

One memorable day, we moved to the basement of another building used in previous times for scream therapy. It was a large room with padded walls, but no furniture or windows. We tucked our clothing in cubbies to experience painting in total darkness while in the nude. Before each of us, as we sat on the floor, was a large piece of paper, one paint brush, a container of water and two cups of acrylic paint, one black and one white. The lights went out. There wasn't even an exit sign to be seen. Loud, rhythmic, fast-paced tribal music flooded out of unseen speakers. There was only one suggestion: Meera's encouragement to "Paint... Keep painting... Paint... Keep painting." She said this in an almost trance-like voice.

I didn't get into a trance; I got a bit bored with painting on paper, and started to paint my body with the black and white paint. The contours were more interesting. It was a surprise when the lights came on, and I was the only one who had painted both on and off the paper. We were told to keep painting, and the law of monkey-see / monkey-do took over. Soon some of us were painting each other. Have you ever had the urge to paint a partner's penis black, or to add color to another body part you would like to accent? Not long after, six of my fellow body painters lifted me up over their heads and paraded me around the room until Meera directed us to the showers. There we played some more, washing and scrubbing each other, leaving our classmates to clean up the cell.

The next day, during our discussion of the previous experiment, Meera commended me for my originality and called me a "volcano ready to explode." Because she was such an outrageously wild and extremely dramatic teacher, I found the remark flattering. Meera admitted she was seldom upstaged.

◇　◇　◇

December is the anniversary month of Osho's passing and a time of cele-bration. The Brazilians were especially visible and at their best orchestrating a Rio-like carnival parade, which took us out the commune's gates and through the streets surrounding it. Their floats and costumes were outstanding, espe-cially the one where they portrayed themselves as wine-worshipping follow-ers of Bacchus celebrating drunkenness. There was enough skin showing, and behavior wild enough, to give the hordes of locals who had gathered to observe the festivities certain proof that we were indeed uninhibited, if not doomed.

For my role as part of Ma Meera's class of mad artists dressed / half-dressed in our paintings, I also made a huge long-handled paintbrush to carry, and wings to wear in an effort to portray myself as a good fairy.

Tapping parade onlookers on the shoulder with my paper brush prop, I wished them well.

"Let there be more color in your life," my fairy self said. Many of the Indians whom I tapped and looked in the eye turned away as if I were invad-ing their space, which I was. The person who was videotaping the parade, however, must have been impressed because he captured me full face and figure, giving me my fifteen (or more likely five) seconds of fame on film. I appreciated my creativity when the video of the parade, with me in it, was shown the following evening in the Buddha Hall.

After that, I thought I'd better get back to a more contemplative space. "Mystic Rose" was purported to be one of the most revolutionary meditation courses Osho ever offered. We met in silence for three morning hours for three weeks, and were expected to remain so outside of the sessions as well. Others respected our space as we wore buttons which read "I am in silence."

Osho emphasized that anything and everything (even emotional release), could become an opportunity for meditation. The first half of each session the first week was spent listening to mood music and allowing ourselves to cry. Sometimes it was forced; mostly it was contagious. The latter half of each session was spent in silent meditation.

The second week was for laughing, which was initiated by making funny faces or weird body movements to bring on a belly laugh. We laughed the hardest on the day when we all tickled and rolled over each other. That probably wasn't what Osho had in mind, but it was my favorite session.

For the third week, we met in a quiet space for the Vipassana silent sitting practice of watching the breath and allowing our thoughts to just pass over. There was so much chatter in my head that it was more like I was observing myself as one of the so-called crazy people seen on the streets talking to themselves. I held high expectations for the experience but was disappointed (again) at not having achieved the promised transformative result. I returned with renewed enthusiasm to doing the regularly scheduled movement meditations on the hour in Buddha Hall.

Despite the "Mystic Rose" disappointment, I was not disenchanted with Osho and his unusual techniques for spiritual growth. After all, didn't he, as the initiator, even laugh at himself and deconstruct his own authority, often declaring his own teaching to be a game or a joke? It didn't matter. I was enjoying playing the game with everybody else.

My next thoughts had to do with the disciple decision. Looking into the process, I felt it was time to interview for the initiation to become a sannyasin, and went to Room 4 in the Osho Meera building to do so.

"The only thing is," I told Ma Prem Amira, the black robed, tousled blonde-crowned interviewer, "as much as I appreciate his teachings and this commune, I can't promise to pledge unwavering devotion to Osho."

Ma just smiled as she looked over my completed single page application which lay on the coffee table between us. I glanced at the guru's hundred or so book titles on the shelves behind her.

"Guru worship is not what it's about," she responded confidently, having heard that statement before. "It's about pledging devotion to freedom and awareness; can you agree to that?"

Affirming "of course" verbally to her was no problem. I was just double-checking to make sure that, as a disciple/sannyasin, I wouldn't have to turn my fortune over to the guru.

Noting my agreement, she continued, "According to your paperwork, you completed three courses here at our Multiversity, not that that is necessary to take sannyas. I am glad to read that you found the class work and our daily hourly meditations in Buddha Hall so inspiring. That's why millions of seekers from around the world come to immerse themselves in the 'energy of the buddhafield,' as it is called. Even though Osho left his body just two years ago, his presence is still here, greater than before, as he said it would be. You will probably feel the collective potency of this unique place even more during and after the ceremony. Shall I put you on the list for the Initiation Celebration next Saturday?" she asked, picking up her clipboard.

Properly registered, I got excited about the upcoming event, especially the spiritual naming part. The shared preface for women was Ma and for the men, Swami. I was hoping to get a Ma Deva rather than a Ma Prem name, knowing that was up to whatever higher power arranged such things. (I had trouble believing Osho picked it out for me personally from beyond the grave.)

On the assigned Saturday morning, I sang as I slipped on the best of my three maroon robes. It was fresh and only slightly faded after being beaten clean on the river rocks and ironed with a non-electric iron filled with hot coals, all for the price of a few rupees. I gave extra attention to my makeup, even put on mascara, and wrapped the new Kashmir shawl, purchased special for the occasion, over my shoulders.

I entered Buddha Hall on that clear January 12th, 1992, where the specifically-created live music moved me more than usual. The fifty or so others who were also taking sannyas also looked quite devoted as they sat listening. I took my assigned seat and pondered Osho's definition of discipleship from the Heart Sutra that got me to this time and place.

"Sannyas is just the seed beginning of a totally different kind of world where people are free to be themselves, where people are not constrained, crippled, paralyzed, where people are not repressed, made to feel guilty, where joy is accepted, where cheerfulness is the rule, where seriousness has disappeared, where a non-serious sincerity or playfulness has entered." Having seen such a lifestyle mirrored around me for the past four months, how could I turn it down?

I pondered that until it was time for me to approach the slight platform. I leaned forward to have the mala placed over my head and around my neck, as well as to receive the blessing from the same Ma Prem Amira who had interviewed me.

With those 108 beads and a picture of Osho over my heart, I heard, "Blessings, Ma Deva Ashni."

I liked the sound of my new name and was told it meant "divine flash of lightning," a reminder of the sweet impermanence of all things. But even that name was impermanent, it appears, for upon looking it up in present time on the Osho website, I learn that Ashni actually means "woman who has been blessed." (It is the name "Asho" that means divine flash of lightning.) Was there a mistake or have I received a new reality to embrace?

What was, was; what is, is. After the ceremony, friends presented flowers; there were hugs all around. We danced and I was giddy.

I also felt quite special until I thought about the concept of pride. The Deva name signified specialness to me, which was a separating thought. So much for Oneness. Reading of others' experiences with the Neo-Sannyas initiation, I judged that I hadn't gotten it: the vision, the commitment, the potentiality. Or did I? I will let St. Peter make that decision at the Pearly Gate. But I was hardly ready for that saintly evaluation. I felt I had miles yet to go on this spiritual journey.

◇ ◇ ◇

Contemplating where to go next, I decided to "ask" Osho and stopped by the area called Samadhi, a six foot long, five-foot-tall marble monument holding Osho's ashes. As I walked into the courtyard, I reviewed one of his quotes about his teachings: "I am not here to convince you about anything. I am not here to give you a dogma, a creed to live by. I am here to take all creeds away from you because only then will life happen to you. I am not giving you anything to live by. I am simply taking all the props away from you, all crutches."

To pay my respects to this deceased self-proclaimed non-teacher, I walked in silence around the imposing burial platform which was surrounded by flowers. A plaque read:

OSHO
Never Born
Never Died
Only Visited this

Planet Earth between
Dec 11 1931 – Jan 19 1990

What did that mean? Was that true only for gurus? I decided when I finally believed the universality of this statement and got closer to my final resting place, that I would request the same never-never message on my memorial. Would I have many more "visits"? Did I even believe in reincarnation? How many years have I left on this "visit"?

Pondering the future, I went over to the Communications Center to check my mail. A letter from my daughter Dianna had just been delivered.

Twenty-One

Dianna in India

"Dear Mom, I want to visit you in India. Can you fit me in your plans? I've decided to come down from my 29th floor perch here in Boston and take a similar job with Coopers in California. Before I leave for the West Coast, though, I would appreciate an Eastern world experience with you."

This unexpected request was my answer as to what to do next. The universe once again provided just what both mother and daughter needed.

It was a delight and a wish come true to greet Dianna in New Delhi a couple of weeks later.

"I have to admit, Mom, that I have been having anxiety attacks. My doctor has put me on Klonopin. The prescription seems to be helping, but what's really healing for me is this trip, and being with you before moving to the new job in San Diego. I plan to have a good time here for four weeks. I especially want to get over my symptoms. Robert is flying over then, and we will head to Butan together to trek."

Because I had experienced such shock on first arriving in the seventh largest country of the world, I did my best to prepare my professional daughter for this sometimes uncomfortable culture by starting out with top tourist attractions. Visiting Agra and the white marble Taj Mahal mausoleum with its reflecting pools and ornamental gardens is always a gift, as is riding an elephant up to the hilltop Amber Fort in the Pink City of Jaipur. (I later realized how unhealthy it is for the elephants.) It was exciting to plan our visit to Pushkar in the colorful state of Rajasthan where the famous Camel Fair is held.

Having ridden a camel in the golden desert there on my previous trip with Joe (neither time in Camel Fair season), I headed directly to a particular stall to hire the gentleman who had taken me on such a marvelous arid and sandy tour the winter before.

"I always thought I wanted to take an overnight trip into the desert on camelback and to camp under the stars," I admitted to Dianna, "but three hours on those hard humps was quite enough. It felt like a true desert experience, just me and the brightly turbaned local who led my camel out on the sands, weaving in and out of the buffalo villages and herds of goats in the hills. Did I ever show you the picture of me at our rest spot where I stretched out on the sand eyeball to eyeball with my camel, who was also so reclined? I loved that moment."

I recognized the stall right away, but my previous guide was not there. "Oh, that old man retired," the young attendant said, "but my partner and I will take you on the same trip for the same price. Come see the camels." We couldn't resist the looks of those beasts of burden, especially after finding one was named "Pepsi Cola" and the other called "Coke."

The problem began soon after we handed over our rupees. First, each of the young men climbed up on the camel behind each of us "for your safety" they said, "just as described in the brochure." (This was different from what I remembered.) Secondly, the camels didn't seem to like the two young, greener guides, disobeyed their directions, and even spat on them. Even before leaving town, the camels, instead of going forward, backed up into prickly bushes, in an attempt to dismount the handlers, I supposed. Neither appeared hurt, but Dianna and I couldn't relax.

Once out in the desert, I got upset when the camels started running; my daughter was terrified. Even the rest stop in the dunes was a failure because, as Dianna recalls, my "Coke" camel rolled over on me as I dismounted. I must have repressed that memory.

After that fiasco, we didn't look back as we sought out some comfort food and started shopping in the colorful stalls along the amazing market road. My eldest spent over two hours happily picking out the perfect handmade meditation-size rug as a gift for her fiancé. The shopkeeper was most attentive and even offered to mail it to Robert in Boston for her. She gave him the address, paid the extra agreed-upon amount for postage, and asked him to pose for a photo holding the chosen 2'x4' carpet, which he did. Dianna and Robert now have the photograph, but not the purchase. It was never shipped. Dishonest of them; naive of us. Not a good day.

◊ ◊ ◊

Happier is our memory of the women of Rajasthan, who, whether working in the fields or in the markets, were most appealing in their brightly-printed, red skirts, mirrored tops, embroidered shawls and heavy silver jewelry. I giggled with delight when we stopped to observe the snake charmer on the corner and pose for a picture with him.

"Would madame like to hold the snake?" Sure she would. Camera snap.

On one of our bus trips, Dianna appeared shocked and displeased with me because I threw a banana peel out the window of the bus.

"I don't care if everybody else litters, I didn't expect it of you," she said. Like the liberal trying to get a point across to a conservative, I replied in my own defense, "It's customary in India to share with the cows and monkeys in this way. See them waiting outside the window."

◊ ◊ ◊

Our only other glitch happened at a train station where, disregarding my suggestion, she decided, "No, we will not buy first class tickets. We'll do what you normally do: simply reserve seats in the women's coach for our trip up north. It'll be fine."

We were the first to board the train for the trip north to the Himalayas, and gladly took seats next to the window and opposite to each other. It wasn't long before our so-called reserved, six-women compartment filled with five Indian women, three children, and what appeared to be their life's possessions. The family men, out in the hall with standing room only tickets, added their packs to the pile. It grew more and more uncomfortable to the point that Dianna wanted to call the porter to complain about the "overbooking."

I convinced her that this is "how it is." I wanted to add, "I told you so" regarding my wish to purchase first class tickets, but I didn't. She was probably thinking about that anyway.

The children were fascinated with their seatmate and couldn't help touching her white cheeks and beautiful hair while trying to make conversation, all while finishing their curry and rice, which they were eating with their hands.

When the men crowded at the door to share the food and greet the children, Dianna teared up, and then started silently sobbing. All I could do was to keep handing her tissue after tissue, which to my surprise she threw out of the window one by one in a disgruntled way.

About an hour later, Dianna simply stopped with the tears and the Kleenex, sat up straight, and even began to communicate with our numerous compartment-mates.

I didn't comment about her behavior until months later when I mentioned the incident, suggesting she initially acted like the ugly, entitled American.

"Mother," she retorted, "I am not that uncouth! I may have acted as you say, but that event was a major transformative experience for me." And so it was. I apologized and really heard her tell that story in her own way.

Traveling further north, we arrived in Dedra Dun, set in the foothills of the Himalayas. Our destination was the Himalayan Institute, a brand-new health facility founded by Swami Rama.

Mother and daughter accepted the invitation to enroll as the only trial guests; the clinic had not yet officially opened. This part of the Swami Rama Ashram was specifically built to support the health of the holy men in the Himalayas, located close as it was to the spiritual sites of Haridwar and Rishikish. For this pre-opening week, however, the new yoga teacher held private sessions for us and the cook experimented on us with his menus. Dianna was glad to consult with the on-staff neurologist about her anxiety attacks and was even given an appointment with Swami Rama's personal homeopath. He recommended a remedy called Tarantula, a first for her. Such intervention was so successful that my healed daughter went on to study that alternative medical method when she moved to London (instead of California) the following year. She became a licensed homeopath, to the benefit of all who know her.

On our return to the south, I planned a stop in Poona to do bank business and to arrange for Dianna to tour the Osho Commune. She was resistant to visiting because she felt it would be condoning the ex-Oregon-renegade-guru Rajneesh (Osho's former persona) who had notoriously gotten in trouble for his excesses.

I gave her the brochure describing the Osho Commune International as "a great experiment in Buddhahood... a pure land, an unworldly world, a paradise on earth which offers ideal conditions for rapid growth," etc, etc. Then I practically insisted she take the hour tour: "I stayed here happily for four months, and I really think this orientation is a way for you to better understand my experience. I'll meet you back at the German Bakery in an hour."

Having reluctantly agreed, she departed and left me drinking tea and nibbling on marzipan. One hour passed and then another as I ordered more tea and an apfelstrudel. Satiated and a bit concerned, I headed to the commune entrance, peeked in the orientation room, and found Dianna immersed in deep conversation with one of the black-robed teachers. When she saw me, she quickly said goodbye to the staff member, and joined me for an unusually uncommunicative train trip back to the outlying village where we had planned another week long "nature cure."

We sat down the next morning to complete the registration when Dianna surprised me. She had changed her mind and wanted to return to Poona and the Osho Commune. I agreed it was a great idea. I had no problem with her going there and my staying at the health spa. A week later, I went to the Commune and found her looking quite fetching in her maroon robe. No, she was not interested in going to Bodhgaya with me for a Vipassana retreat. That was the end of traveling in India with my daughter, which was OK, because I loved seeing my firstborn being kinder to herself.

Dianna stayed at the Osho Commune for a few weeks, taking lots of courses and experimenting as one does at that time in that space. When next I saw her, I found that my anxious and anorexic daughter was now curved and comfortable with her new self. I was fortunate to see her do well performing as one of the Gurdjieff class participants in Buddha Hall.

Shortly after that her fiancé arrived. I waved them off at the train station as they departed for Bhutan. Now married, the two have become three, blessing me with a lovely redheaded granddaughter.

Twenty-Two

Off to Africa

With Dianna and Robert off to Bhutan on their reunion, I decided to make another adventure of the need to renew my visa once again and headed for the great continent of Africa. I would take care of this business at the Indian Embassy in Nairobi, Kenya, on the east coast where I had always wanted to go. On the flight from New Delhi to Nairobi, the capital and largest city, I thought how different our family life would have been if my husband, who was stationed in Frankfurt, Germany at the time of our marriage, had made the decision to accept an African post instead of resigning from the US Foreign Service.

It was important for me to remember, however, that he was not offered Kenya as an assignment, but rather one of the other 54 countries, the land-locked Chad, referred to as the Dead Heart of Africa, due to its distance from the sea and largely semi-desert climate. In the 1960's, long before it became an oil exporting country from which it stood to benefit, Chad was (and reportedly still is) unstable, violent, and poor, mainly stemming from tensions between its Islam and Christian religious factions. Instead of accepting the assignment and settling in what was considered a hardship post, Jerry chose to move our new family of three back to New Hampshire, his home state. I had no objection. Since I didn't see any of Africa then, I felt great about visiting at least a part of the continent now as a single woman, 27 years later.

It was a gift to go to a country at zero-degree latitude on the equator, even if that dividing line or the famous Lake Victoria or Mount Kenya weren't on my itinerary. I planned to do the necessary paperwork and to visit Greta and Jared, the German friends I had made at the Osho Commune, who had invited me to their adopted country.

Disembarking in Nairobi, I headed straight for the Indian Embassy to renew my visa for another six months, the longest period allowed at that time. With the business completed, except for picking up the papers the next day, I headed to the market streets where I looked at and touched everything from soapstone knick-knacks, beaded jewelry, baskets made from sisal and leather, to teak and ebony carved animals. I wanted but didn't buy the brass bells and African drums. I only opened my purse to purchase three cotton sarongs, finding the colorful patterns worn by the African women attractive and irresistible (the prints and dyes however, never quite fit in once leaving their country of origin – until decades later when I discovered African drumming, and wrapped myself in them for class). It was best for me, finding the scene a bit frightening, to be at the hotel by dusk. Nairobi felt too strong, tribal, and masculine for me, compared to what I considered to be the softer feminine energy of India.

On the morning of the third day on this continent, I set out to visit my host couple with whom I had recently shared the NLP/Osho experience. They resided on the Indian Ocean coast, and I was happy to camp in their beachfront yard for a week. The tides were extra low and extra high on the coral barrier reef during this beautiful Easter's full moon time, and I absorbed as much of the sea, sand and sun as my skin could tolerate. Greta shared how to shop for food in the market. Jared convinced me that a Land Rover was superior to a Land Cruiser for *bunda bashig*, off-road driving, which I got to experience during my next venture.

"Naturally, you want to go on safari," my hosts suggested, nominating both Lake Nakuru and the Masai Mara National Parks. Following up on the opportunity to fulfill another long-held dream, I signed up for a five-day trip (much too short) which involved camping out in the bush beneath an abundance of sky. I was reminded of my peaceful nights in New Mexico under canvas, albeit a less magnified version, while listening to the chorus of animal sounds entertaining me.

My safari involved lots of driving in a Land Rover pop-up under clear skies in this normally rainy season. It was a time of drought and that meant much suffering and famine for those residing here. The trips were scheduled early and late in the day, so as to catch both sunrises and sunsets, when the animal sightings were best. We saw pelicans and thousands of pink flamingos by the lake, with baboons on the cliff above.

I'd seen wonderful animal photos and films, but real live eyeball watching was truly awesome. Not threatened by the tourist traffic to which they had become accustomed, the animals went about their lives, to our delight. True to the advertisement, we saw a lioness with a cub in her mouth sauntering down a path, cheetahs feeding, giraffes nibbling on the tree tops, zebras running, impalas bouncing, and a leopard sleeping in a high tree. I heard warthogs snorting, saw a rhino and her baby bathing in a water hole, and watched in wonder as herds of elephants and buffalo moved along their ancient paths.

I had to be told that the strange sculptures I saw were termite mounds, and that the beautiful upside-down trees were called baobabs. The yellow fever trees were especially vibrant, and served as perches for vultures signaling that an animal was feeding nearby. The black male ostrich and brown females walked with flapping wings to keep cool. The slim white egrets rested on feeding buffalo, just as I had first observed in India. I loved seeing the vivid blue swallows and was impressed by the eagle's wingspan. The weaver birds had intriguing hanging nests, which also fascinated me in India. Bougainvilleas were in full bloom, as was the generously flowering African Flame tree. I'm only sorry that such a safari has been just a once-in-a-lifetime experience for me.

One sighting was especially exciting. On this particular early morning tour, a magnificent, graceful cheetah started running alongside the front wheel of our Land Rover, which was not unusual for this particular animal, our guide said. "Che-Che often positions herself like this in order to get closer to her prey before the ambush. Even though she is the fastest cat, she is not capable of a prolonged chase; she has learned this adaptation to ensure food for her cubs. Watch as she dashes out ahead of us, as we get closer to this herd of gazelles." And so it was: we saw enacted in front of us an example of the survival of the fittest or, at least, what it took for this most clever beast.

At this time, the international press horror stories of Kenyan discontent and violence over inflation and the hardships caused by the conflict in the

Middle East, the drought, a shortage of fuel, and the tension of upcoming elections may have been real, but bad as it was, the populace appeared to be carrying on a normal day to day existence. Humans are so adaptable. My life is richer having shared some of theirs.

◁ Twenty-Three ▷

I Do What I Can

It was May, 1992. Being "home-free" in India was feeling really good. The sannyas seed of freedom was still with me; my work ethic was no more. Instead of a career commitment and paying a mortgage, I had only to decide where to go next to save my soul and make the most of my savings.

"I feel flexible in my mind," I told the intake person at a small Hindu ashram in a rural setting near Poona where I decided to commit to the study of hatha yoga. "But I have always been physically quite stiff," I added, arguing for my limitations.

"You have come to the right place," the yogi said, "This is a center which does research on the medical benefits of yoga, besides being a teacher training center. You will find that the instructors meet the needs of all of our students, no matter what their skill level. In the four weeks that you will be in the training program, you will learn the adaptations of hatha yoga postures which are beneficial for all."

I was one of eight Westerners, all middle-aged women, among some sixty Indian students of both genders, most in their twenties. Men and women were taught separately and housed in separate dorms. Since we eight foreigners paid more and probably expected more, we were given single rooms and had a special dining area. We became good friends while practicing and taking long walks in the hills together. Later in the year, some of us met up at other yoga centers.

I found the two hours of asana practice daily as helpful as advertised. The four hours of yogic philosophy, however, offered in the heat of the day, were particularly difficult. Being taught by straight lecture reflected the oral teaching tradition of India, which better suited those students raised as auditory learners. There was one exception: the engaging instructor named Omaja who presented the lectures on Patanjali's Eight Limbs of Yoga, a science which had been around since approximately 200 AD.

Because of Omaja's comprehensible and interesting lecture style (not to mention his yogic presence and bright brown eyes), I began to grasp the Yamas and the Niyams, those universal morals and personal observances, without having them cast in stone like the Ten Commandments (or even written on a chalkboard). He reviewed the reasons for hatha yoga postures (Asana) and breathing (Pranayama) exercises. After being in his classes, I wanted to learn more about inner withdrawal (Pratyahara), Dharana (single pointed focus), Dhanna (absorbed meditation) and union with the Divine (Samadhi), which were the last four limbs of yoga. As good as the lessons were, however, it was not enough for me to even want to attempt to get certified as a yoga teacher. I left a few days early (is there a pattern here?), feeling uninterested in taking the final test required for completion. I was being drawn elsewhere.

I may not have checked off that effort as a total success, but I was aware that no trip to India would be complete without a visit to Varanasi, the oldest and one of the holiest of cities. Observing the purifying rituals along the western bank of Mother Ganga where this religious hub was built felt important to me. Call it macabre curiosity if you will, but I wanted to see the burning *ghats*, the riverside ceremonial cremation platforms on which the bodies were placed. Not believing that death was contagious, I knew I could handle observing others go through their final cremation transformation.

One did not need a tour guide to find a funeral service in the holy city that people were dying to go to. Hindus believed that expiring in Varanasi was auspicious, as it offered moksha, the liberation from the cycle of rebirth. I followed a procession of male mourners, close relatives I was told, down an alleyway. In the lead were eight men dressed all in white carrying a decorated brier on their shoulders. The corpse was said to be dressed in new clothing, which I couldn't vouch for, covered as it was in flowers and garlands. After traveling through a myriad of narrow streets, we arrived at the river and at one of nearly 100 burning ghats on its bank.

The body was placed on the pyre, a raised concrete-looking platform, and covered with wood carried by the processioners to the site. From a respectful distance, I watched as the designated chief mourner circled the body five times, once for each of the elements: air, fire, water, earth and ether, before lighting the fire. As the only woman in the area on this moonlit night, I didn't stay the usual three hours (sometimes longer) that it took for the body's transformation into smouldering ash. I left soon after I was shocked to observe an attendant hit the skull of the deceased with a rock, startled as I was by the loud crack meant to release the spirit to Divinity, unity with Brahman. It would have been quite a sight if I had had the proper vision.

I went back the next morning. While standing on the riverside, a Dutch couple generously offered to take me along in the rowboat they had rented to observe the ghats from the Ganga perspective. We watched the white-garbed caretakers, the so-called lower caste Indians assigned to the cleanup aspects of this ritual, at their labors. My fellow tourists shared what they had learned about the supposed thousands of flesh-eating turtles that were released into the river. Their role was to consume the partially intact bodies of those from families too poor to purchase enough wood to complete the task of cremation. (I learned recently that there are no more turtles in the river because they were all killed by hunters for meat.) As we cruised along, noting how close the bathing ghats were to the burning ones, I decided not to do a ritualistic bath in the waters as the residents and Hindu pilgrims felt blessed to do.

Twenty-Four

Back to the Himalayas

As fascinated as I was with Tibetan Buddhism, far-off Lhasa, Tibet, was not on my list of likely visits, but Dharamsala, India, ranked high and felt more realistic a mission. I made plans to meet Joe there.

I boarded the night train north to the Himalayas, grateful to have a respite from the heat of the lowlands. Wheels followed rails as I caught a bus to this "Tibet in Exile," a Himachal Pradesh hill station where the Dalai Lama, monks, and other displaced Tibetans had taken refuge after escaping from their Chinese-occupied homeland three decades ago. Since Joe knew the ropes from previous visits, I followed his suggestions and shared his enthusiasm for this ancient Buddhist culture.

"We'll stay at McLeodGanj, a pleasant village a few kilometers away, where most Westerners stay while studying Buddhism," Joe decided. It was wise to have brought only a daypack, as we walked up over a hundred steps to get to our hotel in this cantilevered community. En route, we paused for many minutes on the street, enraptured by the chanting of the Gyuto monks who were also housed in this area.

"We can bus back and forth for Tibetan Buddhist classes in Dharamsala if you are interested," Joe suggested. Of course I was, especially as they were offered at the Dalai Lama's mountaintop temple where he was currently in residence. This also afforded many opportunities to circumnavigate the temple on the prayer path which circles His Holiness' home and the monastery which houses many monks.

My steps were meditative, and I felt like we were being blessed as we walked the level, pebbled path as so many had done before us. It was lined by "Chud do," smooth medium and small stone offerings inscribed with chiseled prayers, each letter darkened to stand out. (I resisted pocketing one.)

It was energizing, being in that high altitude ambiance, strolling among the reverent, smiling Tibetans with close-cropped hair, as they fingered their prayer beads while reciting mantras. We observed many of the elderly, all wearing the traditional dress, turning the prayer wheels, spinning their petitions to the heavens multiple times.

We followed the red-robed monks climbing up and down the hills on their way to practice playing their long Tibetan horns at a higher elevation. We sat near them on the grass and took pleasure in listening, while watching the changing cloud formations over the bald peaks of the Himalayan mountains. Angelic are the ancient sounds of these ceremonial trumpets, often compared to the singing of elephants. Before leaving, the monks folded their horns in telescope style to one-quarter their length for transport.

Intermingling easily with the other casually clad Westerners, we trusted that because of the presence of so many of us, the Tibetans would prepare menus to satisfy our palates. Although the porridge, scrambled eggs, and sandwiches looked and tasted good, we were warned that it was not always prepared in the most sanitary conditions. Many got sick, although Joe and I were fortunate not to have any digestive problems.

There was another issue with the restaurant business which was less palatable. Disturbing was the fact that the waiters were always children, some as young as ten. India, with its widening gap between the rich and the poor, is reported to be the home of the largest number of child laborers in the world, according to childlineindia.org.in. Offspring were sent to Dharamsala to support themselves and hopefully send money home to even poorer families in the more rural areas. Accounts from people concerned with the problem reported that many never saw their parents again. The youth remained uneducated and worked 12-14-hour days. Saddened by the situation, we acknowledged their efforts and tipped them well as a gesture to support them (and to alleviate our consciences).

Other than that social-economic situation, I resonated with the culture, finding the people, the geography, the prayer flags and temples beautiful. Joe and I visited the Tibetan Children's School, which was established to care for and educate some of the many orphans and destitute Tibetan children. There the elders taught them to throw pots, to hand-knot carpets, to carve prayers into wood blocks for printing, and to paint intricate tankas on canvas, as well as to create larger mandala paintings on walls. We spent a couple of days just watching these artists. I developed a great appreciation for the dedication of the teachers and students. It was fascinating to be with the artists who concentrated, undisturbed by our staring over their shoulders, while painting the detailed, colorful, holy images on the temple walls.

Joe later commissioned one young artist to paint the image of the teaching Buddha on smooth three-inch oval rocks similar to those from the prayer path. (Not sure where he found them.) He gave me one that I still have on my altar, now resting on a small pouch made of hand-woven Tibetan fabric. I wanted one of everything from the school store, and once again almost wished I was on a shopping trip as well as a spiritual journey. Two exceptions to my "buy-not / carry-not" philosophy were my purchase of a woodcut plaque of the mantra "Om Mani Padme Hum" and a book of line drawings of thangka paintings. When I returned to America years later, I used the pictures as models for fabric wall hangings I created of the Buddha and the Green Tara.

His Holiness was in town, and Joe and I, along with a small group of other visitors, only had to wait a couple of days to be granted an audience with him. He just smiled his sweet smile as he blessed the tiny Buddha statue I carried and a soft white silk scarf that I had presented to him as is the tradition. He first placed it around his own neck before returning it to me. One of his assistants tied a red string around our wrists, which signified having received the Dalai Lama's blessing. In the presence of His Holiness, who is perceived as seeing only the loving and the loveable, I had to ask myself, "Was this loveliness really mine?"

Our stars were aligned just right to allow our presence at His Holiness' 57th birthday celebration on July 6th, 1992 (less than a month after I turned 56). He. presided over a puja ceremony of body, mind and spirit purification with great pomp and circumstance. It was just as pictured in National Geographic magazine or on film: primal, colorful, ethnic and unique – only better because I was standing there on hallowed ground next to devout Tibetans in the energetic aura of the greatest living Buddhist teacher.

The Nangyal temple's high ceiling and pillars were hung with brocaded, silk-tasseled scrolls of thangka paintings. The walls were frescoed with a pantheon of Buddhas, deities, saints and demons brightly pigmented and highlighted with gold paint. In the courtyard, musicians from the local Tibetan Institute of Performing Arts Temple, wearing beautiful fur, brocade, felt and silk costumes, presented a lively song, dance and instrumental program depicting legendary stories, rituals and spiritual teachings. Following that, row after row of monks, seated around the Dalai Lama inside the temple, started chanting, ringing bells and blowing horns, a ritual that went on for hours in clock time but not in Here Now grace.

◇ ◇ ◇

Invigorated by all that inspiration and fresh mountain air, Joe and I, wanting even more, began to practice the Tibetan Five Rites, five energizing exercises that, when done daily, were said to be all that one needed in order to be strong and healthy forever (how's that for a takeaway?). While we were diligently doing what was necessary and waiting for the dramatic increase in physical strength, suppleness and mental activity, we decided to hedge our bets a bit. We welcomed the opportunity to make an appointment with Dr. Yeshi Dhonden, the Dalai Lama's personal physician for years. Tibetan medicine is believed to be empowered by the Blue Medicine Buddha, known as the "Doctor of the World" who cures Dukkha (suffering), using the medicine of his teaching. The pills the doctor prescribed were blessed in preparation by the reciting of mantras to overcome mental, physical and spiritual sickness, and for the purification of negative karma.

We joined other patients in his waiting room. An hour later we were directed to a simple office, where this most renowned and experienced practitioner of Tibetan medicine was sitting next to an interpreter who signaled us to sit down.

"Dr. Dhonden will tell you your constitutional type and prescribe the proper pharmaceuticals simply by reading your pulses."

I observed the kind-looking and busy Tibetan doctor closely as he took my hand and "listened" to the rhythms he felt in my fingers and the rest of my hand. He looked at me only once and asked only a couple of questions about my parents, if I remember correctly. I was confident that his prescription would be exactly what I needed because he was reciting the healing mantra while making his diagnosis.

Joe received that same attention, and we met in an adjoining room to collect our pills. They were carefully counted out and wrapped in paper bags which I marked a.m., noon, p.m. It cost a pittance for a three-month supply, and we were given an address for reorders. We took out our water bottles and consumed our first doses of 20 pills each. Even though the meds came from about three different bottles, they all looked and tasted the same: black and bitter. It never became an acquired taste and, in spite of my good intentions, I didn't even finish the first supply before moving on to another cure-all. (Yes, there is a pattern here.)

Similar to what I've heard about multi-vitamin therapy, it is likely true that most people never follow through long or faithfully enough to either be cured or to cause any harm. I belonged to that fickle clan and thereby retained my unpurified state. Without taking responsibility, I decided it was possible that Tibetan medicine works only for Tibetans.

Later that week marked the beginning of the Tibetan Buddhist classes being taught within the sanctified walls of the monastery's library.

"The Buddha bequeathed countless teachings leading to enlightenment – 84,000 paths corresponding to the 84,000 afflictions of sentient beings," an ancient teaching Lama informed us, "and our studies are for the development of the Bodhi Mind, the aspiration to achieve Buddhahood for the benefit of all sentient beings."

As usual, I was excited to begin a new course of study. However, as sincere as I thought I was about attaining Buddhahood for the benefit of all sentient beings, I found many of the teachings too abstract. I was not enough of an intellectual to grasp their significance, even though it was all laid out in precise lists of categories: five Aggravates representing the body and the mind, six Sense Bases, 18 Dhatus, six Paramitas or stages of spiritual perfection, nine realms, 12 Nidanas, and so on and on.

Nirvana tempted me; the ball and chain relationship between karma and the individual scared me. I attempted to stop grasping and clinging to my "self-identification: I, me, myself," without much success. It would take years for me to begin to understand Non-self (Anatta). More obvious were Suffering (Dukkha) and Impermanence (Anicca). As a layperson, I was willing to take Refuge in the three Jewels: the Buddha, the Dharma and the Sangha. I accepted the Four Noble Truths, beginning with "Life is suffering." It was good to be reminded that craving and attachment were the cause of suffering and that "there is an end to suffering" by following the Eightfold Middle Path.

I needed a bit more effort in that "Eight" department. I practiced observation of the Five Precepts after learning that if I kept them, I would be reborn as a human being. I did not want to come back as a cockroach. (Didn't enter my mind that I might not come back at all...) Those five disciplines of liberation: not to kill, steal, engage in sexual misconduct (I didn't consider being with Joe to be sexual misconduct), lie, or use intoxicants, seemed doable. I was surprised that "no stealing" also meant "not taking anything that is not freely given," which would have been the end of my helping myself at family-style meals. These five were relatively easy compared to the eight or ten precepts (which included no dancing or handling of gold or silver) that each monk took early on his path. Later, tradition required hundreds more rules for fully-ordained monks.

I planned to read *The Tibetan Book of the Dead* to understand the world of the six bardos, which are described as the realms of the afterlife between two incarnations. It appeared to take a lifetime of spiritual practice to maintain equanimity during these transitional states. Just how equanimous could I be with my seemingly endless aversions and desires? It was comforting to imagine that I probably had nearly half a lifetime left to get over them. Or would I add on more A's and D's?

What made the most sense to me at the time was the more familiar Vipassana daily meditation offered by a master named Durrani while sitting on the grass-covered, terraced hillside which we shared with the sheep and goats. The concept of "dependent arising" and the "emptiness inherent in all things" became clearer because of our teacher's presentation. I pondered reincarnation: one's present life being only one in a beginningless series of incarnations, each incarnation determined by one's actions in previous lives. I became curious about this Buddhist equivalent of St. Peter's book for "making a list and checking it twice" as we moved onto the next item on our itinerary.

Twenty-Five

Ajanta and Ellora

Joe and I left Dharamsala and traveled south to the interior Indian state of Maharashtra to visit the man-made caves of Ajanta and Ellora, which are architectural marvels of the world. The resident caves were carved into the side of a 250-foot-high, volcanic rock cliff which is horseshoe shaped around the Waghora River gorge. It was possible to imagine myself as a 2nd Century BC merchant welcoming the opportunity to stay in one of the cave temple monasteries while on my trading ventures. I would have been happy to support the Buddhist monks who took up residence there.

Those travelers had the opportunity to observe the artists painting the frescos on the worship hall walls (as we had in Dharamsala) and perhaps gain merit as they walked around the carvers of the columns, stupas and sculptures in the numerous niches and alcoves. The art of many centuries was preserved there: each of the 26 caves housed a representation of the Buddha, either in painting or carving.

We studied seated Buddhas with hands positioned in teaching mudras, hair in a topknot, which was often jeweled (a "cranial bump" representing expanded wisdom). There were images of the spiritual rebirths of the Buddha, but also a profusion of secular motifs: beautiful murals which portrayed well-formed, uninhibited females with elongated eyes and ample adornment. On the ceilings were decorative floral and ornamental motifs, flying figures of celestial beings, deer, pigeons, hawks, peacocks, golden geese, pink elephants and fighting bulls. Around one corner was a monkey, around another, a mad elephant: so many symbols with so many meanings to fuel my imagination (or better still, enhance spiritual vigor).

Protected from the monsoon rains and sharing the cool darkness of the cave interior, the frescos that the monks painted and the images they sculpted are preserved and maintained at this UNESCO Heritage Site. As I look at today's websites revealing the magic of this site (which was discovered accidentally in 1819), I can only marvel that at the time we visited in 1992, we were practically alone in the caves, without fences, without guards, without kiosks – silent and spacious. The whole ambiance was reverent. It felt right to go deep into the caves and walk through the chambers, praying and hearing the echo of our voices as we chanted "Om mani padme hum."

"It's colossal! Incredible!" was all I could say as we entered Cave 26 and saw the seven meter (23 foot) sculpted reclining Buddha. His head, which was bigger than my entire adult body curled in a fetal position, was resting on a pillow with his eyes closed. As a rendition of his last illness, the esteemed one, about to enter Parinirvana, was surrounded by a group of kings, queens and monks who mourned while celestials rejoiced. It was recorded as being carved between 600-800 AD.

Equally incredible was how Cave 26 was aligned to the East. As we moved into the enclosure, I attempted to visualize what it would be like to be standing there at dawn of the summer solstice when the sculpture of the seated Buddha within an elevated stupa would be illuminated by the rising sun. Cave 19 contained another stupa and Buddha statue, this one aligned with the rising sun of the winter solstice. Imagine the whole cave illuminated at these two times of the year (as if our present experience wasn't enough of a wonder of the world!).

Satiated, almost overwhelmed with it all, we ended our visit at the mouth of Cave 16, famous for its ceiling which carried the contour of beams and rafters which were rock-cut so as to appear wooden. After getting a good view of the river from this vantage point, we headed down the slope to the entrance gate. I let Joe know how much I appreciated his taking me there and introducing me to the beauty of the antiquities.

"And there is more," Joe said, as he hinted at another temple near Ellora we were yet to visit.

◇ ◇ ◇

The next day was even more intriguing. Was I really there? Was I so blessed? The most dramatic of all was the Kailasa Temple, the "greatest excavated architectural wonder of the world." Rock-cut, life-sized, three dimensional elephants greeted us on either side of the entrance of the Kailasa Temple, which was almost twice the area and height of the Athens Parthenon. Perhaps we should have flown over the wondrous monument dedicated to Lord Shiva first, as it was said to be visible even from space.

Was this free-standing Hindu temple created by a culture more evolved than modern society (or perhaps one aided by aliens)? I could only imagine the advanced skills and more "know-how" than chisels, hammers, pickaxes and shovels necessary to carve this perfectly engineered two story structure from the top down out of a solid volcanic rock hillside. How did they carry away the 200,000 to 400,000 tons of cut-off rock? (Who knows for sure, anyway?)

Most tour books agree, Kailasa is a monolithic temple, unsurpassed as the largest and most grandiose of such monuments in India. It is an imitation of a constructed building, complete in its external elevation, from basement to tower, and consisting of sequences of internal spaces, from triple open porches and connecting bridges to enclosed shrines. In an inversion of structural practice, it had to be cut out of solid rock from top to bottom, which demanded a deep trench on four sides to expose the massive block of solid rock no less than 33 meters high, which was then chiseled into a semblance of architectural form.

Sculpture is my art form of choice and I couldn't have been happier with this day's exploration of the interior of the temple as well. The guardians of the four directions and the river goddesses appeared at the gateway to the complex. Durga greeted me on the right with Ganesha on the left in the passageway. On one of the panels, elephants were busy bathing Lakshmi, who was seated in a lotus pool. Narrative friezes revealed the gods and goddesses battling with buffalo and elephant demons and monkey armies, along with plenty of attendant maidens and lounging amorous couples. A dancing eight-armed Shiva was carved on a ceiling. A lingam rested on a circular pedestal. Ravana shook Mount Kailash. Shiva and Parvati played dice. (I felt I won the lottery, just being there.)

We came back the next day to explore as much as we could of the 34 other caves. Always recognized as a holy spot, these mountainside sites extended in a north-south line and were representative of three religions: Caves 1-12 were Buddhist, Caves 13-29 were Hindu monuments, and Caves 30-33 were Jain excavations. I spent a great deal of time in front of a wonderful sculpture of the Buddha under the banyan tree, vowing to myself that I would get to Bodhgaya to visit the site of that representation of his enlightenment experience. We ended our visit outside the caves, resting in the monsoon greenery, delighting in the waterfalls and rock pools, thrilled with what we had shared.

Twenty-Six

What Do I Need to Feel Complete?

T hings changed with time, and "shift happened." Joe and I heard enough of each other's histories, and tolerated enough of each other's eccentricities. I was more than ready to let go of the clinging and aversion which danced throughout our relationship. I needed a cure from what were once healing hippie ways, artist's gaze, and good sex. As grateful as I was for the gifts Joe shared with me, it was time to return to a more solitary and settled path. I set off to do a cleanse and moved into a little stone cottage at a Gandhi ashram in the rural village of Uruli Kanchan, not far from Poona. It felt good to sleep alone again.

Before I signed in, I did a little research on Gandhi ashrams: "organic communalized expressions of the concept of withdrawal and renewal which had inspired Thoreau." Mahatma Gandhi "felt his ashrams were his finest achievements because, while self-realization remained the ultimate goal of the ashramite, active service to society was the means to that end." He was determined to promote the concepts of self-help, self-sufficiency and self-care (even cow care) to the isolated, uneducated villagers and to the untouchables. Nevertheless, Gandhi is more renowned to most of us for his nonviolent interventions, revival of hand-spun cotton, fostering active asceticism, and international political achievements.

Established by Gandhi as a health center in 1946 for the application of simple naturopathy for the sound health and hygienic practices most needed by the rural masses, the Uruli Kanchan Nature Cure was a relatively simple ashram when I was there in the early 1990's. (It is now appealing to the well-healed for its more upscale yet still scrupulous attention to diet and its regimen of enemas, sponge baths, wet-sheet and mud packs for the treatment of chronic diseases.)

I settled in for a six week "fast" and met with the naturopath who recommended that I feast only on carrot and spinach or beet juice between two raw fruit meals which I purchased from street vendors. Since the soils were ideal for growing grapes in this area, I enjoyed the purple variety most often. The rest of the cure consisted of big tub baths (rare in India) each morning. Each noon I rested with mud packs on my abdomen, forehead and eyes. I took steam baths in those old-fashioned, sit-in-closets wearing a cold towel on my head. The 6 a.m. yoga sessions and the daily massage in my cottage felt very indulgent. I was also introduced to the medicinal qualities of drinking one's own urine, recommended as a tonic to cure arthritis and its application as a skin softener... probably just as well that I was sleeping alone.

One evening after the chanting session, I went to the library, which more than met my expectations in my quest for materials to further advance my spiritual goals.

"I see that you are reading J. Krishnamurti's *Freedom From the Known*," I heard a voice behind me say.

"Truth be told, I'm just browsing," I replied. "I am a bit overwhelmed with where to begin with this teacher. Perhaps you have some advice?"

Indeed, Mr. Patel, close to Gandhi as a longtime resident of the ashram, as well as having spent time with Krishnamurti, had many suggestions.

"Many start with *The First and Last Freedom*, which is more logically structured than many of this spiritual philosopher's other works. However, for getting clarity 'with' him, observing him speak rather than reading his works might be a better approach. Would you be interested in viewing some of this guru's videoed talks? Many have found that tuning into him in this way is most powerful."

So began my friendship with this wise elder. We met many times to watch videos together during the next six weeks. I asked a lot of questions and became open to the possibility that all that I'd previously thought might have been wrong.

I never did finish reading any of the guru's books. My immersion was in

Krishnamurti's videoed talks, focusing on his words in an attempt to "jump" (transcend) man-made belief systems, nationalistic sentiment, and sectarianism, as he suggested.

Like many others, I didn't really jump very far, making true his observation: "We don't (jump), unless we 'know' (certainty) what's on the other side of the fog, and that it's safe (security)."

However, I had taken some baby steps, agreeing as I did with this Krishnamurti quote, "It is no measure of health to be well adjusted to a profoundly sick society." There was more to do beyond my quest for a geographical cure for all my perceived lacks on this trip to India.

"Tell me about Gandhi," I asked Mr. Patel, who had worked so closely with this world-famous leader in the past.

"Like many others, my wife and I came to Gandhi to observe and stayed to serve. He taught us by personal example. He wanted to improve the health and sanitation of the poor, so he encouraged us to live with the people in the rural areas as he had done, educating them, sharing their burdens and sorrows. This ashram is an example of his teaching in form, although it's changed over the years."

Mr. Patel also talked about nonviolence and Mahatma's teaching of non-cooperation. The resulting withdrawal of citizen support for the institutions of British government was instrumental in bringing about India's independence from Britain.

"What Gandhi saw so clearly was not a way of escape from the world, but of a freedom from self-interest which enabled one to give one's self totally to God and to the world."

I thanked him profusely for his friendship and his guidance before I left the Naturecure. I also had the courage to ask him one last personal question.

"Why is it that you alone, in this community where diet is so emphasized, seem to pay no mind to what you eat?"

Mr. Patel patiently tried to explain to me once again what he called the "inconsequential nature of matter" – that it's all in your mind.

"The mind that sees illusions thinks them real," he said. "They have existence in that things are thoughts. It is your thoughts alone which cause you pain. Nothing external to your mind can hurt you or injure you in any way.

Your mind is powerful. What it has created, it can uncreate." Was this seed thought the kind of nourishment I needed most? It was like a quote from one of my future teachers, Marianne Williamson: "Why continue to have more faith in the power of cancer to kill than in the power of God to heal?"

In future time beyond this experience, I pondered Mr. Patel's behavior and beliefs. I reflected on the all-encompassing nature of Spirit as presented in *A Course in Miracles (ACIM)* and in Mary Baker Eddy's "Scientific Statement of Being" from her book *Science and Health with Keys to the Scriptures*: "There is no life, truth, intelligence nor substance in matter. All is infinite Mind and its infinite manifestation, for God is All in All..."

I so wanted to be cured by Mind alone, as the Christian Scientists seemed able to do, that I registered for a ten-day Practitioner Training Course at the Mother Church in Boston on one of my family visits to Boston years later. This took place after my second surgery for a cancerous tumor in my thigh and six weeks of radiation as the cure. Since I wasn't planning on ever going back to an oncologist again, I turned to Spirit for reassurance. It was indeed a healing experience to study such truths. (Disclaimer here: As similar as the ideas in Mary Baker Eddy's book are to the *ACIM* text, one of the material differences is that the Miracle minder can also accept medicine when recommended, unlike Christian Science which allows doctoring only for broken bones – a concept it took a study of both to grasp.)

Even later, on becoming a student of *A Course In Miracles* upon my return to the States, such truth was presented again in that text as Recognizing the Spirit: "You see the flesh or recognize the spirit. There is no compromise between the two. What you decide in this determines all that you see and think is real and hold as true."

Why is it so difficult to not compromise?

Reading on in *ACIM*: "Salvation does not ask that you behold the spirit and perceive the body not. It merely asks that this should be your choice." It was my choice as I fudged around (compromised?) with seeing myself within a body, while choosing to believe that I was Spirit having a "woman experience."

Back in time in India, once again I sought the next learning that would make the holy difference in my life, perhaps even find the elusive Savior. I did what seekers do: I signed up for another spiritual practice. I was repeating the game plan of my single student days in Europe (and my sabbatical), moving from distraction to distraction whenever I felt the void. What did I need in order to feel complete? Searching was more fun than paying a mortgage and it sure kept me busy. Obviously, I wasn't ready to "transcend my ego and the quest" as one book suggests.

I instead related to a quote from *If You Meet the Buddha on the Road, Kill Him* by Sheldon Kopp: "The only way to be saved is to spend one's lifetime on a pilgrimage. It is the journey itself that is salvation."

That sounded perfect until the author qualified it with a later remark, "Any path is only a path; all paths are the same – they all lead nowhere."

Sooner or later on this circuitous journey with all its lessons in Hinduism as well as Buddhism, I would recognize this and look to the Buddha within for my answers.

On the other hand, most of the Indian teachers I met taught that there were three rare blessings to be secured (and I felt that I had a good chance):

> - 1st, a human birth, a rare privilege after passing through 8,400,000 births in different species – tick! got that,
> - 2nd, cherishing the desire for liberation from transmigration (as opposed to interest in sense pleasures)– well, maybe, somewhat, and
> - 3rd, securing the company and spiritual guidance of an enlightened soul – the rarest opportunity in life.

It was stressed that those who have secured all three blessings should leave no stone unturned till they achieve liberation.

I touched lots of stones. The latest was joining the lifelong yoga practitioner Cristine, my Austrian friend, at the Vivekananda Kendra Center outside Bangalore.

I found their promotion of "positive health with yoga and detoxification by Ayurveda and Naturopathy set in a serene, tranquil and homey atmosphere" to be true (and so much easier.) Southern India felt more feminine and was less crowded and hectic than the north.

It was in reading a book, *The Master As I Saw Him*, published in London in 1910 by Ninedita, "Sister," that I really grew to appreciate Swami Vivekananda, the inspiration for the Center. The author, by bringing forward pages of his life, said that Swami never quoted anything but Vedic scriptures, the Upanishads, and the Bhagavad Gita. This was my opportunity to get an overview of Hinduism as he taught it to Westerners.

"The materialist is right! There is but One, only he calls that One Matter, and I call it God." (So many handles: Love, Christ/Jesus, Truth, Buddha, Allah, Consciousness, Higher Power, Awareness, The Tao...)

Later, the text states, "The many and the One are the same Reality, perceived by the same mind at different times and from different perspectives."

(I think I get it! God is God, the Highest Power/ Reality that endows each of us, who see ourselves as separate beings, with Free Will to put on and change costumes/ handles/churches at will. At this juncture on my path, I tried on Hinduism. As a child I wore the reality of a Catholic. Later, I would know that "anyone can be a Buddha," or a materialist or whatever. How comforting to know that I/we will never leave the One Truth/the same Reality of Who I Am/ Who God Is, regardless of which label I/we wear in human form.)

In the meantime... I learned that the Swami was called the "prophet of happiness" and that his center seemed to exemplify one of his quotes: "By being pleasant you are closer to God than through prayer." I could do that.

Housing at the Center was once again dormitory style; the atmosphere collegiate. Lessons were experiential. When the demonstration on how to swallow eight feet of cloth and expel it to clean the excretory system was given, I did not need to be told not to attempt to do this at home, or to do it without personal guidance at the ashram. I had no plans to try it in this lifetime.

I did, however, experience success inducing vomiting early one morning after drinking lots of salt water on an empty stomach.

Using the neti pot to clear the sinuses was OK, but I soon chose to forget about pulling the cord in and out of my nostrils.

The eye exercises were new to me and easy, but I didn't do them consistently enough to give up my specs.

I never missed the guided stress-release meditations taught by an incredibly appealing Indian yogi named Sukumar, who spent many evenings with the Westerners sharing his handsome self and wisdom on the cool dorm rooftop.

We also did lots of chanting, which prepared me for the visit to the nearby Sivananda Yoga Institute for Shiva's birthday celebration which began at sunset. I was glad to be alive enough to welcome dawn the next day when we broke fast. We had spent the languid hours of an all-night walking ritual in a long line of yogis circling an altar and chanting "Om Namah Shivaya." As proud as I was of having dragged myself through it, I was happier to go to bed.

◇　◇　◇

For Christmas that year of 1992, Cristine and I headed further south to Shantivanam, the ashram of the Benedictine monk and priest Bede Griffith OSB, whose community was a blend of Western Catholicism and Eastern Spiritualism. Beloved for his wisdom and universal heart, Father Bede had the reputation of setting aside time to meet newcomers as the "spark of God."

Anticipating his celebration of the Eucharist on this holy Feast Day, we arrived there in time for Mass in the tiny chapel dedicated to the Holy Trinity, only to find a young Indian priest making the offering. Father Bede was too ill to see anybody.

The British-born octogenarian, whose life was one of service, study, and search for God, was spending the end of his 86 years of life in prayer in a tiny hut, his home in this jungle near the Karery River. Simply to be at this mystic's ashram and to hold vigil outside his window contemplating his life's God realization at this hospice time was heart-opening.

Warmly welcomed at the Tamil Nadu center, we learned more about Father Bede's life work as a leading thinker in the development of dialogue between Christianity and Hinduism. In his autobiography called *The Golden String*, we learned that the Benedictine priest was also a sannyasin and was named Swami Dayananda, meaning "bliss of compassion."

He wrote of free will, "All men must infallibly obey the will of God because the universe is subject to a law of absolute necessity; but we are free to choose whether we should obey willingly or unwillingly. To discern the Divine Will beneath all the events of daily life and to adhere to it with one's own will is the source of all happiness." (Why, in my dedication to Truth, did I need to hear this verbalized so often?)

Twenty-Seven

The Aurobindo Ashram and Auroville

"We are here for the delight of God," Sri Aurobindo had proclaimed, and that delighted me. Cristina and I headed next to his Hindu ashram in Pondicherry and arrived to find this French-settled town south of Madras still strung with Christmas lights. Cristina suggested we rent rooms at a guesthouse called "The Cottage," which was above an incense factory on a single room dorm-like floor endowed with a sandalwood aroma. How sweet was that!

The next day we took the minibus tour through this old French settlement. Here the intellectual guru and his energetic French companion called "Sweet Mother" had built more of an efficient Western-style community than a traditional Indian spiritual sanctuary. More than 2,000 people lived and worked there, joyful in service, meditating and honoring their masters. In one section of the tree-shaded courtyard was the large villa which was the gurus' home for over 30 years. Nearby was the flower-covered shrine called the Samadhi, where two separate chambers held the mortal remains of the beloved teachers. It was a reverent place to meditate from pre-dawn till late in the evening, Cristina said, having gone there many times.

Outside this gated heart of the community were numerous other properties owned by the ashram. Who could ask for anything more than the guest houses for the many international visitors, schools, factory shops for making paper, pottery, leather shoes, and steel metal products? There was a drop-in dispensary, Ayurveda section, and offices for homeopaths and naturopaths, as well as a vision center where patients are taught to relinquish their eyeglasses.

There were suggestions for sun treatments, reading by candlelight or following the pendulum, but I only followed through with palming, which is a great way to "see no evil." (Having just googled the Aurobindo Eye Exercises to remind me of what they are, I am tempted to try them again.)

Pondicherry town also had a bank, a theater, and the Main Post Office where I expected to find mail forwarded to me by friends from my last residences. I frequented the library, the laundry, and the bakery, but didn't get close to the farm or the dairy.

All my meals, served on locally made steel plates, were taken at the dining hall and outdoor patio inside the gates where everyone seemed to congregate sooner or later. The exact same menu was repeated each week: breakfast, lunch and supper of mild vegetarian food: rice, dahl, steamed carrots, potatoes or cabbage, and yogurt. The food plan hadn't changed for decades as Mother had established it. It was believed that because she ordered it, it must be optimum nutrition. Prepared and ladled out with love at a price even the poorest could afford, it was a taste acquired in traditional silence. (I didn't stay long enough to get malnourished or grow superhuman.)

Because Cristine had been there many times, she soon moved on, but I stayed, anxious to see what Aurobindo's practice of Integral Yoga was all about.

It was not about renunciation of the world. The ashram was said to be a human laboratory where the Supermind was being called down to bring about a super race, a new type of Gnostic beings. This evolution of a higher spiritual cosmic consciousness was for everyone; a goal of perfection not meant for just a few individuals, nor one country. How very democratic...

The teachings were a combination of all the old systems, because the whole being had to be trained to bring the human into a divine life. Herein was the hope for a more harmonious evolving order.

Fascinated and willing to be one of the above superhumans (while remembering being taught that just being human is a rare blessing), I figured I'd win either way.

I went to the library built in a French architectural style to find out more. I picked one of Sri Aurobindo's books from a dark wooden shelf, sat down on a tufted couch facing one of the arched windows, and started to flip through the pages.

Highly intellectual and classically trained, Aurobindo was a prolific poet and author, had a rich Indian cultural heritage, had mastered Sanskrit and many Indian languages, and was steeped in all the great religions as well as being politically conscious. I didn't expect that I would find his writings difficult. His methods did not proceed from any set mental teaching or prescribed forms like mantras and meditation. The study was based on one's aspiration and inward and upward self-concentration.

My intention continued to be to embody a greater life of the Spirit, but I had to admit that Integral Yoga wasn't working with my degree of aspiration and self-concentration. I went back to the dorm to smell the sandalwood. There must be something for me here, I assured myself, because I am here and not planning to abandon the cause. Besides that, attending the ashram theater was fun, even if the esoteric plays were hard to follow. I had no problem at the Dance and Music Halls when a Tabla and Harmonium concert was performed. On other occasions, I took part in devotional singing (called "Bhajans").

One morning while having breakfast, I was pondering whether Aurobindo's Integral Yoga was the right spiritual discipline for me. I sat at the counter imagining all the other diners as having already manifested the perfection that the renowned seer had envisioned.

As I was sipping my tea, I was surprised to see a tall, gray haired, distinguished-looking Westerner walking through the gates, someone who looked like Ram Dass. It couldn't be, I decided, he's too famous – he'd never come alone or be in a situation where fans/disciples weren't surrounding him. He disappeared around a corner, later to reappear exiting the compound just as I was washing my steel plate and spoon.

Deciding to take a chance, I quickly followed and caught up with him as he was walking down a tree-shaded side street.

To my query "Ram Dass?" this Being of Love turned around and greeted me with a hug, as is his nature, which I took as a cue that I could tell him how much I appreciated his teachings.

"I was first with you at your Caribbean St. John retreat a couple of years ago."

He told me that he was in Pondicherry to meet with his friends and to tour Auroville. "Is there anything I can do for you?" he asked.

Trusting his sincerity and thinking he could read my mind and know my wish to visit "the city of dawn" which he'd just mentioned, I had the audacity to ask if I could go with him to tour the nearby international community inspired by visionary Sri Aurobindo.

Ram Dass suggested I give him a call later regarding the details, which I did. Indeed, he had made arrangements for me to meet him and his friend Dr. V at noon the next day.

Arriving at the model self-sustaining experiment close to the Bay of Bengal, the three of us, as pre-arranged, were red-carpeted around the Auroville compound and let in on future plans. I didn't say a word or ask a question during the fascinating presentation, vainly thinking that our guides might be curious about me, the mysterious woman who was with Ram Dass.

"This new city-in-the-making, following the specific guidelines of The Mother, is planned around a huge edifice of spiritual but non-sectarian significance called the Matrimandir, Sanskrit for 'Temple of The Mother.' The foundation of this soul of the city was laid twenty years earlier on The Mother's 93rd birthday," our guide said. (It would be 17 more years before this huge concrete sphere surrounded by 12 petals would be finished and covered by golden discs to reflect the sun.)

I was thrilled when we two plus one were invited to enter the half-completed temple and to spend time under the large dome in the high ceiling meditation hall. In the center was a giant crystal which reflected streaming light in such a way that the whole space seemed to glow as we sat in silence. I don't know how long we meditated there, although I feel certain it was more than the ten minutes the average visitor was allowed to spend in so-called "silent concentration" when it opened to the public years later. I came out more inspired to continue my exploration of Integral Yoga.

On the drive back to Pondicherry, I took the opportunity to ask Ram Dass more about his SEVA selfless service projects. I shared with him how two years previously, after being on his retreat, I had applied for a volunteer position in India with this international organization.

"The letter I received in response politely declined my services, suggesting that a donation was the way I could be most helpful." I went on to explain that even though the SEVA avenue was closed to me, I nevertheless quit my college job as a volunteer coordinator and bought a one-way ticket to India to begin my full-time search for truth.

It was at this point that the guru glanced over at his friend Dr. V. from Aravind Eye Hospital located in Madurai, also in south India.

"Perhaps we could arrange for you to use your skills in working with the volunteers at this fast-growing hospital," Ram Dass suggested, speaking of one of his SEVA projects. (As it turned out, Dr. V. was Govindappa Venkataswamy, MD, an award-winning ophthalmologist and charismatic founder of this much needed Indian eye-cataract-surgery hospital.)

"Inspired by Aurobindo and named in his honor, the treatments are entirely free or heavily subsidized for the poor, with even the well-off flocking to it because of its excellent reputation for eye care. It might be the opportunity you were looking for."

In hindsight, I can hardly believe my response to Ram Dass' suggestion. (Is this my one regret in life? To my ego, yes to my desiring a little fame by association which is why I mention it.)

"Thank you so much, Ram Dass, Dr. V. I am honored to be considered, really I am, but I must decline because I feel my path at this point has become a more contemplative than an active one."

These holy men understood perfectly, and I parted with their blessings for my spiritual journey. How differently my life would have turned out if I had taken that opportunity. Perhaps I had... in a parallel universe.

Was my intention really that lofty? Somehow, wise words I had heard from Ram Dass years before came back to me as we went our separate ways.

"How do you know that what you are doing is from a form of evolving consciousness and not just an ego trip? Until a final moment before enlightenment, I can guarantee that everything is an ego trip. Even spiritual practices are ego trips. They're all ego trips because it's you being somebody thinking you're doing something. That's an ego trip."

Twenty-Eight

More Men and Then...

Contemplative, did I profess? Maybe not. Before yogi Cristina left Pondicherry to return to Vienna, she highly recommended Vivek, her massage therapist.

"Although he's young, in his mid-twenties, I imagine, he's been a long-time resident here and I always have him work on me while I'm here. Shall I ask him to contact you? I'm sure that you will like him." Here begins a tale of two more men and very divergent outcomes.

And so it was that the highly recommended, dashing devotee arrived at my door. I was treated to the best three massages I had ever had. Vivek not only had professional techniques; he seemed to have a special ability to breathe hot breath. It was such a thrill and a rarity that when he concluded his body work by using his hot breath to breathe all over my nude body, I found it to be orgasmic. I was, in fact, so aroused that after my third massage, I asked him if he was coming on to me.

Vivek took that as an invitation, which it was, and we ended up having sex while he was seated in my hard-backed desk chair with me on his lap.

I was sorry I asked. I was even sorrier when, face to face, he commented, "This is strange, having sex with you. You're probably the age of my mother."

I freaked out, not so much related to any reference to the Oedipus complex as with my personal concerns regarding aging. Why didn't I just laugh and accept being a "cougar"? (Was that term even in the vernacular at that time?)

I couldn't and I didn't. That was the end of great massages and the hot breath protocol, but not the end of the story. A second man had, by chance, been an auditory witness to the event.

Rajesh was a young Indian friend whom I'd met earlier at the guesthouse when we sat at lunch together. He had also been with Aurobindo for many years and was well schooled in the practices and the philosophy, which he was happy to share with me. I looked forward to talking about higher principles with him.

Being that Rajesh was walking by my thin-walled room at the time and happened to overhear my cavorting with Vivek, my behavior became the topic of our next philosophical discussion. We spoke more now of the Hindu beliefs about the body and its desires as being a hindrance to the achievement of enlightenment.

Since it is true that what one puts one's attention on grows, I had yet another avenue to explore with regard to sexual pursuits. Living down the hall from me was a well-known Jungian analyst from California named Robert Johnson, who was in Pondy to study and write. With the hopes of talking with him, I reread his 1983 book, *We, Understanding the Psychology of Romantic Love.*

We never did converse, but I got what I needed from his premise that "romantic love has become the greatest single force in our (Western) culture for lack of any other acceptable channel towards wholeness. Since the greatest known force in the psychic universe is a demand for completion, for wholeness, for balance, we Westerners seek that something greater than our egos, that vision of perfection, primarily through romantic love because we do/will not admit to or recognize the option of the religious (spiritual) experience." Thank you, Robert Johnson.

It certainly was time for me to admit once again that I needed something besides hungry-ghosting/obsessing about perfect sex, job, possessions, or even "good causes" to fill my emptiness. Acknowledging the sacred had put me on this wonderfully strange but paradoxical journey.

◇ ◇ ◇

Confused and conflicted by the mixed messages from past Osho opportunities, Jungian wisdom, and Hindu asceticism, I wanted to escape. I contemplated leaving Pondicherry, and pedaled the bike I had rented to the Post Office to pick up my mail at General Delivery before departing.

"Still no mail for you, Ms. Francis," the postman said. Why hadn't I received any Christmas letters from my children? I had provided plenty of postage and envelopes to facilitate the forwarding from my last address. I left upset, with tears in my eyes, feeling lonely and isolated. I was so distraught that I fell off my bike, got a fair share of bruises and gashed my big toe. The next day the toe appeared infected, and I went to the ashram infirmary to be treated.

"This is a dangerous wound. It's best to get a tetanus shot," the doctor said, "and you will need to stay off this foot for three weeks and have the bandage changed daily." I was devastated, even more so when I had a severe reaction to the Indian tetanus vaccine. (Had I received the dosage meant for a horse instead?) I became ill with a high fever, was delirious, and had a horrible headache. I was weak, too weak to get out of bed when I finally got back to the guest house.

Fortunately, the young holy man Rajesh, who lived down the hall, became aware of my condition and came over every day to take care of me. He put cold compresses on my head, provided me with lots of fluids, changed the bandage and consoled me with his company.

This period of my life turned out to be profound. Over the course of three weeks, in that third-floor guesthouse room, I told my life story to Rajesh, mostly grieving losses, until, under his guidance, I began to celebrate my successes and contemplate my future.

I felt that Rajesh was an enlightened being. On another level, I questioned whether that was true and tested his reaction to all the bad stuff I could dig up on myself. I even attempted unsuccessfully to seduce him. (Good God, would I ever give it up?) After laying on all the charm, I released all my venom. He maintained a posture of gentle selflessness and pure love, forgiving my attacks and responding wisely to each of my questions.

One day I challenged him: "Prove to me that you are enlightened."

In his quiet way, he asked, "How do you feel in my presence?"

The answer was that I felt completely at peace.

"What else?"

I could honestly report, "When we meditate together, I achieve total stillness and am engulfed in joy."

"I feel that you are serious about your spirituality," Rajesh affirmed, "and the next step is to truly concentrate on the practices, best achieved by being celibate."

"Wait a minute!" I protested. Before elaborating on this radical step, he asked how many sexual partners I had had.

Until I took time to review, my eyes looking upward and to the left as I was processing my past experiences, I wasn't sure.

When I came up with a surprising number, he further questioned, "Isn't that sufficient? Haven't you dissipated your energy enough in this area?"

Not yet convinced, I asked, "Is celibacy the only way to be truly spiritual?"

"Of course not," Rajesh replied, "If you had been deprived and dormant, I would have suggested yoga or even a committed sexual relationship to awaken the kundalini, but you have already done that."

Nevertheless, the message that I had received, believed and accepted from my conditioning was that to give up sex was to dry up and die. In encouraging me to be celibate, Rajesh asked me to stop using sexual romance as a substitute for Love. He might have added giving up seeing physical health as a substitute for Wholeness, and to begin questioning religious beliefs as a substitute for Truth.

"It has indeed taken a lot of attention to attract sexual partners and much energy to keep them satisfied," I admitted. And Rajesh's recommendation was timely, as I was not too happy with myself, being deeply in the throes of self-judgment as a dirty old woman. I found myself ready to commit.

"Thank you, Rajesh, for your wisdom and advice. I am trying to find truth, love, enlightenment or whatever it's called. If this is to be my next step, so be it. I will be celibate for at least one year."

I left Pondicherry after that commitment and a promise to keep in touch. Rajesh's final suggestion was a quote from Jungian psychologist James Hillman: "You have to give up the life you have in order to get to the life that's waiting for you."

It didn't take more than two days before I was tested. The next holy man I met on the road also impressed me, not only with his higher self, but also with the loving spiritual hug we shared as we parted after an amazing discussion of all things spiritual. We planned to meet the next morning for tea. I cancelled immediately after the second hug which included his hot breath on my forehead, ears and neck. Oh no, not this again, I firmly decided, faithful to my new commitment.

But I must finish the Rajesh story line. I was happy to join him once again at the Aurobindo Ashram in New Delhi before I left Asia. I was true to my vow of celibacy, and he was on his normal holy path. We said our goodbyes and headed off in our different directions to the same goal.

More than a decade later and continents apart, I was surprised when he tracked me down through the internet, and shocked by his email.

"I hope this finds you well," he wrote (after thinking it over for 20 years?): "I want you to know that I now believe that we should have had a sexual as well as a spiritual relationship."

I never responded, annoyed as I was with his change of heart and fall from the grace that I had bestowed on him (or was I mourning the lost opportunity?). It's just another example of man simply being consistent in his inconsistencies, I decided. But I could have given the guy credit for trying the middle path...

Twenty-Nine

Swami Sahajananda

Would there ever be an end to my efforts at Self/self-improvement? Certainly not yet, as I made my next move in striving for perfection. (Just who was there to perfect? Who was I kidding?)

As pre-arranged, my friend and ex-roommate Cristina was already settled into the little thatched-roof hut that we had reserved. I was anxious to begin another cure at the small remote Atheetha Ashram on 12 acres of land outside of Bangalore in southern India. We had registered for 15 days with an option to stay longer. This time it was a fasting/yoga retreat developed by a Hindu healer named Swami Sahajananda. This total fasting cleanse, my first, began with five days of silence. The fast was meant to give my body an opportunity to heal itself and be rejuvenated. We were to stay in our rooms for mandatory bed rest with only water to drink.

Having absolutely no energy, bed rest worked for me. However, wrestling with my dark side in that small windowed thatched-roof hut felt anything but good during that fast. (If you'd rather not have me turn into a grouch, feed me.) Our teacher came daily to check on us, the only time we were encouraged to speak.

Cristina, a long-time yoga teacher, reacted differently to the regimen, sat like a Buddha, and was given permission to do yoga twice a day because she felt so energized.

In my extremely negative state, I used the dialogue opportunity with Swami to express anger and to complain about my inability to cope. The wise man listened carefully. His response?

"How wonderful! How fortunate for you that all your Christmas mail was lost, that you had an infected toe and got a tetanus shot. What a gift that you have arthritis." He constantly stressed that all problems could lead us to giving up attachments. As he saw it, the lost letters were a message to further let go of my children; the vaccine led to celibacy; the arthritis was to encourage me to do yoga and take care of myself.

Fortunately, the following five days, with broth added to the menu, were better. We started each day with yoga, followed by a lecture on the Bhagavad Gita.

"If the human being does not understand that Center within which is limitless, then he is caught in thinking he is limited. He is in bondage. He is suffering. Understand that limitation is self-imposed by one's own thinking. Pain and misery can be transcended by being non-attached, without ownership over the fruits of our actions or objects of the world."

My head and body may have been cleared by the cleanse and the yoga, but I was still "attached." Regardless of how much pranayama I did or how many bhajans I chanted, I was still an expert at self-imposed limitation.

After the first ten days, we were served a non-spicy, vegan lunch: rice, dahl, and overcooked vegetables – raw was not wise in India. Such a sattvic diet was common in most ashrams so as not to stimulate the senses. Only food considered "pure, essential, natural, vital, energy-containing, clean, conscious, true, honest, and wise" was offered. I survived and thrived.

In the afternoon, we had a talk on health, followed by sessions with a Reiki Master Teacher, a Canadian therapist called Skye, who offered to certify us in the three degrees.

Such energy work fascinated me, being unlike massage therapy and other healing techniques which required some kind of diagnosis by the practitioner, something I found frustrating and beyond me with my doubts about being accurate. I made a resolution to practice trusting Divine Guidance.

My teacher spoke about Reiki, an ancient Japanese healing technique where the practitioners/healers, after being taught particular symbols and mantras, are merely a channel for divine energy. With one hand open, they receive the divine energy which flows through their body into their other hand, which is placed on the receiver's body in the assigned positions. Skye taught that the energy flow continues from the Divine through us to the client and back, a circle of energy.

"Let go of worrying about the outcome. The client will only absorb as much energy as he or she is ready for," she said.

The symbols, considered secret at the time, were taught when we were in the second- and third-degree levels. Learning to draw them correctly (mentally and in the air over the client) was important, as were the Japanese language mantras. But most critical was their activation, their empowerment, which happened after our teacher's Attunement ceremony for each of us. We were declared ready to serve and began to give treatments to daily visitors to the ashram.

Reiki became a meditative practice which I most often was able to perform without expectations for outcomes, since it was not up to the practitioner how the therapy was received. However, it felt curious that on one day when I was feeling particularly endowed, the client rose from the table professing having felt nothing. On another occasion, when I was distracted, the session ended with the client feeling "transformed." I had to remind myself that healing has nothing to do with me, a channel only.

I impressed myself and my daughter a few years later when, after I did Reiki on her malfunctioning car, the vintage vehicle worked well. In another instance, a crying grandchild calmed down.

Today, though, I use a Reiki symbol and the (once secret) mantra, Cho Ku Rei, habitually as a kind of blessing where needed and always when an ambulance or rescue vehicle sirens by.

◇ ◇ ◇

Very satisfied with what we were learning, Cristina and I remained for further instruction. During the second month, Swami Sahajananda introduced us to Pranic Healing, which appeared to have miraculous effects on his patients; a skill we hoped to emulate.

Motivated to add to his repertoire of healing and the sharing of his skills, Swami traveled to the Philippines for an initiation with Jun Labo, considered to be the "No.1 psychic surgeon" in the world at that time. There he was introduced to a Spiritualist medical practice and observed the healer's painless, barehanded surgery for the removal of pathological matter from a patient, an operation requiring no instruments and leaving no sign of invasion in the body. Many have verified such miracles.

Upon his return, we enjoyed Swami's stories of his first trip out of India and his first airplane ride. This big man with long black hair tied in a bun on top of his head, dressed only in a full-length orange cloth around his waist and another over his bare shoulders, must have turned a lot of heads at the Manila airport.

"When I first met Jun Labo," Swami said, "the surgeon and his interns 'looked' at me with heads bowed slightly as I entered the room. This 'third eye diagnosis' was to check out my aura, a technique said to lead to a diagnosis of any possible present or future disease in the observed."

Swami amazed us with details of unusual healings he had witnessed, and we were even more excited when he offered to begin another course of study with us. He was on fire with enthusiasm and healing energy.

After a week of teaching, however, he started to suffer from terrible headaches, suddenly stopped all activity, and took to his bed, deathly ill. The routines of the ashram came to a halt as this powerful man got more and more ill, was treated by one practitioner after another, did a good deal of fasting, and even spent time at another nature cure center.

He eventually entered and left a hospital, refusing chemo and radiation when cancer was diagnosed. As painful as it was for him to be moved, Swami requested coming home to Atheetha Ashram near the end of his life. I stayed on at the ashram as visitors came from near and far to hold devotional round-the-clock healing ceremonies.

Chanting became the main practice, and I spent hours with mostly old women hypnotized by the repetition of the mantras. My favorite was the Gayatri Mantra, a meditative worship of the Creator and petition for understanding: "Om bhur bhuva swaha, Tat savitur varenyam, Bhargo devasya dhimahi, Dhiyo yonah prachodayat."

Swami spent his last days consoling his visitors who were distraught over his illness. He continued to heal them as they held vigil by his bedside, somehow able to overcome his unrelenting pain as he greeted them. For whatever reason, I didn't visit him. After a month and a half, he died at age 58 of cancer, a disease that was neither diagnosed, revealed, nor cured by the third-eye focus of the famous psychic surgeon in the Philippines.

It made me question, among other things, why Swami seemed unable to protect himself from sickness, as we were taught to do by energy healers: shielding ourselves with light, flicking the germs off our hands, or bathing in salt water, etc.

Perhaps he chose to take on another's illness as a spiritual practice, in order to heal that individual, being altruistic in his calling. I knew Swami considered his cancer karmic and accepted it as "his problem being his greatest gift." It was the philosophy he lived by. I was told by his beloved disciple Ma Atheetha that he was often at peace, but admitted, when racked with uncontrollable pain, "I am frightened when I forget my true limitless Center and seem to be in a body."

Not comfortable staying or even visiting the patient, but somehow unable to leave until just before Swami died, I hung out and observed the reverent ceremony of the comings and goings, while trying to make myself useful in the garden or the kitchen.

One of the visitors who befriended me was a naturopath and yoga teacher, a quiet man in every way. I later learned he was a world champion in yoga. He visited the sick room daily, and somehow started to join me for walks at sunset. We hardly spoke as we circled the almost dried-up Lake Ubbanur bordering the property. I found it somewhat strange spending all that time together without conversing, but continued with our ritual for almost a month. Before I left, he sincerely declared me ready to do serious meditation work and encouraged me to register for a ten-day silent sitting practice, something I had strongly resisted up to that point. I began to consciously consider it as a remedy for my lethargic state, but still wondered why I always needed a man to set my course.

Thirty

Goenka's Noble Silence

editation was to become my rudder in this uncharted time. I first had to overcome my resistance and my memories of how hard it was to do sitting meditation practices. I remembered instead, as fondly as I could, sitting with Ruth Dennison in the Joshua Tree high desert of California (letting go of the fact that I hadn't finished the ten scheduled days). This commitment to Vipassana, the "universal remedy for universal ills," would be different, I firmly decided and so it was.

I completed four ten-days and one 20-day Vipassana retreat in four different countries over the next few months. It was equanimity I was seeking, but there were many distractions and diversions, all wonders of life, along the path.

I loved sitting with the Nepalese people at a center outside of Kathmandu and feeling the crispness of the mountain air. I remember the warmth of the coconut grove on a hot springs river in Thailand, where I sat at an international dharma center called Wat Suan Mokkh. I was oblivious to the dangers as I flew into Colombo, Sri Lanka, and bussed out to a mountainside retreat center during a curfew at the time of an election and civil war massacres in that country. I relished the taste of salt on my lips from the day-long ferry boat ride to the Thai island of Koh Phangan before beginning a retreat there. I so wanted to be converted, as thousands before me, "from misery to happiness, from bondage to liberation, from cruelty to compassion."

Beginning at the beginning, I traveled to Hyderabad in central India for my first ten-day retreat based on the meditation methods of S.N. Goenka of

Burma. Although he was not present and I never met him, his highly respected teachings were presented through talks he had recorded, a pleasure to listen to because of his captivating voice. The sessions were monitored by hand-picked devotees who followed his instructions to the letter, in order to keep the teachings uniform at the many Goenka Centers around the world. He emphasized the secular, non-religious aspect of the Dharma/teachings, thus attracting many people to meditation who might have otherwise resisted.

Goenka did stress what I had heard before: "Anyone can become a Buddha." He said that when anyone takes refuge in the Buddha, she/he is not in a subservient role, only basking in the qualities of the personification of enlightenment.

"I'm an anyone," I declared, and once again stated to the universe, "I want to become a Buddha and bask in the qualities of equanimity and peace by letting go of attachment and aversion. Enough of bourgeois life."

Goenka's "noble silent" Vipassana retreats involved eight hour-long sitting and walking meditations each day, plus a dharma talk imparting the wisdom of the Buddha in the evening. I found none of it easy as I perched, knees tucked under a foldable meditation bench made of the finest blessed wood available.

I attempted, without success, to give up comparison of different meditation methods. S.N. Goenka stressed absolute stillness in the posture, which was quite the opposite of Ruth's Joshua Tree style, which had us making micro-movements, encouraging wakefulness and attention to sensation. At this center, the monitor seated at the front of a hot, humid room watched to make sure we didn't stretch or scratch. It was also unique that the only questions he encouraged were those having to do with posture. No other problems were to be addressed.

Could I have gotten my practices mixed up? Somehow, just a few hours into the retreat, this mind and body became more of a Shaker than a Buddhist, as I was beset with tremors. I couldn't stop shaking as I knelt, seriously focusing, as directed, on developing an awareness of physical sensations. I was told that by being aware of the impermanent nature of sensations, I could break my habitual reactions to craving and aversion.

This sensation of shaking was not as impermanent as I wanted it to be. I felt aversion to being out of control and had a strong craving for relief. "You are releasing emotional blocks with each shiver you experience," the hall monitor said. "Your tremors, however, are disturbing to the rest of the group and you must stop."

After hours of this distraction and my inability to control my body, I requested a solitary cell so as not to trouble (annoy?) the others as they meditated.

"Impossible," our guide said, "The cells are only for advanced students." He had to succumb to my wish the next day, however, being as I was such a mess.

After two days in solitary, the assigned Cell D on the second floor, I emerged cured. For the rest of the retreat, I sat still as stone, even as my mind was drifting, racing, swirling into the past and future.

There are also more pleasant memories, namely the generosity. It was the tradition to offer "dana," a gift to the teacher at the end of a retreat. Each participant contributed what he or she could to support the next students, and paid the small fee requested for simple shelter and meals. I remember standing behind an ancient Indian woman at the Nepal retreat who marked her X signature on the intake form, leaving a fruit as dana. She may have been practicing for decades or been a beginner like me, welcome either way.

At other retreats, I recall glancing at my watch or across a crowded room, and fantasizing about living happily ever after with the saintly man in the corner. I remember the urge to break the silence or read a book, read anything, even a notice in the bathroom. I became greedy about getting just the right cushion for comfort, or planning to sit in the perfect spot to catch a bit of a breeze. I mentally celebrated a "good sit" even though we were taught there was no such thing as a "bad" one. It was the act of meditation itself which was of value.

I remember the sessions when I caught myself nodding or fell asleep, the times I went to the late-night meditations just to have the cookies served at the end. Sometimes I shed tears of joy upon connecting with Goenka's deep insights. I recall how disappointed I was with myself at the times I watched boredom come up and stay as I concentrated during the 45-minute walking meditation, back and forth over the same 12-foot path. I felt dull and anxious for more action, so I watched those thoughts as I continued moving with a "lift-carry-place" awareness of my feet.

Why was simply being alive not enough? As positively as I could, I mechanically affirmed, "I do enough. I have enough. I am enough."

It was important to quiet the mind in meditation, not to follow the storyline in the head, thereby losing the here and now. I had no trouble desiring to end negative narratives, but when I got into a juicy script of thoughts, I didn't want to sacrifice a morsel.

I was once told that I didn't have enough tenacity, and I have been persistently trying to make up for it ever since.

From India, I moved on to Thailand. Steven and Rosemary Weissman, an American and an Australian, were my teachers for the silent stay at the secluded Mountain Cave Monastery at Wat Kow Tahm on the southern Thai island of Koh Phangan. Schooled in the Theravada tradition, these popular Western teachers stressed the development of compassionate understanding for others and for themselves. I also became convinced through their example, of the value and the importance of increasing my moment-to-moment awareness while eating, bathing and doing chores.

I found them most empathetic during the one-on-one sessions, three of which took place throughout the ten days. At first, I sat in Rosemary's presence crying and feeling ashamed until she asked, "If you met another woman your age who, divorced after 25 years of marriage, gave up her home and her career, and sacrificed as you did to get here, wouldn't you be sorry for her?"

"No," I replied. "I don't believe I deserve any sympathy. I hadn't had it that bad." Then why was I feeling sadness and suffering? The Buddha, the Dharma, and the Sangha had the answer to the cause of suffering: greed, selfishness and stupidity. Surely, my next retreat had to be the lightning rod I needed to overcome these three vices. Sainthood, I'm on my way.

Thirty-One

Under the Bodhi Tree

The Buddha got enlightened in Bodhgaya. Could I?

I flew back to India, to Calcutta (without visiting Mother Teresa), and bussed from there to Bodhgaya: Mecca and Jerusalem for Buddhists. Considered to be the birthplace of Buddhism, it is in the north-eastern state of Bihar and was built up around the temple which surrounds the Bodhi Tree where I sat outside that famous fenced-in tree, unable to fetch a highly prized fallen leaf.

I pondered how Prince Siddhartha had given up his palace for study and ascetic self-torture, and finally let go of it all to sit under that banyan tree until he arrived at Realization. I pictured him meditating there cross-legged, left hand palm upward on his lap, and right hand touching the earth, at the moment of enlightenment. The posture didn't work for me on day one, but I knew I would return to give it another try.

January is an exciting time to be in Bodhgaya because it is considered an auspicious month for a pilgrimage and retreat. The Japanese go to the Japanese temple; the Koreans go to the Korean temple; the Tibetans go to the Tibetan temple; and the Indians go to the Indian temple. I made my way through the throngs and the vendors crowding the old world's unpaved streets to the gates of the Thai monastery. There I joined other Westerners to begin a ten-day-Vipassana retreat, with an option to extend to 20 days.

Over 75 of us settled into the limited space. I was able to arrange my mat and sleeping bag on the porch next to a wall under a window, not expecting to be so cold. I didn't complain because it was primarily a silent retreat. I was all ears for evening dharma talks by the acclaimed teacher Christopher Titmus from England, who was assisted by three other instructors. These four met with the participants in smaller group sessions daily, where we were gathered to discuss what came up for us in our meditations, and in the discourses which reached to the depths of Westerners' minds. Unlike the Goenka practice, we were encouraged to sincerely reveal ourselves psychologically and spiritually; and the sharings were often juicy as well as prophetic.

I found it all so productive that I registered for the second ten-day retreat, immediately following one evening off. A group of us took that time to head over to another temple to hear Gangaji, another well-known teacher, address devotees in an overflowing hall. Learning that this American woman received a transmission from my favorite guru Poonjaji, I appreciated her presentation even more and hoped to see her again.

It was the final dharma talk by Christopher Titmus on the last night of my 20 days in retreat that brought the vision of my next move into focus.

"I want to honor you here who are 'homeless by choice' in the pursuit of truth," he said. "I appreciate your willingness to give up your usual reference points and resting places with their addictions, compulsions and attachments to personal identity. I encourage you to continue your personal searches as unencumbered as possible, until you reach the Truth."

I felt he was talking to me, of course. It's always about me. I listened even more carefully as he went on to speak of people who made a difference. One in particular resonated with me: a Japanese Buddhist monk named Sasamori Dhoni.

"This humble man has led many pilgrimages for peace," Christopher said, "and next year, 1995, he is planning an international nine-month walk from Auschwitz to Hiroshima to mark the 50th anniversary of the end of World War II."

Our teacher concluded his talk, announcing that he was headed back to the UK to his retreat house in Devon, an organic farm and meditation center where he taught when he was not on the road.

"You are welcome to visit me in Totnes, even take up residence if you wish at 'The Barn' where 12 residents practice living the dharma together."

With that invitation, I was hooked. "The Barn" was my opportunity for a long-term retreat and the pilgrimage was the time-space to make a contri-bution to peace. I knew what I would be doing for the next year and a half.

Thirty-Two

The Barn

Both my daughters were living in London in the late spring of 1994 when I left India to travel to the retreat center in Devon. The time spent with them in their two homes not far apart in Notting Hill felt so good! Michelle had just had her first child in addition to her busy career, and Dianna and her partner were also happily pursuing their livelihoods. I remember how delightful it was being back with family and being introduced to my first granddaughter after all that time in Asia, while knowing that more separation was ahead.

They were good to me. After that month of basking in familial love and big city treats, I pulled myself away to take the scenic six-hour train ride from London to Devon to begin a five-month commitment at "The Barn." Set on a hillside overlooking the Dart River, and a 45-minute walk to the town of Totnes, this small meditation center/organic farm was the brainchild of Vipassana teacher Christopher Titmus, who had been my teacher in India. He felt that the layperson needed a place to practice long-term.

It was not a monastery in that no vows were taken, but it was expected that the 12 residents would meditate together three hours a day, work four hours a day in the gardens, and attend weekly house meetings. We also met for two teaching sessions a week with the dharma teachers: Steven or Martine Batchelor as well as Christopher, rounding out a schedule of immersion in Body-Mind-Spirit. Each interaction within the sangha/community was a lesson in trust and a teaching in cooperation since communal living offered its share of challenges even among like-minded people.

Mostly, I got along just fine as the oldest among the mostly British population there, a laid-back group, and really enjoyed meal times and the shared cooking experience. But I put on weight on the lacto-ovo-vegetarian diet: too much peanut butter and jelly on homemade bread, and lots of eggs and cheese. I also managed to create a conflict in the kitchen having to do with clean-up.

One young Southie went out of her way to avoid contributing. Because I had raised my children to clean up after themselves, I slipped back into the motivator role, and Anna and I soon began to act out mother-daughter power struggles. I seemed to be the only one in the community to confront her. We had a number of house meetings about this issue. Anne shared that for 19 years she had not helped her single parent mother with household chores; that was who she was and I was not allowing her to be herself. Since no one else was concerned about the situation, I alone was unloving, saw her as an adversary, and myself as a failure at unconditional love. It didn't feel good. Hadn't I learned anything from all the mantras, retreats and cures?

On the plus side, I had a ready-made family (which felt better after the Southie left), and we had a lot of contact with the teachers. As often as I could, I would do the 45-minute hike to Sharpham College for more Buddhist instruction. I learned more about organic gardening and had the best early morning job of watering in the greenhouse. The geese were the lesson in that task. As the new person walking through their turf every morning on my way to play and pray with the plants, the geese saw me as a threat. Their nature being to intimidate trespassers on their tract, they did scare me. With necks stretched forward, beak in attack mode, they approached as I ran backwards shooing them off.

Not wanting to give up my favored, light morning assignment, I sought advice.

"What you have to do, Laurel, is show them who's boss. As the lead goose approaches, hold your ground, and when he is close enough, reach over his head and grab his outstretched neck. He will then pull away and when you finally release him, he will have learned his lesson and never bother you again."

The guidance worked in spite of how terrified I was to do it that one and only time it was necessary.

I walked as much as I could on the weekends. My goal of 11 miles on Saturdays was my attempt at training for the 18-20-kilometer daily walks I would be undertaking on the pilgrimage the following year. Getting lost on hedge-rowed one lane roads and on marked trails bordered by stone walls, I crossed lots of fields of grazing sheep. One morning a sheep dog tried to round me up. On another occasion, when I was coming back from Totnes late one starlit night, I got a bit lost and tripped over a cow in the darkness. Somehow, I missed ending up in manure.

Autumn arrived at The Barn.

"Let's have a Halloween party and celebrate the harvest," one of my peers suggested, "It's also timely to contemplate the dissolution of the body, which we have been concentrating on with our teachers. Bring out the ghosts in your mental closets and whatever other fears you have about death and dying."

Having seen a few cremations in India and Nepal, I took this as an opportunity to act out attending my own funeral to celebrate my life and death, and to be cremated in effigy. With the help of a housemate, I made a cot of sticks tied together with rope and a "body" of wood scraps wrapped in a shroud of odd outfits from the share box. Placed in the center of the meditation room and being life size, "my body" looked quite authentic (and certainly weird). I was grateful that my fellow retreaters went along with having the "corpse" surrounded by candles as the central prop for three different meditations on the holiday, a kind of "wake" before the "cremation" at an evening bonfire.

Since I would soon be embarking on a peace pilgrimage in areas of past and present war zones, I felt it necessary to contemplate the possibility of dying while on the trek. I used the time to review my life and prepare – whatever that meant – for my death. I wrote my own funeral service.

My costumed housemates (such cool Brits) cooperated with my fantasy, realizing, as I made sure they did, that I would be walking in areas of conflict in Bosnia, across unhappy neighbors in Israel and Palestine, into Iraq, and later through the war zone in Cambodia.

No one in this community was interested in going to Auschwitz and staying overnight in the death camps, as was scheduled for the orientation. I was more than ready to do what I believed I had to do to be part of the solution instead of the problem. To undertake the pilgrimage was also to be my restitution for having birthed a son who chose to be a member of the military.

Still I contemplate: Who dies? It certainly looks like everybody does, and every "body" does eventually disappear as new bodies appear to be born.

But what is it that is never born and never dies? I often forget that death is a space-time experience, busy as I am experiencing as much of space and time as I can imagine.

Who am I, that is doing the experiencing? Years later, I read a teaching from Dr. Deepak Chopra professing that there are no nouns: all is a verb: sensing, imaging, feeling, or thinking. The idea not to be captive in a body-noun was comforting. All (that's all?) I had to give up was believing in a world made of matter. Until then, Now, as always, is the time for whatever "That I Am" to move along, ideally flowing in the spaciousness of experiencing. Why were there so many more bumps on the banks while going with the flow?

Peace Pilgrimage

9 Months, 17 Countries, 10,000 Miles, (2,000 on Foot)

Thirty-Three

The Convocation at Auschwitz

A fter five months of retreating at The Barn, the mother in me was revitalized by hanging with my daughters and new granddaughter Guinevere in England's capital city before embarking on the peace walk. I felt torn and cried when on December 1st, 1994, Dianna and Michelle saw me off at London Paddington Station with a ticket to Krakow, Poland in hand.

I must be mad, I muttered to myself as I waved out the window and blew kisses as my beloveds ran alongside the train as it accelerated.

Conjuring up some composure, I concentrated on loosening the laces of my new all-leather hiking boots (a gift from my son-in-law Robert) and stashing my backpack under the seat. I congratulated myself for packing only trekker essentials. (But would I really be able to get used to sleeping on a ¾ length self-inflating sleeping mat?)

Hours later, I slipped into my red wool-lined waterproof jacket, jockeyed my French beret over my ears, and hesitantly stepped out of the warmth of the train onto the platform of the Polish city where my father's parents (and Pope John Paul II) were born. I shivered from both anticipation and apprehension until I was relieved to miraculously arrive at the hotel where other pilgrims had gathered for the night. We introduced ourselves over supper, perhaps too road-weary to do much more.

The next morning I got acquainted with Californians Dan and Elizabeth Turner, peers who inspired me with their decades of peace activism as we bussed into Auschwitz, the Holocaust camp which preserves the nightmare memory of Nazi atrocities. This hell-realm was the setting for the Convocation, a week-long orientation, and our first steps of the "International Interfaith Pilgrimage of Peace and Light, 1995."

That evening we were introduced to Reverend Gyoshu Sasamori, the Japanese Buddhist monk of the Nipponzan Myohoji order that my Vipassana teacher had told us about. This "man who made a difference" was a slight yet strong-looking monk in his early forties who wore a white two-piece tunic with an orange robe draped over one shoulder. Active in his order for many years, he worked for world peace by building Peace Pagodas around the world as well as organizing pilgrimages. For the previous two years, travelling to the countries in which we would walk, he made contact with humanitarian groups willing to provide shelter and food for the pilgrims numbering in the double digits or hundreds.

Through his efforts and the help of countless activists, this was the launch of the most ambitious pilgrimage ever, one that would take us through 17 countries, covering nearly 10,000 miles (2,000 of them by foot) over a nine-month period, to commemorate the 50th anniversary of the end of World War II.

Sasamorishonin or Sasamori, as he liked to be called, welcomed some 200 of us from around the world, our own version of the United Nations, with warmth and wonder and gratitude that so many chose to be there at that moment.

"We start our journey here at Auschwitz," he said, "one of the most tragic places of the war, where there was a massive killing industry. We will end it at Hiroshima where the first atomic bomb was dropped on human beings, ushering in the possibility that all humankind and the Earth herself could be destroyed.

"We walk on pilgrimage to offer prayers for the victims of all wars. We will listen open heartedly to the voices of victims, voices of survivors, and voices from the war zones, voices from areas of conflict. All these voices, overcome with sorrow, seek hope.

"I believe that if we face the painful facts of history unflinchingly and convey the lessons drawn from them to future generations, we will be able to bring peace to the souls of those who died in anguish in time of war. From the loss of their precious lives, we can establish new values today and for the future." (an excerpt from *Ashes & Light, Auschwitz to Hiroshima*, published by Nipponzan Myohoji, Leverett, MA. 1996)

We were to follow his example, to follow in his footsteps. I felt blessed to have such a guide on this journey, trusting that Sasamori would be the best leader one could have for such a Gandhi-like journey to wherever there currently was, or had been, war and conflict. We would walk in reverence, while beating out a rhythm on a Japanese hand drum and chanting the mantra: Na Mu Myo Ho Ren Ge Kyo. The chant has been translated as "All life is sacred, all beings are related," and is universally recognized as a prayer for peace.

This practice of prolonged chanting while walking for peace is said "to reduce suffering by eradicating negative karma along with reducing karmic punishments from previous and present lifetimes with the goal to attain perfect and complete awakening." (Sounded like a kind of heavenly award after purgatory cleansing, do you agree?)

That was a lofty goal. I planned to put one foot in front of the other, to observe what did happen and what is happening around the world in my attempt to be part of a solution instead of the problem. It was also the fulfillment of a dream I had had many years before when I wanted to take an early sabbatical to walk across America in peaceful protest of our military-industrial complex, one of the walks this Buddhist order had organized. (I never did that trek because when I told my husband of my wish, he said, "If you go, I won't be here when you get back" – but there was nobody to stop me now.)

The requirements to be part of the pilgrimage were few: make a commitment to morning prayer together; be willing and able to physically walk 20 kilometers a day; cover our expenses (expected to be $5 a day plus airfares); and restrain from using alcohol or drugs. We were to be responsible for our own security in places of conflict, but this did not mean being armed. (Time to bring out the white light.)

Cash outlay was minimal because we were generously hosted by families and organizations along the route, thanks to the volunteer coordinators who had worked over a year to pave the way. Most often this meant we slept on church floors, and either cooked our own food in a community kitchen or ate in a school dining hall. Sometimes we stayed with individual families, but this was harder to schedule as our numbers waxed and waned depending on the country visited and the commitments of the pilgrims. I was ready to go the distance, but in the here and now, I begin at the beginning.

Day Two: I needed the prayers we said upon waking in the halls of a building that had once been the Gestapo barracks. It was just outside the concentration/extermination camp gates noted for their infamous sign: "Arbeit Macht Frei," which ironically translates to "Work makes you free."

The entire atmosphere was bleak: barb-wired, bare of color, bitter cold. Later that evening, we trudged through a few inches of dirty snow from the barracks down the tracks to the selection platform where we held our first ceremony on this last night of Chanukah. Lighting candles in the darkness created an opportunity to offer the light of life to those who breathed their last bit of fresh air on this site, before being directed into the crematorium, or assigned to a slower death of forced labor.

Day Three: Hypnotized by the horror, I couldn't turn my eyes from the so-called "Material Evidence of Crime" as we entered the barracks, which have been converted to house the last possessions of the 1.1 million prisoners of all nationalities whose lives ended here.

It was Block 5 that displayed the toddlers' shoes, size four hand-made sweaters, even rubber nipples, as testament to the children who were not spared. Glass cases in Blocks 4, 6 and 7 preserved prisoner mugshots, stacks of baskets for meager belongings and suitcases with owners' names on them, 43,000 pairs of shoes (one pair of red leather high heels), artificial limbs and crutches, hair and toothbrushes, eyeglasses and jewelry. There were also entire walls with piles of the clothing and darned and patched prayer shawls belonging to the old, young and sick victims temporarily housed in Barrack 13.

There were bags of hair cut from the heads and shaved from the bodies of workers who had bunked in Auschwitz 1. It was even more difficult to glance at the gas chambers where so many died from lethal showers, while others lingered longer in the camps enduring starvation, forced labor, infectious diseases, or medical experiments.

It was in this ambience of pain that we began our offering. My feelings intensified for the women who suffered at Auschwitz. What could I have done? What could I do now?

Motivated by a pilgrim named Sang Hee, I decided to have my hair cut off as an act of empathy. I reached out to this Zen nun, American by birth but a Korean citizen by choice, for help. This "benevolent and pleasant one" performed the task as a ceremony, sharing the razor she used to keep her own head shaved. It felt like a profound gesture and a humbling one for me, as I was sure it would reveal the stitches and the vanity of the face-lift operation I had had a few years previously. Such a procedure might have made for friendly cocktail party conversation about my bald head with lady friends, but I felt ashamed of myself on this much less of an ego trip. I wore an Indian cap continuously until the weather warmed and my hair grew a few inches.

Where was the peace and light we were here to profess as interfaith pilgrims in this atmosphere of fear and guilt? Forgiveness seemed difficult; was it even possible? Was reconciliation possible?

Against the backdrop of darkness of this setting, Rosalie from an organization called "One By One" took center stage. She spoke of how, over the previous two years, the children of Holocaust survivors and children of Nazi SS perpetrators came together, as adults, to heal their histories. We were all encouraged when two of the members, both victims of their dualistic pasts, stepped forward to recount the stories of how they grieved and grew past it all together.

After being buffeted between the atrocities of war, man's inhumanity to man, and the miracles of forgiveness and reconciliation for a week, evening fell on the last night of the Convocation. We all danced the hora. Gays and lesbians who had spoken of the Third Reich and present-day oppression stayed to dance with us. Long-suffering elders, who had made their way there to mourn their dead ancestors, also moved among us.

Dennis Banks, long active in the American Indian Movement, demonstrated one of his traditional rituals. He encouraged us to go the distance, promising to meet us in Japan to present Long Walker patches to those completing the journey. Atsuko, a Japanese high school student, at first too shy to join the others in the circle, but brave enough to leave home and family, joined us as our youngest walker. Olga from Chile and her 18-year-old son had long planned to walk this as their second pilgrimage, and had plenty of energy and enthusiasm for every opportunity to play and pray.

Thirty-Four

First Steps and a Misstep

Day Ten, December 10th, 1994, marked the end of the Convocation and the beginning of the Pilgrimage, our first toe touch east to the Czech border. Freezing rain slashed through fog when eighty of us self-declared pilgrims, and some of our Polish neighbors, said farewell to the other participants. With one glance back at Auschwitz, we started trudging down the right side of the highway behind the banner bearer and the drumming and chanting monks, to whom we responded in kind. We were all in single file except for the blind man who touched the sleeve of his partner. Some tread a token first mile; others stayed until we entered the first village. Cars of uninterested travelers raced past, creating sprays of slush. Knowing that we had seven days of walking before a rest day felt like almost too much of a challenge, once I put my heavy hiking boots to the ground. I began to question my will as I observed others drop out.

Dark and dank dreary as those first days were, my mood lifted when we entered the little eastern European towns where welcoming committees arranged for the church bells to be ringing as we wove through the narrow streets. Smiling villagers strode beside us en route to the square where the mayor and members of the clergy greeted us. Being the Christmas season, the holiday decorations brightened our spirits. Aproned matrons offered sweet hot tea or strong coffee, and rosy-cheeked children passed plentiful pastries after the welcoming talks and our mission statements.

An unforgettable early stop was in a small Polish town where we arrived on a Saturday evening, just as the Catholic priest was beginning to celebrate

Mass. Being told of our presence, Father Josef welcomed us into the warmth of the candlelit cathedral with a greeting in broken English, and invited all of us to come forward to receive the symbolic body and blood of Christ.

At first, falling back into the beliefs of my childhood, I was shocked that non-Catholics and even the non-Christian Buddhists would receive the sacrament of Holy Communion. Somewhat surprised that I seemed to care, I noted my breath when I realized that the bread and wine had not yet been "sanctified," therefore theoretically not a sacrament. The gesture was gracious and generous, and not against Church law and ritual.

Advancing behind the ten monks clad in orange robes over white winter garments made an unforgettable impression on me as they led us forward to the altar to partake. Local nuns garbed in traditional black gowns, big hoods and starched white bibs came up afterwards to shake our hands and offer their blessings. They reminded me of my early Catholic school days when the Sisters of Mercy were my teachers, in the era before Western orders gave up the penguin-like uniforms.

I tripped and twisted my ankle on the 15th mile of the fifth day as we trudged along a Czech Republic highway where the melting ice had frozen into creviced tracks. Realizing that I couldn't put weight on it, I completed the rest of the trek in the comfort of a police car.

That evening, Sang Hee, the Zen monk healer, put acupuncture needles in my ears and used moxa on my ankle to ease the pain, but I still could not walk on it. I travelled with the luggage until the day when the priest who was hosting us offered to take me to the hospital for x-rays.

Being the celebrity pilgrim that I was/we were, I was advanced ahead of nine people in the waiting room and came out two hours later with a gigantic plaster of paris cast from my toes to my right knee. I was told I had to rest for six weeks and restrict activity. My ankle was fractured. I had to accept that I could not walk the next leg of the journey. How did I feel about that? I wish I could have responded as J. Krishnamurti did when sharing his secret to well-being: "I don't mind what happens."

◇ ◇ ◇

Similarly, a Buddhist story comes to mind. An old man had a wonderful horse, so beautiful that the king offered him one third of his kingdom in exchange for it.

"Aren't you lucky!" the old man's neighbors said.

"I don't know if I'm lucky or not," the ancient one replied, "All I know is that the king has offered a fortune for my horse and I do not want to sell her."

"Such ignorance," expressed the neighbors.

The next day the horse ran away and the observers once again called him a fool for not selling his horse while he still had it and had an offer.

"I don't know if I am a fool or not," said the old man, "All I know is that I didn't sell my horse to the king and it has now run away." The next day the horse returned to the farm with another even more wonderful companion horse.

"Aren't you fortunate!" the neighbors said, "You now have two horses instead of one."

The old man once again replied, "I don't know if I am fortunate or not. I just know that my horse ran away and returned with another horse and I now have two."

The story continues like that. I chose to relate to my injury with "I don't know if I am lucky or not. I only know that I have fractured my ankle, and am not able to be part of the pilgrimage through war-torn Bosnia, Croatia, and Serbia." Having said that, I nevertheless pondered whether I had, or even could have, prepared enough for these challenges, for the long trek, for the bitter cold, for the tragic tales being heard.

After bidding adieu to the hardy ones and being put on a bus, I arrived in Austria ahead of time at the pilgrims' next stop after Serbia, a monastery located on the outskirts of Vienna on the Danube (which was too iced over to be blue). I spent the following couple of weeks resting with my foot raised. It was in this position that I got to be helpful by mending the monks' robes there, my ankle healing on its own. There was plenty of activity going on as the monk in charge was preparing to welcome the pilgrims for Christmas and New Year. Arrangements had to be made for the 60 people currently on the walk.

I felt like an added burden and found it difficult to stay put after finishing all the projects I could do sitting down. Fortunately Cristina, the Austrian citizen I knew from the yoga ashrams in India, lived in a little town nearby and invited me over to heal at her mountainside home for the holidays. It was a real treasure to be with her again, to meet her partner and to share in her lifestyle (without joining her in daily hatha yoga practice).

"We never go into Vienna for the New Year's Eve celebration any more," she said, "although the street concerts and fireworks are outstanding, not to mention the fancy ball opportunities. However, we would be glad to show you the city and walk the empty streets on New Year's Day when the partiers are sleeping it off. Want to go?"

Picture January 1st in Vienna, my first visit. The streets were in fact deserted; no stores were open, but the holiday decorations still did their best. The central square was shockingly memorable because the entire area was covered with an inch or two of broken glass. Walking was practically impossible. I visualized the revelers enjoying the fireworks and toasting at the midnight hour after a sedate evening at Symphony Hall or wild extravagances everywhere else. Evidence from a drink and fling ritual was underfoot: the sharp remains of champagne glasses and broken bottles emptied and tossed as part of the celebration. "A once-a-year release opportunity," Cristina said. "Most cultures seem to need their Mardi Gras."

Life in her village was much more sedate. Her partner Lucas was kind. He declared my broken bone set, and judging that I needed relief from the heavy cast I was carrying around, offered to saw it off. (To have it removed in a doctor's office in Austria would have been expensive, although the casting in the Czech Republic was done as an act of generosity for a pilgrim.) My flip-floundering around on the floor was quite a funny and contorting experience as Lucus cut, sawed and gently hammered away at the top, sides, and back of my rock-hard, thick plaster shackle. We roared with relief to see my leg again, though I hardly recognized it for its leanness. I relished being able to take a tub bath. Physical therapy would have helped as I practiced how to walk again with a balanced gait.

After spending that comfortable time with Cristina and Lucas, it was hard to say goodbye or express enough gratitude to them as I departed on my own again for Athens, my lone stopover before Israel. This second visit to ancient Greece would be nothing like my first in the 1960's when I was a young woman traveling on my own and wooed and romanced there by my husband-to-be. Soon after, I fled the country after being raped by a wiley opportunist. These three decades later, my Greek friend Demetrius from Poona days had expressed interest in welcoming me there. (He had no desire to arrange for the entire pilgrimage, as I had suggested.)

It was obvious that I couldn't step into the same river twice, not that I had expected or wanted to do so. Neither this former lover nor I were the people we had been at the Osho Commune the year before. The two days I spent with him felt uncomfortable, as pleasant as we were with each other. However, I hadn't told him in advance that I had committed to celibacy and was a monk-bald hobbler.

Demetrius introduced me to his best friend, but I wasn't impressed by this medical doctor who made his fortune performing illegal abortions as a practice. (I pictured blood on his nitrile-gloved hands and a dead fetus in the surgical tray.) It wasn't until much later that it dawned on me that the doctor was actually putting himself at risk to provide an important service for endangered women in a place where abortion was prohibited. How could I have forgotten how fortunate I was not to have been impregnated by that Greek who sexually abused me decades before? What if I had been faced with the illegal abortion decision like other women in cases of rape? I thanked God I was spared that bodily wound and heart wounding faced by some of my peers.

I left concentrating on the good parts of our friendship and made flight arrangements for Israel, looking forward to being back with the pilgrims on our mission, anxious to stride again in spite of one leg being weaker and skinnier than the other.

Thirty-Five

The Holy and the Not so Holy Land

It was January 1995, and the pilgrimage was reassembling in Israel to begin the Middle East portion of the Pilgrimage. After flying into Tel Aviv, I bused to Jerusalem. I was delighted to be back with the dedicated group again, and to hear from those who spoke of their experiences in the former Yugoslavia: the war zones of Croatia, Serbia, and Bosnia. My friend Sue from New England had taken over driving an ancient green VW van, which served as backup for the walkers, when the usual driver got ill. She filled me in about the pilgrims having to dumpster-dive for food for their daily one pot soup du jour, having to scrounge around for a deep well for water, and adding tabs to make it potable.

Others told of the hardships of those living there, who said that, of all the groups that had come to observe, the pilgrims were the only ones who had come to pray. I applauded their efforts, so important in letting the combatants know that someone was watching, and the civilians know that somebody cared.

It was mind-boggling to be back in Israel where I'd visited as a student in the 1960's when it felt like an exciting frontier land. I remembered staying in a kibbutz before hanging out with an artist and her friends in Jerusalem. It had seemed almost biblical visiting Bethlehem, hiking in the Judean hills, and swimming in the Sea of Galilee (after failing to walk on water). This visit was different. I was quite shocked, naively so, with the changes that had taken place over three decades.

We pilgrims stayed at the Faisal Hostel in the Arab quarter just outside the Old Town. After the cold of the continent, we were all pleased to be experiencing the milder winter weather on this side of the Mediterranean.

The underlying heat of the conflict between the Israelis and Palestinians was not so pleasant. We had only to step outside the door and cross the street to the Damascus Gate to become aware of the heavily charged military atmosphere. Well-armed Israeli soldiers, male and female, young and tall and gorgeous as they were, behaved as hardened professionals as they manned checkpoints and severely restricted the movements of their Palestinian neighbors. So much of the interaction was angry, fearful and brutal, as each defense seemed to bring more attack, and each attack brought more defense.

The fear was in the airwaves too; radios and TV's were always "on" for minute-to-minute reports of suicide bombings. It was chilling, when travelling by public bus one day, to hear everyone's cell phones start to ring one after another. (Wireless service was new and not without disruption, but still a desired item in 1995 in Israel.) Excited conversations ensued as family members called each other to be reassured of each other's safety upon hearing that a bombing had taken place.

The Arab-Jew tension in Israel was mirrored as well by the dissension among the Jews themselves, and between Jews and non-Jews. One-fifth of the population practiced as Orthodox Jews, their large families easy to identify: the men, bearded with side-curls, wearing tall black hats, and their pregnant wives managing many offspring. Others considered themselves to be "Reformed" or lived more secular lives, many claiming to be Israeli but not Jewish.

"Welcome to Israel," a radical rabbi who had joined us from California said, "the home of the most dysfunctional family in the world." The schizophrenia of the society affected each pilgrim as our historical perspectives and prejudices were brought to the surface and explored. Sometimes it felt awkward to even open one's mouth. There was much to contemplate and pray about as we spent much of our structured time meeting with groups from different factions. We listened to many troubling speeches from the different mindsets of professors, families, soldiers, clergy, and workers in the fields, at kibbutzim, settlements, refugee camps, and places of worship.

"What can we do about this dichotomy, these extremes in perceptions?" an American teacher named Josh asked Reverend Sasamori.

Bringing it all into perspective, the monk answered, "We didn't come here to judge. We come here to listen and to offer our prayers. These people show us their pain and their suffering; their rage and bitterness is their truth. We didn't come to hear what we wanted to hear. We come to hear their stories. Listen to their suffering, not their words. We come to offer our compassion to all the people in Israel and Palestine."

These words set the tone for the rest of the journey. Attitudes also softened after sitting with conciliatory groups of Palestinians and Israelis who were cooperating on peace efforts.

Our hearts warmed as we visited an Oasis of Peace (called Neve Shalom in Hebrew and Wahat Al-Salam in Arabic) launched by a Benedictine monk named Father Bruno, truly a holy man. Here a cooperative village of 26 families, Jews and Arab-Israelis, built a "house of prayer" to worship together and operate a school dedicated to breaking down barriers, where children from both camps were educated side-by-side, honoring both languages and traditions.

In Galilee near Bethlehem, we attended an encouraging workshop at the "Palestinian Center for Rapprochement Between People" which worked for equality, human rights, and democracy by protesting, educating, divesting, and boycotting internationally.

There was also a center called Ulpan Akiva Netanya, twice nominated for a Nobel Peace Prize, where both Hebrew and Arabic languages were taught to those interested in growing to appreciate each other's cultures by learning each other's mother tongue,

We walked mostly in Gaza and parts of the West Bank, very undeveloped in comparison to the much modernized Jewish state. (There is controversy as to how the US aid sent to the Middle East is used.) Because of the conflict with Jewish settlements being built on Arab/Palestine mandated land, borders are contested and often closed. It was revealing how Palestinians carry on their lives in spite of curfews and identity cards and border checks not to mention overcrowded schools, high unemployment and an economy in shambles. As we walked through their villages, they appeared truly delighted to greet us, to wave their flag, to feast us, and to dance with us.

While visiting a military base in the Gaza strip, we were hosted by Chairman Arafat's soldiers in a huge tent, invited to sit on plump pillows on a multi-carpeted floor, and served incredibly strong, dirt-thick coffee. It was mostly through nonverbal communication (and surgery treats) that we gradually became comfortable enough to forget the soldiers' day jobs, and to see them as the peaceful people they wished to be.

Meeting with officials of the Palestine Liberation Organization, we heard speeches from activists that revealed how desperate they were about their lack of statehood; how they felt that their historic claims to land and self-determination were not being honored. The peace process was then at a deadlock, and it did indeed seem that their pleas for independence were futile.

It was all so complicated. Both sides held the image of themselves as the innocent victim of a cruel enemy, and each side was seen as a threat to the other. It certainly seemed that the Israelis had the upper hand. Was it because of being supported by massive US foreign aid and weaponry?

I wanted to see Israel as the Holy Land I envisioned her to be, building on the visits to the biblical sites that I had experienced many years before when traveling in my post-grad years.

Our Arab quarter trip began with entering through the Damascus Gate into the Old City, which was a classic Middle Eastern Muslim market. The stone streets were where Jesus supposedly walked "the way of the cross," the Via Dolorosa. We hadn't started early enough to do all the fourteen Stations because the higher the sun rose, the bigger became the crowds who came to shop or pray.

On a wall of one lane which was less than eight feet wide, a placard read, "This is the spot where Jesus met the women on his way to Calvary while carrying the cross."

The other Stations on this way of suffering were marked by signs on major places of worship: a Polish Catholic Church, an Armenian Orthodox oratory, an Ethiopian and Coptic Monastery, a Franciscan Chapel, and a Greek Orthodox Monastery. The culmination of the walk was at the Church of the Holy Sepulchre, where each of the major religions is responsible for a certain portion. I crouched to touch the rock on which the crucifixion supposedly took place as we reached the holy site of the four last Stations where

Jesus is recorded to have been scourged and crucified, where he died and was buried.

At the Mount of Olives, I pondered the judgments and conflicts which continue among the major religions. The Jews, Muslims and Christians live and worship and quarrel on revered earth they all claim as their own religious turf. It all crescendos to a feverish level, especially on holy days.

Our bags were checked and all our movements watched by numerous soldiers as we visited the Wailing Wall, which served as an open-air synagogue. Devoted swaying and praying Jews left their petitions on slips of paper stuffed between the stones. As I approached the women's side of the Wall on the left with my handwritten prayer for peace, I thought of the Muslims doing their rituals at the al-Aqsa Mosque on the other side of that wall of both petition and partition.

I then heard the call to prayer coming from a loudspeaker at the top of a tall spiral minaret there, a call made five times a day, seven days a week. I would have liked to visit that mosque, being most impressed that such a large population prays together so often and every day. I also appreciated the beauty of the Arabic inscriptions from the Koran and the geometric artwork, beautiful and unique, without images of any human or animal form.

When we departed the divided city of contrasts with its holy and not so holy sights, I felt freer. One night we had a beautiful view of Jerusalem while staying at a Catholic hostel called Maison d'Abraham, old enough to have a long history of hosting pilgrims. I took memories from the walled old city with its one square kilometer of Arab bazaars alive with exotic sights, sounds and smells, domes and spires which were so different from the modern office building skyline and shopping malls of West Jerusalem.

Another highlight was February 14th, the day we visited a Greek Orthodox Monastery. I accepted an invitation along with 13 other pilgrims to make the five-hour trek to St. George's Monastery, located between Jerusalem and Jericho and was glad I did. We walked through the Valley of the Shadow of Death (Psalm 23) on the dusty road through Bedouin lands where the tent-dwelling Arab nomads herded sheep and goats. I thought of

Jesus here on his way to Galilee and looked for the Good Samaritan on this barren and rocky biblical path.

On our way up and down through the Jordan River Valley Canyon, we were inspired when we sighted hermit caves and refreshed when crossing streams en route to our monastery destination. This Fourth Century cliff-hanging complex overlooked a lush garden with olive and cypress trees. (Unlike an ultra-orthodox monastery on a Greek island, this holy place allowed female animals, and permitted females to visit.)

The few monks living there warmly welcomed us to tour the three levels and visit the two churches rich with embellished icons, paintings and mosaics in this West Bank wonder. The abbot was pleased to speak of a predecessor who revitalized the St. George's Monastery congregation. He directed us to the tomb of St. John (1913-1960) to view the holy man's intact enlightened body revealed in a glass coffin, something to be seen to be believed.

In Tiberius, many of us slept out on the balcony of the Church of Scotland Hostel overlooking the Jordan/Golan Heights and Sea of Galilee. We pilgrims spent much of the next day bathing in the earliest known thermal hot springs nearby, most welcome after the trek.

Our last stop before departing the Holy Land was the Dead Sea. How fortunate was I, who had hung out in the heights of the Himalayas, to now visit the lowest point on earth and the saltiest body of water in the world.

A few of us couldn't resist spending our last night out under the stars. We slept on a dry riverbed outside a wild game preserve in this desert setting with beautiful views of the barren mountains on the Jordanian side of the unusual lake. The next morning we got to experience floating in the Dead Sea, that fishless (hence called dead) "balmy brine," which was surprisingly very cold water. (It was just long enough of a dip to say we did it.)

Thirty-Six

Jordan

"As you know, American citizens are forbidden to travel in Iraq," warned the Middle East organizer as we were about to exit Israel for Jordan en route to Iraq. "There are dangers in visiting Iraq even though the so-called Gulf War is over. It's your personal decision as to whether or not you continue with the Pilgrimage at that point. Plan now for passport controls before we cross into Jordan. Iraq and Israel are implacable foes; their relationship is hostile, with no diplomatic relations since 1948. Pilgrims planning to go on to Iraq must NOT have an exit stamp from Israel put on your passport. Request the exit stamp separate from your passport, as was the entrance one, or you will be denied entry to Iraq after travelling through Jordan."

Forbidden and dangerous or not, a determined 25 of us dutifully did as directed and crossed the border walking, drumming and chanting near Salt City, Jordan. Because of Ramadan, we skipped lunch and were discreet about snacking and even drinking, out of respect for the Muslims' requirement to fast with no food or drink from dawn until dusk during this holy month. I found it debilitating (how did they do it?) and cheated, nibbling only enough to survive.

Upon reaching the capital city of Amman, we were housed in a dormitory at the prestigious New English School and briefed for our trip to Iraq. We spoke to some of the students from prominent Jordanian families who expressed both pro and con views towards Israel and reconciliation. They invited us to use their Olympic-sized swimming pool, which refreshed our spirits, free from pondering that prevalent dichotomy during that baptism-like immersion.

Renowned peace activist John Schuchardt (one of the Plowshare Eight along with the Berrigans) later addressed our group. This ex-Marine officer and most sincere patriot and his wife Carrie were founders of the stateside House of Peace, a home for young refugees from war zones. (Carrie was not present on this trip, but I met her and the children sharing their home the following year in Massachusetts.)

It was through Schuchardt's efforts, along with the former U.S. Attorney General Ramsey Clark, that we came to learn for ourselves what really happened during the Gulf War, and have this opportunity to see firsthand the effects on the general Iraqi population of the five years of imposed sanctions. John introduced us to Ramsey Clark's book, *War Crimes: A Report of U.S. War Crimes Against Iraq*, a documentation that throws light on the negative influence our military intervention has had around the world. The more we learned, the more committed we became to educating people on the dangers of any military-industrialized country.

We departed Jordan by chartered bus for the 24-hour drive across the great desert on our way to Iraq. The thousand-mile trip west from Amman to Baghdad was calm as we drove past Bedouin camps and camels, but felt more threatening when we had to pull far off the road to let military convoys pass.

We saw tented refugee camps, buffeted by the wind and sand, drove through numerous checkpoints, and passed bombed-out carcasses of military equipment left to rust along with the broken-down cars of broken-down people. We shared the road with fuel tankers, merchants (perhaps smugglers), military supply trucks, and rental cars carrying workers returning home to Iraq on visits to their families with much-needed supplies.

Thirty-Seven

Ten Days in Iraq

On February 26th, 1995, our international group of 25 pilgrims arrived in Baghdad, where we were hosted by the Iraqi government which had arranged for our stay in the eight-storied Baghdad Hotel. Here, on the eastern bank of the Tigris River, each of us was assigned a single room, an almost unbelievable rarity for the likes of pilgrims. On opening the door to #307, I was surprised that it, like all the other rooms, had its own bath. (That was an incredible luxury as the general population suffered from a lack of clean water.)

It was a well-known hotel, famous in the 1950's when westerners had felt safer traveling there. As a citizen of a country without diplomatic relations with Iraq, I was disinclined to broadcast my origins in a hotel mostly occupied by members of the Iraq Governing Council. It was also booked by journalists assigned to cover the complications of bombing and sabotage campaigns by insurgents. Arab-Arab conflicts and consequent military border buildups, the issue of "weapons of mass destruction," and Saddam Hussein's rule which was characterized as a mixture of megalomania and paranoia were also headlines. Some might say the gatherings we pilgrims attended in the hotel's meeting rooms were brainwashing sessions. Were we being lobbied for the removal of sanctions: a near total financial and trade embargo imposed on Iraq by UN Security Resolution 661 after Iraq's invasion of Kuwait?

The ten days spent in this war-torn country (considered by some to have been the biblical Garden of Eden and later site of the Tower of Babel) were difficult to observe, but nothing in comparison to what the locals were experiencing. We saw firsthand the effects the sanctions had on the general populace: the hungry people, the sick without medicine, and the ill-clad elderly. We visited the Children's Hospital where preemies were dying due to a lack of incubators. Only 340 beds were available for over a thousand patients, many contorted in unmanageable pain. What could we do for those who cried out or moaned as they suffered such distress? I gave one of the highly trained doctors my kit of first aid homeopathic remedies, a gift from my daughter, to offer whatever immediate relief I could.

Just because Saddam Hussein exhibited undoubtedly criminal behavior, was it necessary to make an impossible, steady warring situation worse? Did we have to respond in kind?

UNICEF reported that at that time sanctions had caused the deaths of half a million people in Iraq. How much longer, Lord?

Probably "as long as 'our' oil is under their soil" appeared to be the view of the western powers. I learned what imperialism meant and how brainwashing and sanctions affect us all: two sides to every story.

"The American people are also under sanctions, albeit a different kind, in the form of an embargo against information and against the truth," John Schuchardt said. "Our media is doing more than brainwashing – it does brain poisoning. How else would it be so easy to inflict harm on others?"

(I also had to look at my personal dependence on Shell and Exxon and the need for oil to fuel our flights between countries even while on this Pilgrimage.)

One morning we were bused to the Kuwaiti-Iraqi border to view what was left of the 60 miles of the infamous coast Highway 80, used by Iraqi armored divisions for the 1990 invasion of Kuwait, and renamed "The Highway of Death" because of what took place there in February of 1991.

Withdrawing on these six lanes, after the acceptance of a cease-fire proposal, were Iraqi combat soldiers as well as exiting foreign workers, mostly from Palestine, Sudan, and Egypt. A "disproportionate use of force" is the term used to describe this Operation Desert Storm. It was a controversial President George H.W. Bush-directed, US-led UN coalition of aircraft using cluster bombs and napalm on those driving out of Kuwait on those tragic dates. Bombardment from above disabled vehicles at the front and rear of the convoy, resulting in the massive vehicle column becoming sitting targets stalled in a traffic jam. Those escaping across the desert became individual targets. Wrecked and charred military tanks, trucks, civilian cars and buses filled with corpses became the widely viewed media visuals of the condemned devastation.

The best antidote for persecution that we pilgrims had was prayer. We prayed beside what was left of that six-lane highway: a 12-foot-deep trench shouldered by mountains of dirt. It was a kind of monument for the fleeing thousands bombed into pieces without any rituals of burial. We mourned in solidarity with the grieving family members who had lost their loved ones there. Formed in a circle of peaceful prayer, our petitions, chanting and drumming, however, were made inaudible as a UN helicopter hovered over-head, stirred up the dust, and drowned out our sounds with the grim staccato thumps of its rotor blades.

That's how it looked in 1995. The warring history of the highway was to continue, however, as this very same stretch of highway was later repaired and used by the US and British forces during the 2003 invasion of Iraq. That American attack on Iraq was instigated by the second Bush president, George W., and was allegedly fought "to disarm Iraq of [non-existent] weapons of mass destruction, end Saddam Hussein's support of terrorism, and free the Iraqi people."

Just as World War 1, "the war to end all wars," didn't accomplish what it proclaimed, this military operation simply set the stage for even more war-ring. The inhumanely pathetic policies haven't changed; we continue to try to bomb our way into "peace," mainly to protect our "vital interests" (meaning oil, arms deals, and other mega-corporate profits).

Journal Entry:
Baghdad, Iraq March 6, 1995

Today we fasted and prayed at Public Shelter No. 25, a huge air raid shelter turned inferno, scene of the St. Valentine's Day Massacre, now a memorial in the quiet middle class Ammariyah district of Baghdad. It was heart-wrenching as we entered the two-story concrete structure built to be a safe and secure refuge from aerial bombing attacks carried out for 42 days and nights in February 1991.

It wasn't the military command post that NATO intelligence profiled it to be. Just one week after the horrendous war crime, they admitted that it had been a mistake to target it. Nevertheless, no compensation was ever given to the families of the victims, mostly women and children who died as the men slept outside to give the women their privacy.

Umm Greya, a woman who lost seven of her eight children there, made it her remaining life's mission to honor them by serving as a guide to the place which had become a memorial to the hundreds who died there.

"I stay home that night to work. Much heavy bombing all week. I had much to do. Early in morning, I hear two bombs. I run to shelter. Heavy doors sealed shut. Smoke everywhere coming from hole in roof. Shrapnel in surrounding buildings. My children among the 408 corpses. I scream, I cry. I stay. Others clean up. Four years I stay with my dead. I pray with neighbors. I show pictures." She pointed out pictures of the burnt bodies alongside photos of these same women and children smiling in earlier family scenes.

"I bring flowers. I not forget."

A whiskered, middle-aged man approached and interrupted her. We stepped back, taken aback as he grimaced, waved his arms about and shouted, "My mother died here. My sisters died here. I hate Americans. My sons hate Americans. We know, we remember what the Americans did. We will never forget or forgive."

We pilgrims knelt to pray with Umm under the gaping hole where the first of the two laser-guided bombs pierced through the ten-foot-reinforced concrete ceiling. This was followed by the second 2,000-pound bomb which exploded inside, suffocating and incinerating those sleeping on the upper floor with its heat. Boiling water from the destroyed water tanks on the lower level killed the others taking refuge there. The black, incinerated hands of some victims remained fused to the concrete ceiling. Silhouettes of people reduced to mere shadows were frozen in time on the stone walls.

Earlier that morning, as we approached the shelter, school children had stood in straight lines on the side of the road, silently observing the pilgrimage as we passed. Before school closed later in the afternoon, we visited a few of their classrooms in a nearby school. The children shared cramped spaces, were taught without enough essential paper, pencils and books, but sang the songs they had learned: patriotic Iraqi songs as well as repetitious anti-American chants. Here, where students equated the words "democracy" and "human rights" and "George Bush" with pain, destruction and death, there was a constant emphasis on "we will not forget."

The youth indeed had reason to hate Americans. With history unfolding as it has and is, the enemy is me and mine. There is little evidence to show that the minds of those children would have changed since that visit.

I experienced more animosity towards my country while walking down Baghdad Street with a friend the next day. We stopped to buy Muslim prayer beads from a sidewalk vendor who appeared excited to talk to us as there were few customers in the area.

"Where are you from?" he asked Jeff, who answered "Canada" and made a half turn to show the red and white flag on his backpack.

"And you?" he inquired, addressing me. Within seconds, he lowered his head, closed up his suitcase and hurried away, no longer interested in making a sale if it meant earning tainted American dollars. (I contemplated hiding my shame by stitching a Canadian maple leaf flag on my bag.)

Quite the opposite was a flashback to my "good old days" of the 1960's when, as a student, I worked and traveled in Europe and was greeted with gratitude by those who remembered the Marshall Plan. This 1948-52 European Recovery Program following WWII was an initiative under President Harry S. Truman "to aid in the rebuilding of war-devastated regions, to remove trade barriers, modernize industry, and prevent the spread of Communism in Western Europe."

I toured Germany, France and Italy feeling safe and proud of being from a country which seemed to help, rather than further abuse, those who were defeated. I never encountered those who considered the Marshall Plan to be mostly about American "economic imperialism" (as some have declared).

Every story has at least two sides. Why couldn't we repeat the generosity part in Iraq?

I was less than generous myself, as I was never able to fulfill a promise (mea culpa) made to a courageous Iraqi mother and scholar named Nasard, who asked me to help get her book published.

Here's the CliffsNotes: "I was one of 200 women who were attempting to bring a cargo of foods and medicines to Iraq after the first five months of the Naval Blockade. We were beaten and I was made deaf in one ear when some 400 Marines attacked our Women's Ship of Peace in December 1990. We were not permitted to proceed into port. Even now," she said, "humanitarian groups are harassed, fined, and worse, because of their efforts to help those civilians hurt by the sanctions."

I felt helpless, discouraged, and exhausted by these happenings in spite of all our prayer, good intentions, and support of one another.

◇ ◇ ◇

After departing Iraq and arriving in India, I decided to break from the pilgrimage for the first ten days. Been there and done that. I had witnessed the poverty, injustices. extravagances, kindnesses and devotional nature of the natives but needed alone time. Planning to join again in New Delhi, I hopped on a night bus to Goa and spent the one-and-a-half weeks in a little beach hut in almost complete solitude, analyzing my experiences in an effort to reconcile my perceptions with my spiritual beliefs.

There I pondered duality. I reviewed my projection of the image of the enemy. I knew I had been present, was "here-now" with what we had seen. But where was Presence?

I heard the age-old question: "Why does God let bad things happen to good people?"

I knew the answer. Only a god made in the image and likeness of man would allow such deeds done under his reign. What I call Divinity does not involve an anthropomorphic idea of God who rewards and punishes. That white-bearded grandfatherly one in the sky is comforting to many and a disappointment to others. So, it is in a world of duality.

I act in a world of duality... until I don't. What was my part in creating this particular perpetrator-victim reality? I had a choice and I chose to see "man's inhumanity to man" and its repercussions. Having seen it, could I forgive it, see it differently? Or would I judge, condemn and react in revenge? Hadn't there been enough of "an eye for an eye?" It's only enough, forgiven, and finished when I go to a greater Reality, praying without ceasing to let go of separate goals and separate interests, separation itself.

I floated in the Arabian Sea, striving to fathom the biblical concept of being *in the world but not of it.* I pondered the Buddhist teaching of The Four Noble Truths: "Life is suffering. There is an end to suffering. There is a path to the end of suffering. Follow the eightfold path." Where was I in relation to right understanding, thought, speech, conduct, livelihood, mental attitude, mindfulness and meditation, the ideal Middle Way? (Buddha, where are you?)

Thirty-Eight

India / Malaysia / Thailand Pilgrimage

"I remain an optimist, not that there is any evidence that I can give that right is going to prosper, but because of an unflinching faith that right must prosper in the end," the Dalai Lama said, quoting Mahatma Gandhi, "My optimism rests on my belief in the infinite possibilities of the individual to develop nonviolence." (This loving message welcomed me back.)

The occasion was the 125th Birth Anniversary of Mahatma Gandhi. Forty pilgrims joined the multitudes in New Delhi for the ceremonies. We congregated for the opening speech by the most revered Lama, whose wisdom was a blessing for us all. His Holiness spoke of Mahatma's relentless and unshakable optimism, the gift of every outstanding personality, whether philosopher or statesman, since ancient times.

We were hosted by local peace activists who reinforced their beloved leader's beliefs and devoted their lives to spreading Gandhi's ideas of Non-Violent Non-Cooperation. They emphasized his wisdom, courage, tact and foresight. I appreciated being reminded how he was able to inspire such an unparalleled nonviolent atmosphere. These committed followers of Gandhi were able to see the rose in the dung heap as they proclaimed that "the very intensity of the efforts the Government put forth to suppress Gandhi's movement was proof of the strength the movement had attained."

◊ ◊ ◊

Next stop was Malaysia. We walkers left India pondering that quote regarding the "intensity of the efforts" on both sides. It served as an example of Newton's Third Law of Motion: every action has an equal and opposite reaction. Forces come in pairs: violence and nonviolence; war and peace. How is it possible to rise above that duality?

On the personal level, the law of cause and effect means I am accountable for my actions. What actions am I willing to take to create the reactions and life circumstances I desire?

I welcomed returning to walking for peace.

We spent only a brief time in Malaysia, a much more prosperous country than I had imagined. It surprised me that they were preparing to host an international marathon.

After attending a ceremony at the Second World War Memorial in Penang, we learned of the efforts of the Malaysian Buddhist Association who hosted us. They educated their people and us about the environmental dangers of their country's rapid industrial growth, and how best to deal with the consumer culture left in its wake. Those goals became even more familiar as we continued our pilgrimage.

One day, between sessions, we went swimming in the Straits of Malacca off the coast. I was stung by a stingray (or was it a jellyfish – not sure.) Ignorant of potential complications, I refused to see a doctor, satisfied when a bystander shared from a bottle of vinegar, liquid which relieved the pain somewhat. The biggest challenge for me was getting back into the sea one more time before we moved on. (At least, I succeeded at that.)

As we crossed the Malay-Thai border, hundreds of Thai citizens, one mayor, and 50 young monks welcomed us with beautiful flowers and bottles of water. The pace quickened immediately, as officials from Non-Governmental Organizations (NGOs) had planned a most comprehensive trip, primarily by bus, to cover as much of Thailand as possible in the weeks we were there. Our walking was more symbolic than strenuous, although the subject matter couldn't have been more somber or severe. At the many scheduled fact filled meetings both in Bangkok and in small towns, professionals volunteered their time to inform us of the challenges they faced from commercial land grabs and capitalistic, consumer-driven development. Religious and secular speakers shared their visions for peace and listened to our reflections as pilgrims. Our hosts and guides were most hospitable and determined as well that we became familiar with the many battlefields, border changes, and political complexities of their beloved country.

Were there ghosts accompanying us as we marched along the railroad track leading to the bridge over the River Kwai? Something haunted me as we covered just ten kilometers of it on foot and made aware of the tens of thousands of Allied POWs and conscripted civilians who died and were buried along the 419 kilometers of the "Death Railway." I recoiled at picturing them forced to work at bayonet point and under bamboo lash. These victims were reported to have taken many risks to sabotage this Japanese project built to support their invasion of Burma during WWII.

The bridge itself was narrow, with platforms built off to the side for standing when a train approached. We continued to drum and chant as we crossed over the river. On the other side, we visited the Death War Museum that housed historical photos and drawings and paintings done by ex-POWs, morbid depictions of what the work camps were like. We saw a full skeleton laid out on a table, and rooms full of machine guns and bomb shells as remnants of horrific encounters. Entering the rows of thatched-roofed, open walled huts, we paid silent witness to honor those who labored, suffered, and died in this camp. We prayed as we walked along the rows of headstones at the Kanchanaburi War Cemetery.

We were educated about the even more inhumane living conditions of the unpaid labor gangs who laid the natural gas line through the rainforest. We walked near the Three Pagoda Pass at the Burmese border, where we prayed for the victims of that government's repression.

"This pass has been the main land route into western Thailand since ancient times. It is believed to be the point at which Buddhist teachings reached this country from India in the Third Century," the Theravada Buddhist monk acting as our leader told us, offering a positive point of the route's history. We stayed overnight at his monastery, and on our pilgrimage the next morning we learned of a wise and clever act:

"The virgin forest you are walking through is here because it was saved from clear-cutting by an action of forest monks. They 'ordained' these trees as monks by wrapping them in orange robes. Would-be woodcutters honor monks, and this action reminded them of the sacredness of this life form, and hence they left this land untouched."

Trudging our way along a steep nine-kilometer road rutted by the four-wheel drive vehicles used to travel it, we needed many breaks because of the 104 degree Fahrenheit temperature on the way to our weekend destination, a beautiful indigenous settlement.

These Karen border people were unwilling to live as refugees in either Burma or Thailand. Unaccepted by both countries, they set about to maintain a community life in harmony with Mother Nature in a place where political borders were continually being drawn, then destroyed at the whim of those in power.

It was refreshing to enter into this pristine village where family ties were strong and life was simple and close to nature. After accepting an invitation to cool off in the river, we were addressed by an elder who spoke of their belief that everything is related, and that we are all sisters and brothers together.

We relished the pleasure of being served a traditional meal of spiced rice and jackfruit, a first for me, and drank tea from sections of bamboo. After sunset, we smiled and applauded the women and children doing Siamese dancing accompanied by men playing mandolins, flutes and drums.

We could only pray that the Karen people be allowed to maintain their lifestyle and continue to resist so-called progress.

A corner of my mind hated to think how modern communications could change their community so quickly, were satellite TV to be introduced. Would it enter their homes the way I had witnessed in a far-flung Indian village? When I visited a family in their one room dirt-floored hut, I saw both a bare bottomed toddler and the family goat staring into a television screen. Even so, I realized that I had no right to hold the Karens to their simple lifestyle that I both appreciated and romanticized. It was their choice.

Conflicts and contrasts were on the roadmap. We headed into Bangkok, where we got to view Thailand's royalty in person, after seeing so many portraits of them in every home and shop. The popular King Bhumibol and Queen Sirikit were among the world's richest royals during their reign, the so-called Golden Age of Thailand. The pomp and circumstance surrounding this particular celebration was something our hosts wished to share with us, a chance to view the admiration of the citizens who indeed saw the king as divine. He was widely renowned for his efforts for the common man; dissenters weren't present. (I was dismayed by the duality of the situation upon learning that criticism of the King or the institution resulted in imprisonment, even exile.)

Moving from west to east, we traveled from Thailand's Burma/Myanmar border to our last stop in Thailand which was at the Cambodian border. Once again, as in other provinces, we were hosted by Theravada Buddhist monks at their Wat (temple).

After a simple supper served with loving presence, we prepared our sleeping spots and freshened up. The most common bathing practice consisted of cupping water from 50 -allon gender-segregated drums over our dusty bodies before and after soaping up under our wraps. Sitting by the river at dusk was the breath before the next eye-opening painful plunge.

The pilgrimage had touched 13 countries in six months, and we were about to undertake the most difficult and dangerous part of the journey of peace and light. We gathered in the dining hall for an important meeting.

Thirty-Nine

Preparation for the War Zone

"Listen up!" hollered Roger. The Danish shaved-headed organizer for the month-long walk through Cambodia stepped forward to get the attention of the 25 pilgrims gathered on the southern Thai-Cambodian border for the orientation.

"I have been on two of our previous three Dhammayietra (Cambodian Walk for Peace and Reconciliation), and I know from experience the challenges you will be facing walking through Cambodia. Each of you must make the decision tonight as to whether or not you feel called to undertake the most difficult portion of the entire pilgrimage, the very dangerous first ten days. It is imperative that you are fully aware of the risks ahead. Consider six important factors."

(I took a deep breath as Roger began.)

"Number One: This will be the fourth annual Dhammayietra through contested Cambodian territory. The first ten days are through a war zone. Last year, we came under heavy fire and two walkers were killed and five injured in crossfire between the Khmer Rouge and government troops. Any government troops we see are not, I repeat, NOT there to protect us. Our pilgrimage is a peaceful, nonviolent one, and walking nonviolently means not taking sides."

(How brave we are, I thought, and then pictured myself defenseless on the road.)

"Number Two: Because we are traversing a war-torn zone that has been in conflict for decades, the area has been heavily land mined. Supposedly the roads have been cleared, but there is no guarantee that new mines have not been planted."

(I recalled hearing of the international efforts to ban landmines. Cambodia had the largest amputee population in the world because of these hidden dangers. I remembered seeing the Red Cross poster that pictured victims of all ages, which read "The military can't tell us where they left the landmines, but these people can.")

"Number Three: May is pre-monsoon time, when combatants often have final shootouts. It is also the hottest time of the year, with temperatures around 100 degrees Fahrenheit. We will be walking approximately 15 to 20 kilometers a day through deforested areas in the blazing sun. Wake-up call is 4 a.m., with a 5 a.m. departure, which allows for a three-hour rest at lunchtime before proceeding to the next temple.

"Number Four: Sanitary conditions are primitive: very few toilets and little running water. Regardless of how many inoculations you may have had, the viruses are so exotic here that no one will be fully protected from disease. If someone does get ill or injured, or is a casualty due to gunfire, evacuation to a hospital can only be done by way of helicopter. The cost to the victim is in the $4,000 ballpark. It will be wise to share ICE (In Case of Emergency) information with a fellow pilgrim."

(I started to shake with growing anxiety. What would I tell my family?)

"Number Five: One small backpack per person is allowed for transporting your personal mats and mosquito nets required for sleeping on temple grounds. You must downsize. A truck accompanying us will transport these packs from temple to temple along with non-potable water. Please team up to share responsibility for filtering the water to meet your needs."

(Dehydration was a real danger, especially in the heat. And I already carried next to nothing in my backpack. Could I get along without my journal, my book of Rumi, family pictures, address book, passport, first-aid kit, changes of clothing, toiletries?)

"Number Six: The Cambodian farmers living along the way welcome pilgrims every year and provide us with food from their larders. You can expect dried fish and rice for lunch, and a simple hot meal at night provided by our hosts. Since our interfaith group is joining over 500 monks and nuns on this journey, conditions are crowded and resources scarce."

(Oh my God, what if the cooks don't wash their hands! I knew we would be accompanied by others, but 500 of them? Fearful of scarcity and feeling so insignificant in such a crowd, self-pity arose in me.)

"Those are the facts," Roger concluded. "Each of you must decide for yourself whether you will cross the border or not. Any questions?"

Feeling so disturbed by what I'd just heard, and disappointed in myself for being weak and weepy, I reactively put up my hand and admitted, "I can't do it. I'm too soft. I don't feel strong enough."

Others expressed their concerns and intentions, and one attempted to console me. I felt even worse when he said, "I understand, Laurel. It's OK. You can rejoin the pilgrimage in ten days or when we get to Vietnam."

The room quieted down when Sasamorishonin, our brave leader, stepped forward to beseech us.

"Search your soul and look deep within your heart to know if you really are ready to risk your health, your emotional fortitude, perhaps your life, on this portion of the pilgrimage. Go to bed now. Tomorrow morning we will make final preparations, after I have spoken to each of you individually."

I left the room in tears, anxious to hide my shame and wallow in my regret. The full moon kindly lit up the area surrounding the meeting hall. I stumbled to a grassy knoll by the river where I had laid out my mat and tied my mosquito net between two perfectly spaced trees. Not even bothering to undress, I curled up under the sheet in a fetal position, fretting and fuming about being such a coward.

This pilgrimage was important to me as the mother of a son who chose to be a military man. I knew Christopher had made the decision to join, as many young people do, to have his higher education paid for. He committed himself to nine years in the Air Force. I had not succeeded in instilling pacifism in him, and was determined to amend and balance that out by committing these nine months to peace.

So much for intention. I couldn't convince myself that it would be OK to just skip out when the going got tough, even if that was ten days in a war zone. I started crying again.

After forever, the sound of the rushing river consoled me and I stretched out. Becoming conscious of my breathing, I started to meditate. My thoughts quieted down. My breathing slowed. I asked for help; I surrendered; and dropped off to sleep. Sometime later, I felt myself being gently roused, and opened my eyes to a bright light, too bright to be the moonlight filtering through the trees.

I became aware of a voice addressing me and heard, "Cross the border, Laurel, for you are divinely guided and protected. You have set an intention and you will complete the pilgrimage as you have planned. All is well. All will be well." There were no more words as the light faded to moon glow.

Awestruck, I pondered the reassurance I had received in a manner completely foreign to me, and rested in gratitude.

The next morning I met with Sasamori as he requested. I told him about receiving higher counsel regarding my next steps.

"Now I know in my heart that it is not the personal 'I' that is undertaking this portion of the pilgrimage, and that it won't be the egoic me that completes it. All this is a meditation, and I can and will do the entire walk through Cambodia and beyond. I am feeling confident and unconflicted."

Our dedicated leader nodded in agreement and bowed as the Japanese do. I bowed back.

Others also had second thoughts. Some decided to take a different route to Battambang City, the capital city at the other end of the war zone, and departed that day with plans to rejoin the pilgrimage in ten days' time. Two of the Vietnam vets who were most excited about going the distance were denied permission by Sasamori, who recognized that they had been too conditioned as warriors to be able to walk defenselessly. They were most disappointed, but accepted his decision and left with the others.

The committed 14 of us, ten westerners and four monks, met to form teams to fulfill the filtered water requirement. Dan and Elizabeth Turner invited me to buddy up with them. I was so grateful to have this former priest and nun, longtime activists in nonviolent encounters, be my support team. Their calming presence had often reassured me in the past few months. We vowed to take care of each other, exchanged emergency forms, and shared about our families. It made me realize how much I missed my children.

Taking advantage of an opportunity to use the one public phone at the *wat*, I decided to call my daughter Dianna in Boston to tell her of my plans. I got to use the last minutes of a friend's international phone card and waited my turn to make the call. It was around noon, her Eastern Standard Time, when we connected. Delighted to find my first-born at home and hear her voice, I melted into motherly concern for her before relating where I was, and what I felt I had to do.

She cried as she said, "I don't care about peace. I just want my Mommy safe."

I had to trust that telling her about the Voice and the night-time message reassured her. Promising to call again from Battambang, I requested she relay the message to her sister and brother. I then asked about what was going on in her life.

"MOM, you just told me that you are about to start walking in a war zone. You may be killed and you are asking me what I am having for lunch?"

Interested, I asked, "What are you having for lunch?"

We both laughed, and she opened up about her plans, delighting me with stories of simple pleasures and big ideas. As the operator did the minutes' cut-off countdown, we lovingly said goodbye after reciting together, as we had done so many times before: "May all beings be happy, may all beings be free, may all beings live lives of peace and harmony."

Forty

First Footsteps in Cambodia

I t was noon the next day and 110 degrees Fahrenheit, as we waited at the border while immigration officials processed our passports. Two hours later, we were allowed to proceed with the Thai exit stamp, cross over the invisible line, and then move on for the Cambodian entrance visa. Once on the other side, the energy was high as we were joined by the other Cambodia walkers, some 500 Buddhist monks and nuns. We were energized as we got our first look at the "Gandhi of Cambodia."

More than a thousand eyes were focused on the Venerable Maha Ghosananda, the 1966 Nobel Prize nominee, who was the momentum behind the movement. This revered monk, wearing a Buddha smile on his round face and a saffron robe over a rather frail body, blessed the retinue, and gave his heartfelt message to welcome us as the international delegation on the Dhammayietra VI.

"Our journey for peace begins today and every day. Each step is a prayer, each step is a meditation, each step will build a bridge." It was a privilege to be in his presence and to know that he would be walking with us for at least part of this pilgrimage.

"Peace is always a part of departure and arrival. That is why we must always begin again, step by step. Panna (wisdom) will be our weapon, metta (loving-kindness) and karuna (compassion) our bullets, and sati (mindfulness) our armor. We walk until the whole world is peaceful."

After this mission statement, our first footprints in Cambodia were with Maha and Sasamori. Our international delegation led the way around a rotary, away from the border. Stronger, younger pilgrims took turns carrying the peace banners for visual impact; the rest of us offered the beating of the hand drums and/or chanting to attract the ears of onlookers (and God, just in case S/He didn't notice).

Our multinational presence of 14 was dwarfed by the hundreds of Cambodian monks and nuns who were the impetus behind this Dhammayietra. As we wove our way into Poipet, it was reassuring to look back at those local spiritual practitioners who would be our companions as we walked across Cambodia.

Never having been much of a history buff, I knew little beyond hearing there was a movie called *The Killing Fields* about the atrocities the Khmer Rouge (the name given Cambodian communists) had committed in Cambodia. More than one and a half million people were starved, worked to death, or executed under the Communist dictatorship of Pol Pot. The leadership specifically annihilated the educated and the religious orders, killing those who wore glasses or had soft hands. These acts throughout the so-called Year Zero had as their goal the return of Cambodia to its agrarian past, which nevertheless failed without proper irrigation or educational practices.

I had read next to nothing about America's part in setting the stage for the Khmer Rouge takeover. My country, in its bombing efforts to destroy North Vietnamese military installations and supply lines along the Ho Chi Minh Trail, wreaked havoc on what remained of Cambodia's rural border population and agrarian economy.

Even with the spraying of the poison Agent Orange in this over-spilling of the Vietnam war, the "Blood Road" continued to function. On the quest to eliminate so-called Vietnamese Communists, even more voracious US bombings destroyed marketplaces, rice fields and villages in neutral Cambodia, causing further social disintegration, which later turned into a civil war.

Maha Ghosananda, in petitioning for peace, said he did not question that loving one's oppressors – the Cambodians loving the Khmer Rouge – may be the most difficult attitude to achieve.

Nevertheless, "It is the law of the universe that retaliation, hatred and revenge only continue the cycle. Reconciliation means we see ourselves as the opponent. For what is the opponent but a being in ignorance? And we ourselves are also ignorant of many things." I sighed as a being in ignorance, and tried as a pilgrim to be present with peace and reconciliation.

Arriving at Poipet, the border market town with its shops pockmarked by shelling, I turned my attention to the Cambodian pilgrims: perhaps 300 saffron-robed monks, mostly teenaged, and a couple of hundred nuns who were much older women, mostly widows, many toothless but nevertheless firm-limbed. The nuns were all wearing white blouses and black skirts; their uniform was part of the spiritual sisterhood. All had shaved heads.

These were the oppressed whom Maha Ghosananda had brought back to the solace of Buddhism, the religion that their families had embraced before the Khmer Rouge desecrated 3,600 of their Buddhist temples. Only 3,000 of the 60,000 Buddhist priests escaped being forced to disrobe (renounce their priesthood), or be tortured or murdered.

The revival of the religion began in 1979 when, as a Theravaden monk from a Thailand forest hermitage, Ghosananda trekked from one refugee camp to another along the Thailand border, and ministered to the disheartened Cambodians. He chanted ancient and familiar sutras, and distributed photocopied Buddhist scriptures. Against the orders of the Thai military, he rebuilt historically established *wats* and ordained new monks.

By 1988, he was known as the supreme Buddhist patriarch who inspired all without taking sides, putting himself only in the lap of the Buddha. Living up to his name, which means "great joyful proclaimer," Maha Ghosananda made teaching about the Buddha very much a part of his mission to the masses. (Hence, many locals joined us for his lessons each evening at our stops along the 74 miles between Poipet and Battambamg.)

Standing out in every crowd towered the six and a half foot tall, red-headed Bob Maat, an American monk who had served in Cambodia for years working on behalf of the victims of the conflict. Present with us in Auschwitz at the beginning of the pilgrimage, he encouraged our efforts for peace as pilgrims, and bid us to join him in his adopted homeland. I had doubts when we learned that the year before, he had been taken prisoner by the Khmer Rouge, questioned and released. I sincerely hoped that that would not be anyone's fate this year.

Here we met again. Wearing a T-shirt and jeans and the same size 12 flip-flops he wore in the snow in Poland, he flashed a big smile on his sunburned face and stated how happy he was that we had come so far. I was equally pleased to see him again, greeted him personally, and then rejoined the women.

Using lots of sign language on our part, and the little broken English known by the nuns, a few of us got somewhat acquainted on this, our first night in Cambodia. A small round-faced nun named Asvina offered me one of her white blouses to wear over my brightly colored rayon dress.

Take it, she gestured, thinking that we should wear white tops like they wore so as not to stand out. I was most touched and gratified by her generosity. We exchanged addresses and I promised to write when I returned home. I did as promised, sending money and pictures to Sister Asvina as the correspondence continued. (I later had to write and ask Bob Maat to intervene, to apologize to the nun for me, and to convince her that I really could not continue to honor her requests for dollars.)

We five western women were assigned a ramshackle dirt floored dining hall as our dorm. It was full of wooden picnic tables, which we used as platforms for our sleeping mats. We hung our mosquito nets from the rafters before going out again.

We lined up with the nuns waiting to share a curtained-off shower head for washing up while our feet got rinsed in the runoff. They stared at us curiously as we smiled awkwardly. After some time, a translator appeared and invited the five of us elsewhere to use a bathhouse. Gratefully and a little sheepish, we accepted and were led to what turned out to be the residence of a better-off woman in this impoverished community. Although still primitive by western standards, the facility was an upgrade from the muddy area we had just left, and we soaped, shampooed and showered in hot water. We never met our benefactor, so my curiosity about her life was not satisfied. I attempted to forgive my judgmental thoughts about this house, and the reputation I imagined it had, as I relished in its comforts and fantasized the owner's right livelihood.

Clean and relaxed, we retired early to our platforms, but it was impossible to sleep because of the revelry of the locals. I crawled off my camping mat, out of my mosquito net, slipped on my dress and new-to-me blouse, strapped on my tevas, and went outside to see what was going on.

I followed the bright lights and piercing sounds to a huge open area. Maha Ghosananda was seated on a platform teaching the dharma, perhaps the Four Noble Truths, to the multitude gathered at his feet. These peasants, living isolated lives with few educational opportunities because of the war and the murder of bespectacled and soft-handed professionals, were hungry for the spiritual messages of hope and this yearly change of pace. It was a festive occasion. Music was broadcasting from scratchy loudspeakers set on poles, blaring out the ten top tunes of the time. Often a message interrupted: repetitive requests to the villagers to bring food for the pilgrims to the *wats* where we stopped for lunch or overnights.

One of the goals of the pilgrimage was to bring attention to the serious problem of landmines, and to efforts to help those affected. Booths set up by grassroots Non-Government Organizations had displays to educate us all.

"Mines fight on long after those who laid them pass on. Grandchildren of combatants can be victims of their grandfathers' wars." There were picture posters of a skull and the words in English and Cambodian which read, "Every twenty minutes, someone somewhere in the world is killed or maimed by a landmine!" Videos were played and materials were available on how to spot landmines, and how to contact minesweepers to clear the fields.

The NGO was also recruiting sweepers to remove mines, a painstaking and dangerous job. For each inch of dirt swept, an indentation had to be made with a stick to test it for mines, before moving on to the next inch to be inspected, and cleared if necessary. Each monsoon season, with one fast approaching, brought more of these persistent civilian-killers to the surface, hence the removal was never completed. Still more discouraging was the fact that even though millions of landmines had been removed, twice as many were currently being laid down by warring parties somewhere.

Some 20,000 signatures were collected on a petition to promote the International Campaign to Ban Landmines, an effort started in 1991, aimed at eliminating anti-personnel landmines in use since World War II.

Since Cambodia had the highest number of amputees in the world, even more had to be done. The Red Cross had videotaped programs which drew the most interest from these amputees and their families. They revealed good news: help was available for them to acquire prostheses. There was new hope and much joy as arrangements were made to bring the affected parties together with the medical suppliers. Was it enough?

Maha Gossanda reminded us all that "To make peace, we must remove the landmines of hatred, greed and delusion from our own hearts, which keep us from making peace."

It was still difficult to sleep when I returned to the women's quarters. I admit I was annoyed by the loud scratching noise until I learned that the sounds which disturbed our rest that night and for the next nine nights were purposeful. The broadcasted music and videos from the speakers also served as a means of protection. They informed both sides that it was a truce time, as the Dhammayietra was on site. The noise came with the hope and a kind of unspoken contract: there would be no attacks or shelling during this period from either side such as had occurred in previous weeks in these areas. Better to hear loud music and videos droning on through the night than the sound of artillery at these yearly gatherings, a time of nonviolence as well as an opportunity to educate. I fell asleep with Maha Ghosananda's words in my mind:

"Peace begins with you. The suffering of the Cambodians has been deep. From this suffering comes great compassion. Compassion makes a peaceful person. A peaceful person makes a peaceful family. A peaceful family makes a peaceful country. A peaceful country makes a peaceful world. May all beings live in happiness and peace."

Forty-One

Buddha on the Battlefields

It was 4 a.m. and my companions' flashlights beamed around the platforms at wake-up call. Pull off nightie, drape on dress; mindlessly habitual by now. Disengaging the mosquito net took two thoughts. While folding my mat, sheet and net, I had three consultations in my half-awake, half-asleep state: there was no need to put on makeup, just sunscreen; a rest stop was scheduled in the afternoon; and this sacrifice of mine would surely save the world.

By 5 a.m. we set out to tread on a road made visible only by flickering candles held by farmers and villagers who lined it on both sides to light our way. Families ventured miles down the hills to receive a blessing from Maha Ghosananda and celebrate our arrival. As their supreme patriarch approached leading the pilgrimage, devotees knelt beside buckets of water decorated with flowers while holding smoldering incense sticks, a symbol of war, as well as their candles. Using a palm frond which he dipped into the water, the Cambodian Gandhi showered the faithful with waves and words of peace. He always smiled. The children squealed with delight when this loving father figure, in a playful cooling act, picked up the whole pail and dumped it over their little heads. Two monks assisted by dipping the incense into water to symbolically put out the fires of war.

The pilgrimage moved along at this pace for the few hours that Maha was with us for ten days in the war zone. First in line after the honorable one and his helpers was Sasamorishonin, along with the three Nipponzan monks who took turns carrying a banner with the mantra Na Ma Nyo Ho Ren Ge

Kyo ("All life is sacred") written in Japanese. I felt carried along as one of the ten internationals who continued to drum and chant, following Sasamori, who led the call and response. Walking through and among the hundreds of Cambodian precept takers doing their walking meditation last in line was their much-loved Brother Bob Maat, who supported and encouraged his adopted countrymen as he had done for many years. Those watching our walking statement of hope and nonviolence seemed to enjoy our presence, our attention, our intentions for their safety and happiness. It was as if peace had come. And so it was here and now.

I took my turn drumming in the early morning hours before putting up my sun umbrella, then continued to chant and drift in a kind of daze. By 11 a.m. I was glad to collapse and rest, sometimes on temple land, often just roadside where we shared what little shade there was on a stretch declared free of landmines. There were very few trees, as the extent of deforestation meant miles and miles of only fields to pass, which nobody worked, where no animals roamed. A few narrow paths had been cleared through those barren lands, which were potentially full of landmines. These single file lanes led into the hills where most of the farmers lived and worked their small plots, which they hoped were mine-cleared. While welcoming the monsoon season, they also feared that the rains would bring to the surface more of the indiscriminate weapons which had maimed so many of their neighbors.

On days when we spent the 11 a.m. – 2 p.m. lunch and rest stop on temple grounds, I usually napped, but others didn't. I honored the stamina and willingness of Heidrun from Germany, a veteran of many peace marches across the US and Europe, who interacted most of the time with the children, teaching them to fold the origami paper peace cranes. She was magnificent, as was Peter from New Zealand, who took the opportunity to entertain those surrounding him with his juggling.

Our noon meals most often consisted of a bag of white rice flavored with dried fish, perhaps a fried insect or two, gifted to us by the farmers. We saw them walking down the trails to meet us carrying their donations, which they put into the truck for later distribution. I first blessed and then ate whatever was offered, with gratitude. We pilgrims would end our 15-20-kilometer days at host *wats* just before the sun set.

Since the monks slept in the temple proper and the nuns in the dining hall, the rest of us would scurry around the unfamiliar grounds to find a place for our mats and mosquito nets. At one site the only open space was in the burial grounds. The Asians had fearful ideas about the spirits in such places, thoughts which we didn't share (or have the luxury of entertaining that night), as we set up our bedding between the mounds. This also happened to be one of the few nights we heard persistent sounds of artillery shells booming across the countryside from a distant battle between the army and Khmer Rouge guerrillas. A chilling night that was...

To speak of a lack of toilets was an understatement. Three-sided walls around holes in the ground did provide one level of privacy, but the stench was enough to risk constipation. Having to relieve oneself while on the way was tricky business. Nothing to do but squat in plain sight on those roads with shoulders declared landmine contaminated. They were marked with a black skull and crossbones image on a hot red colored background. My semi-flared skirt provided the only degree of modesty.

Interesting, the water bit. We never had to filter water as expected because our luggage transport truck carried cases and cases of plastic bottled water. This gift showed up as a donation from a well-heeled Cambodian who walked along with us for part of the week. Being western educated, he befriended the English speakers and updated us on world news. He also invited us to share the sumptuous evening meals delivered to him for the three days that we had his company. Lots of vegetables, even desserts, were served on porcelain plates with proper cutlery; purified water arrived in glass bottles.

The plastic water bottles gifted to the walkers were emptied and immediately dropped along the way. Such disposal was a problem only for those of us conscious of littering and recycling. We tried to exemplify saving the bottles by collecting as many as we could and putting them into the back of the transport truck, but to no avail. A trail of plastic bottles was left like litter on a wave's wake on the side of the road by the pilgrims. Perhaps the locals found a use for them. Later, I noticed streamers of them hanging from flagpoles.

◇ ◇ ◇

"A boy has been killed." This sad, bone-chilling news was related to the intermittent shelling we'd heard the day before.

"He was wounded by a shell fragment and died while being driven to the hospital." This tragedy brought to mind the fate of the two pilgrims who were killed the previous year. It served as a reminder that we were still in the war zone, which made our actions and interactions even more poignant.

In spite of this loss and the deaths of his family members, friends and fellow monks in the war, Maha, sometimes called the "Buddha of the Battlefields," was consistent in his message. Whenever he addressed the gatherers, this genuinely peaceful monk preached from Buddha's words of love, the Metta Sutra:

> *"With boundless heart*
> *Shall one cherish all living beings,*
> *Radiating love over the entire world,*
> *Spreading upwards into the sky,*
> *And onward into the depths..."*

The leader's aura of peace and calm reinforced his messages: "Hate can never be appeased by hate; hate shall only be appeased by love."

The peace march arrived in Battambang, the capital of this western province, on May 12th. We were greeted by thousands of people and six interfaith colleagues who rejoined us there, and were given an amazing reception by the locals who had waited for hours in the rain for our arrival. They lined the roads to receive the ritual blessing of peace as they had in the previous three years. Everyone wanted peace. Even armed military men here put down their guns as Maha passed, just as we had seen other soldiers manning roadside defenses do. They bowed for his blessing and to declare their wish for the end of conflict as well. In speaking of them later, Maha said, "The soldiers pray with us. They pray that their bullets will not kill the Khmer Rouge because they are their brothers."

◇ ◇ ◇

I found it more difficult to walk through the noise and tuk-tuk traffic as we entered the business district. Battambang, once the prime target of the

Khmer Rouge insurgency, was now repopulating and reclaiming some of its riverside charm. We passed some faded but still lovely buildings in the French colonial architectural style. The population just wanted to get on with normal lives, which included feasting on the king of the fruits. Mango was in season, and we ate it greedily like sheep at the trough, not just to boost our immunity, which it did, but because it was plentiful and exotic and sweet and juicy and ad-picture perfect.

We stayed overnight at Wat Kanthal before launching into 11 more days of walking through rural countryside en route to Phnom Penh. For three days, the wide roads were shaded by coconut palms which offered fresh coconut water to drink from the road vendors. On the following three days the scenery was the same, but only Coke or Pepsi were available for sale in the stalls. Unaware that Cola Wars were going on internationally between the two soft drink producers, I didn't realize these liquids were often more available than potable water. Even though I promised myself to take only what was freely given (or offered for sale), I broke the precept and asked a local man for coconut water. He was happy to climb a tree to pick one to accommodate me, and wouldn't accept money for it. Another random act of kindness among many.

Dhammayietra IV was over. We were all safe. We had completed the 21-day mission across Cambodia, a country still devastated by a killing war. A different reality lay ahead. There was a bit of confusion at the Cambodian-Vietnamese border as we transitioned into an industrialized country which sought to enter the world economy while still maintaining its traditions.

Forty-Two

Scars of War / Vietnam

mericans called it the Vietnam War; Vietnamese called it the American War. Either way, it was hell.

However, the Vietnam we saw in 1995 was like a phoenix, risen from the ashes of decades-long conflicts in spite of repression of the press and other communist controls. Permission to enter was granted us at the last minute, only because one of the pilgrims, who joined us at the border, knew the Vice President. There was a stipulation, however. "The powers that be" would plan our trip and book our hotel and transportation. Almost no walking would be permitted. We were not, however, discouraged from drumming and praying publicly at cemeteries and memorials, of which there were many.

My first memory of the Vietnam conflict in the late 1950's was during my college days when I dated a big guy named Moose, one of the early returning soldiers. Having served as so-called "early advisors" in Vietnam, these vets were mature and exciting to me. They were happy to be able to afford a higher education because of the GI Bill. Later, after college, when working as a civilian with the US Army in Germany in the early 1960's, I remember meeting some GIs who were volunteering to go into the jungles of Vietnam to fight the VietCong rather than stay in the chill of America's Cold War with Russia.

Back in "the land of the round door knobs" (as the GIs called the US) during the rest of the sixties, I was barefoot and pregnant and loving my babies. Starting back to work in the early 1970's while raising our children, I paid as little attention as possible to the horrors of napalm, body counts, the Gulf of Tonkin incident, Operation Rolling Thunder, the Tet Offensive, the Mai

Lai Massacre, Agent Orange, and the Kent State killings. But I was attracted to the Beatles – who wasn't? – and the "flower children." I sang along with the protest songs: "Where have all the flowers gone?" and "Blowing in the Wind." I started wearing more colors and a t-shirt with a marijuana leaf on it, a gift from a friend who had a good laugh knowing that I didn't realize what I was promoting. It was a shock to me when I found out, and I never wore it again. (I would now, nature girl that I am.)

I finally woke up enough to allow myself to feel the angst. After placarding as "Another Mother for Peace," I campaigned and voted in allegiance with the anti-war movement during this turbulent period.

I volunteered as a "Beyond War" facilitator in the eighties, a dream child of academicians from the San Francisco peninsula. Being as terrified as many others about the stockpiles of nuclear weapons nightmare in the world, my small effort (with a partner as two of 23,000 others across 23 states) to encourage political action, was by educating groups about these dangers and its potential global catastrophe. The most dramatic part of the presentation was when my partner and I would slowly pour thousands of BB's into a tin garbage can to represent the number of bombs stockpiled. It took quite a while and made lots of noise. I hate to imagine how those piles of nuclear weapons of mass destruction have grown and are still growing exponentially in sophistication and proliferation in this present-day. (Some suggest that there are now countwise fewer nuclear weapons. How few is few enough?)

On this pilgrimage, being given the opportunity to make up for my historical lapses, I discovered early on that I had (and still have) a lot to learn and unlearn, with so many erroneous or half-baked beliefs based on the media's fact/fake reporting.

One of our most heart-wrenching tours was of the American War Museum in Ho Chi Minh City (Saigon), later renamed the War Remnants Museum. Some called it propaganda because it concentrated only on US acts and tools of aggression. I had difficulty looking at the gruesome, almost life size photographs of the deeds of war-deranged soldiers, the effects on civilians from the US use of napalm and phosphorus bombs, and scenes of the dead and those who wished-they-were-dead. Seeing the photo of controversial counterculture icon Jane Fonda sitting on an anti-aircraft gun in Hanoi and smiling, implying she approved of the shooting down of US pilots, made me aware of how any act, naïve or otherwise, can be used to promote either side of a cause. Eventually, these very same photos, along with many others, served to redirect public attention in the US, and were instrumental in bringing an end to America's involvement in the war. The horror and cost of the annihilation could no longer be ignored.

In the museum we also saw a display of rows upon rows of US pilot helmets, along with a sculpture of welded-together parts of downed US boats and planes. These graphically portrayed the magnitude of the destruction in the war that the US and South Vietnamese lost. Regardless of how many battles we may claim we won, the reunification of North and South Vietnam was under Communist control, as the country became the Socialist Republic of Vietnam in 1976. Even two decades later when we pilgrims arrived, there was a lack of real reconciliation between the north and the south, in spite of newfound prosperity resulting from the lifting of the trade embargo by the US the previous year. War has no winners.

We pilgrims, known as "The Delegation," departed Ho Chi Minh City (still called Saigon by many) by train on the fourth day. We continued north to the capital city of Hanoi on an official 12-day tour of historic spots. Sitting on hard, straight backed benches on a train called the Reunification Express, it took 25 hours to travel from the former South Vietnam capital of Saigon to the 17th Parallel and the demilitarized zone (DMZ) dividing line in Quang Tri Province. Here was the scene of the heaviest fighting during the war, the land still highly contaminated with unexploded ordinances.

We were bused to the Truong Son National Cemetery where Buddhist monks led us in a ritual to liberate the battlefields. Set on 202 acres and holding 10,000 graves, a fraction of the 300,000 North Vietnamese soldiers missing in action, each grave had a martyr inscription. As at all military cemeteries, Ho Chi Minh's words were inscribed on the monument: "There is nothing compared to freedom and independence." (Is combat and destruction the only way to get freedom and independence?)

Along the way, four pilgrims who were veterans of the Vietnam War met with some of their former enemies and invited us to sit in on the discussion. I was especially moved by the interaction between an American bombardier gunner upon meeting a VC pilot. They spoke to each other calmly, each in hopes of forgiving and making peace with the other. Acceptance and kindness, not anger, were the norm in all of our interactions with the Vietnamese people, in spite of the disfigurations of their bodies and their geography, and the loss of life and livelihood we had inflicted on them.

In this area of most intense conflict, tens of thousands of kilometers of dense jungle were destroyed. This ecosystem that had still supported wild elephants and tigers in the mid-sixties was defoliated by Agent Orange. People rebuilt their lives as best they could in spite of all the suffering; but I can't help wondering: where did the animals go?

We tread silently around wide and deep bomb craters on this land where a ratio of seven tons of bombs per person had been dropped. We climbed down into some of the 30-meters-deep underground tunnels. Entrances were camouflaged where entire villages had taken shelter from the intense B-52 bombings and the chemical warfare. This elaborate network of tunnels was a 120-kilometer complex which housed the villagers with public and private spaces, plus serving as supply routes for the resistance. Those living below ground endured a difficult life. Air, food, and water were scarce; they shared space with ants, centipedes, spiders, scorpions and vermin; many were stricken with malaria.

I visualized GIs walking the surface on night patrol and being ambushed by Viet Cong guerrillas coming up through trap doors to engage in battle. I heard about soldiers called "tunnel rats" who were assigned to enter and "investigate" the entrances they found. Their casualties were great because of the booby traps at those openings. (Trained dogs took over the tasks with equally high mortality.)

War is hell. As poet Robert Burns said, "Man's inhumanity to man makes countless thousands mourn!"

◇ ◇ ◇

Back on the northbound train for another 15 hours of travel before arriving in Hanoi (in so-called North Vietnam), we crossed the Ben Hai River, once the middle of the DMZ. Railroading through once ravaged rice paddies, bulldozed swatches of jungle and razed villages, we now viewed renewal. We passed rice farmers walking with hands on wooden plows being pulled by giant water buffalo. There were fish being farmed, and shrimp being cultivated. S-shaped Vietnam with its central highlands, spectacular mountain scenery, and over 3,000 kilometers of coastline was a beautiful country, as were its people.

Leaving the stunning wilderness of the countryside, we entered the cosmopolitan capital city of Hanoi, which turned out to be a fascinating blend of East and West, of Sino (Chinese)-Vietnamese motifs and European flair. There were French-style villas, shady lanes, and busy streets. We got caught in a swirl of cars with honking horns weaving around families on scooters, men on motorbikes, cyclos (pedicabs), casual pedestrians, vendors in conical hats, and pretty women on bicycles. How did these petite women manage to look so lovely, while tenuously balancing the bamboo poles slung over their shoulders with huge bundles hanging off either side?

Our government-directed tour continued as we passed by the Ho Chi Minh Mausoleum where the famous Communist leader (1890-1969) had his final resting place in plain view under glass. This was quite a contrast to our next event, the Water Puppet Theater, where the puppeteers stood in waist deep water behind a screen. They danced and glided the hand carved puppets, created out of fig wood, on the surface of the water which was the stage. This traditional reenactment is their often-repeated story about a king and a dragon (another type of conflict). We were surprised by the ability of the dragon to be a firebreather. Its creator put fireworks inside the puppet to create the effect.

That was the extent of our official visit, which concluded with a meal of whatever looked good, purchased from vendors on the street. It might have been duck blood soup or fried frog, but it was delicious and cheap. How casually we ate whatever was available. Picky eaters we were not. We had other fish to fry.

◇ ◇ ◇

We did make one more stop in Vietnam as a Pilgrimage, which turned out to be one of my favorite holy places. At a tenth century Buddhist pagoda, reverent monks and nuns greeted us. This One Pillar Pagoda, rebuilt not long before we arrived, was decorated for our visit. After feeding us a delicious lunch of nuts, pungent fruit, cakes sweetened with coconut milk, and tea, they led us through an unusual ceremony. In single file, we walked joyfully into the temple holding a long, wide train of red cloth up over our heads. It was believed that by holding the red cloth we were gaining great merit as we honored the Goddess of Money to whom the temple was dedicated. I imagined the merit there and then, the shekels to arrive later.

As it turned out, 1995 was an important year in American – Vietnamese relations, a good year to visit. Diplomatic relations were restored between the United States and the Socialist Republic of Vietnam, with the opening of an American Embassy in the capital city of Hanoi. After noting such activities marking the 20th anniversary of the "no way to win" end of the Vietnam/ American War, we 18 pilgrims flew to the Philippines.

Forty-Three

The Philippines

The view from the Manila Airport / City Center shuttle bus was the extent of my sightseeing, enough to imprint on my mind the sprawling, polluted, noisy nature of this densely populated capital city. We passed slums next to streams, beside factories and in dumps, even next to mansions. I doubted there would be space for us until sequestered in a hotel. I was glad to close my eyes for our overnight stay after the initial orientation and a short press conference about the purpose of our Pilgrimage.

Our bus the next morning headed north. Seven hours later we arrived in Baguio, the cooler Summer Capital in this mountainous area. There we received a warm welcome as we were joined by 12 other pilgrims, mostly new people but some reuniting ones.

Our journey from north to south, walking for some 300 miles when not on public transport, was organized by the "Initiators for International Dialogue," as they called themselves, who orchestrated more than adequate care, food and shelter for us over the entire four weeks. Most of our hosts were happy charismatic Christian groups and most generous about sharing whatever they had. Many of their young and energetic members walked with us and entertained us with their music and dance. Wise elders taught us history lessons about American colonialism.

Having only a vague knowledge of World War II in the Philippines, I was shocked once again by the effects of my country's military actions during that period, as well as the present day effects of developmental policies made for the benefit of transnational and multinational corporations. (How does one balance environmental damage done with trickle-down job creating opportunities?)

The Pilgrimage took on this additional economic/environmental focus for us all. The lush rainforest that had once covered this archipelago was now devastated by legal and illegal clear cutting, some for crop cultivation, but mostly for the sale of lumber to international markets, with the US being one of the biggest. After becoming aware of this, I never again looked at wood in quite the same way and took it as a call to ask myself, when making a purchase of something made of wood, especially exotic wood, if it was truly necessary. (It's no sacrifice to give up buying a teak headboard for a bed, but would I desire or be tempted to accept a gifted jewelry box with custom ebony inlay? I was somewhat relieved to learn that acoustic piano keys are most often now "Ivorite" plastic for whites and hardwood stained black for the other 36 keys, small comfort that it is.)

The indigenous Aeta people believed trees were much more than a commodity. As one woman expressed, "My people believe that each person has a tree companion for life. The tree's spirit intertwines with the spirit of the person, so that whatever happens to the person happens to the tree. They are interconnected; both are sacred."

If being sacred were not enough, trees left standing could have prevented at least some of the monsoon and typhoon water damage in the event and aftermath of the 1991 eruption of Mount Pinatubo, another area we visited.

We learned that 364 communities and 2.1 million people were affected by the volcano's activity. The indigenous Aeta people were hit the hardest with the destruction of their mountainous homelands by the aroused dragon. Even these four years later, it felt as if we were on another planet as we walked on miles of cement-like earth over the buried infrastructure. We ferried across deep streams between villages in the provinces most affected by the volcanic disaster. We saw first-hand the ongoing damage caused by the continuous flow of so-called "labar," a mix of volcanic ash, sand and water.

Ash from the sides of the volcano was re-mobilized by the yearly monsoons and frequent typhoons. It became an incredible tonnage which added feet every year to the ground level.

Wasteland though it was, it was also homeland. Some villagers chose to build new homes using the hard covered rooftops of their previous houses as the foundation. In other places, we saw only rooftops resting in a desert environment.

Little more than the dome and the belfry remained visible of the San Guillermo Roman Catholic Church, a once impressive cathedral. The priest there offered a memorial service at an altar in what used to be the choir loft. We sat facing him on white plastic chairs on uneven sand-packed earth, hardened "labar," level to the top of the stained-glass windows. The sound of the big brass bell, now so close to the ground, reverberated with shock waves across the empty landscape, where once there were groves of bamboo and fields of rice. I personally needed those prayers to cope with what we had seen, and for what we were yet to encounter.

Most of the people displaced by the volcano had been moved to government-organized resettlement sites such as San Fernando, where we were invited to spend an overnight in the new homes of those recent arrivals. They were simple houses laid out on a grid, and the population, though comfortable, was bored and listless, and would much rather have been living on their own small farms. Our hosts wanted to converse, to share stories of what had been and what was ahead, to get our opinions and to give us theirs. It was hard for them to adjust to semi-city ways so unlike what they had known. We listened to their stories about the rivers where they had fished, the groves of exotic wood or bamboo forests that had shaded them, and the acres of rice and vegetable fields where they once worked tending to crops, poultry and livestock. They spoke about their strong Catholic beliefs, and about unemployment, dull days, and alcoholism. We heard the wishes of the young men whose greatest desire was "to go to America to get rich."

"Enough talk," said the teens who wanted to introduce us to their rock music. "You gotta hear The Eraserheads. You don't know the Philippines if you don't know the Eheads. Best band ever, the Beatles of the Philippines. They have songs to make us laugh, cry, be aware of things, and dance." And so the evening ended with their vocals and gyrations along with their legendary band, their "Brown Music" counterpart to American Black Music blasting from a boombox. Not long after, our hosts directed us to their beds which they vacated for the night to give us a place to sleep. The less they had, the more they shared.

The next morning we moved 37 kilometers south, where we studied a big city scene in Olongapo City, site of the only recently closed US Subic Bay Naval Base. We met with Father Shay Cullen, a Catholic missionary priest with a thick Irish brogue, who stressed that "Childhood is for Children." That was what he called his efforts on behalf of the hundreds of children that his PREDA foundation had rescued from brothels, domestic abuse, and worse. Here, in his adopted homeland, he had started this humanitarian effort with two locals in 1974. We joined Father Shay at the loving orphanage he had founded in a comfortable setting high on a hill overlooking the bay, where the Seventh Fleet both brought in and sailed away with the fathers of these "Amerasian" children.

We then meandered down (chanting? probably not) the long strip row of bars in the town's red-light district reactivated as a sex tourist industry now that the naval base was no longer in operation. The nearby US Clark Air Force Base was also closed in the early 1990's, removing what many thought of as a vestige of colonialism, but leaving behind toxic contaminants and negative norms. Local women, many underage, hosted servicemen on R&R when called in from the impoverished rural areas to act as "bar girls" whenever a ship came in. They did what they felt necessary to help support their families.

The military establishment supposedly took steps to assure that prostitutes received regular check-ups for STDs. However, should a woman get pregnant, the military did not consider that to be any of their business. Often, these children were sooner or later abandoned by their parents. Soldiers were, in fact, actively discouraged from marrying their Filipino sweethearts, with such messages as "She won't fit in back home." Father Shay had recently worked with an association of 720 mothers who brought a class action suit in an effort to gain compensation for those children deserted by their fathers.

Even if the mother did try to raise an offspring, these Filipino-American children were not accepted by either culture. Discriminated against, abused, dirt poor, living on the street, neglected, uneducated, often imprisoned and stigmatized, they became victims of child prostitution rings and human trafficking. The odds were against women who worked at what appeared to be their one and only available trade.

Precedent being set, the district still housed profitable bar businesses, many run by former US servicemen. Lax and corrupt law enforcement was what Father Shay fought against for decades in his efforts to protect the vulnerable and put the pedophiles out of business. He also started health education programs to prevent the spread of the AIDS epidemic, and job-creating recycling industries for the unemployed. It was an honor to meet with him twice before moving on.

◇ ◇ ◇

Was I wrong to perceive that walking part of the route of the Bataan Death March was more difficult for the Japanese delegation on the Pilgrimage because of the Japanese War Crime it represented? Some estimated 60,000 Filipino and 9,000 American POWs had surrendered after being defeated in the 1942 Battle of Bataan by the Japanese Imperial Army. These weakened, sick and starved combatants were forced to walk some 64 miles to internment Camp O'Donnell under most arduous conditions, bayoneted and beaten if too weak to walk. When news and visuals of this reached the American public, a graphic photograph became propaganda. A recruitment poster with bold print read: "What are you going to do about it? Stay on the job until every *murdering jap* is wiped out."

Our role as pilgrims was the opposite: we chanted for those left dead by the side of the road or buried in mass graves there.

Revenge for the doomed defense of Bataan was the aftermath which Supreme Allied Commander General Douglas MacArthur exemplified when he kept his "I shall return" promise on October 20,1944. He commanded combined naval, marine, and air forces (225,000 troops and 600 ships) for the invasion of the island, resulting in the recapture and liberation of the Philippines from the Japanese. We chanted and drummed as we walked this same Red (blood-spilled) Beach of Leyte where MacArthur and Allied commanders waded to shore, a highly memorialized (later rehearsed reenactment?) event. War is so dramatic a hell on earth which mankind can't seem to live without.

Distressing as well was the visit to the fortress island of Corregidor, another historical/hysterical destination pockmarked with a war-ruined, mile long barracks, seacoast guns and abandoned weapons in a "rust in peace" environment. There were more memorials to chant around and the Malinta Tunnel, the well-shielded solid rock Allied headquarters, to walk through while hearing our chanting echoed back to us.

On our pilgrimage back to the capital city, even before we heard about the 100,000 civilians who perished there in the last days of the war, I realized that I couldn't, or didn't want to, learn much more about the madness. I started to ask myself, "Haven't I done enough penance? Why hasn't mankind learned to be kind? When will we ever learn? Is it true what that veteran said about it being only the dead who will know no more war? I want to go home. But I don't have a home."

The tales and the trials continued, however, as we heard about the bloody Manila Massacre, the so-called liberation that destroyed this once "Queen of the Pacific." Determined to keep my grip and finish what I had started, I fasted and prayed with the others in the city center called Intramuros, which was once an ancient architectural and cultural wonder "within the walls."

Soon after and yet again, I was relieved to move on and fly to Japan for the grand finale, the last month of the pilgrimage. Others must have felt finale fever also, as our core group of 12 Westerners and five monks swelled to over 100 walkers soon after we arrived in Hiroshima for the 50th anniversary commemoration of the US bombings.

Forty-Four

Japan:
50th Anniversary of the End of WWII

Once in Japan, I realized I needed three boxes in which to file my attitude toward the Japanese. I buried the one labeled the "Militaristic Japs" who were guilty of such atrocious war crimes as were recorded in Cambodia and the Philippines, and heaven knows where else. (Not that any American should throw the first stone.) In box #2, I held in high esteem the Nipponzan Myohoji Buddhist monks who led the pilgrimage. The third box was for the country and the countrymen I met in their homeland: modern, neat, polite and prosperous – judging from the lush toilets.

Can a country's affluence be measured by its toilets? Skip Schiel, a long-time activist from Boston with a sense of the absurd and one of my favorite fellow pilgrims, had that realization and gave me ideas for this report of the luxurious facilities in Japan (1995).

The squat toilets which were common in countries just visited – most often outhouses, limited in number and sans toilet paper – were sometimes flushable if not backed up because of low water pressure. My experience with the squatting variety available in Japan's public spaces found them always clean, well-watered, and stocked with paper. The sit-down style in some hotels and homes was often positioned side-by-side with a bidet. (I laugh as I remember that spring of water treat from the bidet in the Crocodile Dundee movie.)

On the Super Express train, where a choice of "thrones" – western style or Japanese style – was available, there were never quite enough Ladies Rooms (like most anywhere in the world), although unisex toilets helped shorten the lines. Men could also use the urinal behind a Gentlemen door.

There were high technology toilets, with written instructions understandable if you read Japanese or experimented with the novel control buttons off to the side. Some had heated seats and variable water rates and temperatures, even hand washing bowls attached. (Was I anxious to get back to America and see if the self-closing lids were available? It reminded me of the time I shared my ignorant belief, when I was a student in Denmark in the 1960's, that "everybody in America had central heating." I had only to visit West Virginia hill country soon after to learn of mostly pot belly stoves and outhouses.)

Japan was prosperous, yes, and also expensive. It cost more for the seven-day Rail Pass "Bullet Train" ticket than I had spent in the previous month. It was, however, an impressive adventure, maybe my once-in-a-lifetime, and a relative bargain as well. After flying into Osaka, we boarded the high-speed train (275 mph), a bullet-looking wonder. Within hours, we were in Kyoto. To maintain that speed required separate tracks, (off-limits to other trains) which had minimum curves as the train went through tunnels and over viaducts, not around obstacles. There was also no slowing down while crossing roads, being no road crossings at grade.

At the Kyoto stop, Sasamori wanted us to experience one of the world's most beautiful temples in this city of 10,000 shrines. He hired cabs for our tribe of 12 Westerners and five monks, given our brief stopover. We taxied past palaces, impressive gardens and amazing architecture, before arriving with just enough time to touch the earth, enter the magnificent temple, view the oriental garden, and say one prayer before re-boarding. I was awestruck at this reverent and beautiful introduction to Japan, but sorry for not buying a postcard identifying which of the most famous of the famous temples we visited.

When we returned to Kyoto at the end of the pilgrimage, we were again inspired by the Buddhist religion upon visiting the Sofukuji Temple, a Chinese Zen temple of Ming Dynasty architecture, which featured a giant cauldron used by the temple monks to feed up to 3,000 people in a 17th Century famine. (Food kitchens are not a recent phenomenon.)

After three hours at 275 mph by train on August 3rd, 1995, we arrived in Hiroshima where a 100 more walkers joined us for the offerings. Our Japanese hosts planned delicious meals which we (sometimes, sorta) helped prepare. We shared facilities, sleeping side-by-side in a huge hall, while newcomers camped outside in tents. The next few days were booked with meetings with town officials and walking, chanting and drumming, banners flying, as we made our way through the busy high end shopping district with a police escort. That was a challenge to my ego. I felt we were unseen, if not ignored. I observed all the extremely well-dressed pedestrians and compared our life choices. I had to have a good talk to myself and refocus on miracle-mindedness, after realizing how quickly I had become a materialist again.

It remained more stressful than prayerful to me until we got to the Peace Park to hold a ceremony at the Children's Peace Monument, where a young girl named Sadako Sasaki was immortalized in bronze. She was cast standing tall holding a gold wire crane above her head, the symbol that inspires children and adults around the world to hold and share her vision. Sadako was two years old and two miles away when "Bomb Little Boy" was dropped on Hiroshima. At ten years old, she was diagnosed with leukemia, the "atomic bomb disease." While hospitalized with so many others suffering from radiation poisoning, this child spent her last days folding origami cranes before dying at the age of 12. She had hoped to make 1,000 peace cranes in order to earn a legendary promise of the fulfillment of one wish upon completion. Her desire was that no one, especially children, would ever have to suffer from war again. The tradition of making peace cranes to share or present at her shrine and elsewhere continues to this day. Heidrun, our energetic pilgrim from Germany, respectfully hung the chain of 1,000 cranes we had made with the help of many others she had involved in the origami folding along our way.

Later that afternoon, we strolled through a bamboo forest to the Peace Pagoda at another Nipponzan Myohoji Temple which was even more conducive to prayer and meditation from its hillside site above the city. We returned there in the evening for a candlelight ceremony where monks placed 100 candles, one for most of us, on different levels of the pagoda, which illuminated its beauty against the dark blanket of the night sky.

On August 5th, we fasted, and viewed and prayed at the only edifice left near the epicenter of the A-Bomb blast. The Atomic Bomb Dome with its gaping hole in the roof, now a skeletal structure of steel ribs, was all that was left intact. Once the Product Exhibition Hall building, it retained much of its original intent as it continued to serve as an art and educational exhibit. Even in its destruction, it became a sculptural symbol of death and the resurgence of life for the city of Hiroshima.

The YMCA International Hall served as our meetup with the Native American leader Dennis Banks, whom we'd met at Auschwitz. I was pleased to receive one of the "Long Walker" patches from him. Others were presented with "Long Runner" recognition for having just run the length of Japan with him, all of us like-minded in our efforts for peace.

A Paper Lantern Ceremony took place on the eve of the 50th anniversary of the first war time atomic bombing. Many of us were drawn back to the epicenter at nightfall for this dramatic event in memory of the Hiroshima civilians whose lives were lost even as the war was ending. In what became an annual event, thousands of colorful paper lanterns were released on a finger of the Ohta River, each floating vessel to represent someone who died there. A lit candle, set in the middle of a simple wooden eight-inch square frame (as base for four sticks wrapped in a paper coat of many colors as windshield), was launched from stairs ending at river height. I purchased two, one to float in solidarity and one as a memento, even though I didn't need a souvenir to remind me what it must have been like for the victims. Without warning, they experienced an intense blinding flash of light, followed by a blast of hot air, darkened sky, falling buildings, and temporary unconsciousness if not instant annihilation. We were told that as victims regained consciousness, it was to find their bodies burning hot. Begging for water, without refuge, no sanctuary and nobody to help, they tore at their burnt skin. Thousands jumped into the river hoping for relief, or to escape a raging firestorm which lasted three days after the fireball.

Effects long surpassed the immediate devastation, to voice the obvious. It remains difficult to this day for me, for most, to recount the horror of that nuclear date with hell. Others, nevertheless, are stimulated to build even more powerful bombs and larger stockpiles as a "deterrence." But are they really a deterrent? Unfortunately, history has shown that all new weapons, each more devastating than its predecessor, have eventually been used in warfare. When first invented, the machine gun and the airplane, for example, were believed to be too terrible to ever be used in warfare, but unfathomable as it was, they were eventually engaged in the wages of war. That thought contributes to the overly-nervous system of many of us.

On the actual 50th anniversary of the Hiroshima nuclear holocaust, we returned early to the Peace Park along with 60,000 people from around the world for the city sponsored Peace Ceremony. Bells were rung and sirens wailed just before the moment of silence from 8:15 to 8:16 a.m., the exact time of the explosion of the bomb on August 6th 1945, 50 years earlier.

Other than that, the atmosphere was festive as camcorders whirled and bands played. Citizens were glad to be alive and grateful for the physical and economic recovery that they witnessed. The reality check came later at the noontime address by Mayor Takashi Hiraoka of Hiroshima. We listened carefully to his highly anticipated speech about events a half-century before. We heard him apologize "for the unbearable suffering that Japanese colonial domination and war inflicted on so many people."

When a reporter asked me if I had heard the apology, I replied, "Of course, but I feel equally inclined to request forgiveness for my country's part in the war, for the dropping of the bombs which annihilated 200,000 civilians."

While later repeating my apology in a small discussion group with Hiroshima survivors, one Japanese man said, "Oh no, it was wonderful what America did; it was necessary. The bomb was the only thing that could have brought about the collapse of the entrenched feudal system in Japan and allow the phoenix of the new civilization of Japan to rise from the ashes."

Others spoke of how it was better to have the resulting US influence over Japan, rather than that of the Soviet Union or China. Another said it destroyed the patriarchy and allowed women more freedom.

Upon hearing those comments, I was both horrified and more confused than ever as to who was right, and what was necessary. Was it possible that even in war things are meant to be and work out for betterment?

Again I asked myself, "Who is the enemy?" Or even, "Who is the winner?"

As Jean-Paul Sartre said, "Once you've heard the details of victory, it is hard to distinguish victory from defeat."

In spite of the moral implications, and presumably because the Hiroshima bomb did not elicit immediate Japanese surrender, another B-29 bomber dropped an even more complex and powerful bomb on Nagasaki three days after the first city was destroyed. More instantaneous and early deaths, long term illnesses, pulverized buildings, and carbonized animals resulted from the "Fat Man" bomb dropped at 11:00 a.m. on August 9th, 1945.

President Harry S. Truman told the American public and the world that this was necessary to "shorten the agony of war and to break the enemy morale." The question remains about the nature of this atrocity: was it the lesser of two evils or a war crime? Isn't all war criminal?

Hard as it is, I came to accept, as a result of the pilgrimage dedicated to hearing both sides of any conflict, that each party did what they believed they had to do to protect their families, their country, and their "way of life" (whether for the common good or for feathering one's own nest). Each partner in the dance of war believed that they were right, and were convinced that they would be victims if they did otherwise. Some justified revenge at any cost. Yet most people wanted to live ordinary lives in peace, and tended to blame governments and the military-industrial complex for the wars.

What is my individual responsibility in allowing such sour cream to rise to the top and make these big life and death decisions that affect us all so negatively? Could it possibly be as simple as "love our neighbor as ourselves" and my not loving enough? But if I feel guilty about what I have or have not done, what do I do with that guilt? Projecting it outward is a problem leading to more conflict, in the world and of it.

But what if there is no personal responsibility?

Haven't I been taught that there's no one home in a body? That the answer to "Who am I?" is not a name, rank or serial number? That this "me" is not controlling the blood and guts and breath that keep this particular bodywork activated? That it's only wishful thinking that I can always control my thoughts and behaviors? That I spend most of life on automatic and in conditioned reaction? That the so-called world seems to carry on without my managing it?

Personal responsibility implies an individual entity. Feeling like a separate self, going it alone, is scary and requires armour. Defend or attack. Attack or defend.

In Non-duality, when Aware, there is no separation, only One in consciousness, and only Love without defense. Thus, as Advaita teacher Rupert Spira expresses in his teachings, "In line with totality, we serve the totality." (View "The Essence of Non-duality," on YouTube: Scienceandduality.com.) Could that esoteric lesson in "not-two" be true? Would I someday realize the illusion, the maya, the mirage of separation?

I resolved that this realization was the moment to stop resenting my son's decision to be a warrior, to forgive myself for not recognizing that his choices were right for him (and were part of our believing in being in a material world). The time to heal our relationship had arrived. I longed for his forgiveness too.

I needed to go back to the *Bhagavad Gita* for spiritual help with this military mentality dilemma which still confronts us in the present day, 4,000 years later. This Hindu Vedic scripture's dialogue between Krishna (as God) and Arjuna (as military commander) has been interpreted as teaching that true peace is beyond this material world. War is a reflection of the ethical and moral struggle of human life, an allegory of the battle raging between good and evil.

This could serve as a righteous defense of the duty of the warrior class to fight a "just war," killing when necessary for the betterment of society, conducting the fight which is transcendent (beyond karma) in the service of good over evil. But are there not forces for good as well as evil on both sides? For whom do you fight? Can any human have the ability to be aware of all the facets of any situation?

Ah, duality. And non-duality. Could it be true that if it's not love, it's not happening? That while the body acts, the soul does nothing? That nobody dies? Can it be that simple when it is so complicated? It remained a koan.

That persistent dilemma drained the mojo out of me. It wasn't enough to deplore the devastation; I could not ignore the consequences. I drifted, dissociated, while struggling to be present.

◇ ◇ ◇

We left Hiroshima by bullet train and arrived at seaside Nagasaki after swishing through a landscape of bright green rice paddies, small villages, and mountain views. We were comfortably hosted by the Nakamachi Catholic Church in what was known as an unusually pious city, culturally and religiously diverse. Even though the casualties from the nuclear bombing were equally atrocious, Nagasaki city and harbor seemed to hold smaller and more understated ceremonies and war memorials, although one of the museums displayed exhibits as powerful arguments against nuclear proliferation. (I had used those facts as a Beyond War facilitator years before.)

We participated in the August 9th ceremonies at the Peace Park and Atomic Bomb Memorial at the hypocenter of that second blast. The exact 11:02 a.m. anniversary moment was marked by the sound of a wailing woman's voice over a loudspeaker, and the sight of a sea of bodies of young people who fell to the ground as if to join those who perished there.

The eeriness of the portrayal woke me up. I returned to our chant and echo ritual with fervor. Indigenous people from the Philippines invited us to individually ring a huge peace bell made from bomb casings that they had brought to Japan for the occasion. Its resonance made each step of waiting my turn in line into a prayer.

While resting on a park bench with some fellow pilgrims after our offering and the speeches, we were approached by one of our Nipponzan monks who introduced us to an elderly, wizened Japanese nun. He interpreted that she wished to meet each of the twelve pilgrims who had come the entire distance from Poland. We bowed and thanked her as she gave each of us an envelope to show her appreciation. Inside was a gift, the yen equivalent of 100 American dollars. (Was this the universe's way of returning to me the money that I had earlier or later donated to the Cambodian nun?)

We decided to blow it on dinner, a rarity for pilgrims who usually bought market food and prepared our own meals when we were not hosted. Restaurant windows displayed realistic plastic replicas of the meals served inside. Pointing to the mouth-watering items of our choice was easier than trying to read menus printed in Japanese. Even though we were unsure of what we ate (except the noodles, of course), we went back to the park satisfied with the splurge.

We arrived in time for the evening's Lantern Floating Ceremony on the river, which engaged me once again. Symbolic, traditional and beautiful, it was a ritual to remember and to affirm "never again." This time-honored Buddhist rite was believed to comfort the spirits of the dead and to ferry these spirits "from the sea of delusion to the shores of salvation."

En route from the historic sites in Kyoto back to Tokyo for the wrap-up of the pilgrimage, I robotically followed through five days with more walks, peace vigils, forums, and a visit to Mount Aso, the volcanic area and birth-place of Fujii Guruji, most venerable founder of the Nipponzan Myohoji Order. We had home stays where we slept on mats and squatted at low tables for traditional rice and tofu meals. Everyone was so generous. (Was I too exhausted to take it all in and appreciate the gifts? A bit of regret here.)

It was a full moon night when we visited the town of Beppu, situated between the bay of the Inland Sea and two dormant volcanoes. It was famous for its hot springs as well as being beautiful. Relaxation was the primary goal there for both posh vacationers and locals returning from work. We used the public baths, not the mixed-gender one for this tribe, washing and rinsing well before entering the springs, cleanliness being next to godliness, as well as mandatory.

We slept on mats again in Zen-like homes when we returned to Kyoto for another gracious home stay and a visit to two alternative/Community schools.

Elementary and junior high school education is compulsory, and most students attend these public schools. High schools are private and charge tuition. Since Japan is known to have the highest-educated workforce in the scientific and technological areas, schooling is intense, with the burden of highly competitive entrance exams for university admission. Being as not all students fit or can adjust to that mold, there is a more diversified, less struc-tured education available in Community Schools, most important in lessen-ing the pressure on the young, allowing more freedom of choice and more parental input as well.

My nephew Patrick and his Japanese wife had started such a school in Tokyo. Called the Nishimachi International School, it was/is successful in attracting the children of foreign diplomats and business people because of its forward-thinking curriculum, global perspective, English language instruction, and sports opportunities.

I soon had a chance to tell my sister Gini in person how impressed I was with her son's success as she had timed a visit with Patrick and his family to coincide with my arrival on the Pilgrimage in Tokyo. We also had other business to confirm.

"Let's do it," we agreed as we reunited with kisses and hugs and happy antics. The plot we had discussed for years and across many miles was soon to be reality.

"We're getting Mummy out of the nursing home in Indiana. Enough of her Midwestern living! We three will make a new home somewhere near the sea. Imagine mother and daughters united again. My moving back to the States will end our decades of East-West-coast separation and my galavanting around the world."

The family visit was short, but future plans were in the works and my spirits were lifted. It was a time to rejoice after a final walk in Tokyo and attendance at an "International Peoples Forum: Native Vision for the 21st Century," where we interacted with the Ainu people from Hokkaido at the University of Tokyo. Two celebrations followed.

A generous benefactor treated both pilgrims and monks to dinner and a night at Toshimaen Amusement Park. We cleaned our palettes after the fine dining with sake. This 15% alcoholic beverage was served in small cups to be emptied quickly to preserve the flavor. As a result, both monks and pilgrims got very happy. We weren't excessively happy, but rambunctious enough that the elder nun who accompanied us (and even floated with us through the tunnel of love) decided to step in. On the subway back to the Shibuya Dojo where we were staying, she made the young monks get out of the train two stops early. This holy woman was not going to have us walking into the temple together in our giggly state.

The next night, at our last full gathering, even our most reverent Sasamori celebrated with us, and loosened up a bit after the farewell speeches and lots of toasts. I reawakened to gratitude as songs were sung and tears were shed. Our peace posse exchanged even more addresses, certain that we would keep in touch after sharing so much on these many months and 10,000 miles of pilgrimage. Another adventure was over and we departed for different corners of the world.

Was it all perfect? Yes and No. It was WabiSabi: the embracing of the beauty of being imperfect, impermanent, and incomplete. (Would I have the privilege of living long enough to accept the beauty of the imperfection, the impermanence and never-done nature of my life?)

Would I do it again? Would I recommend it to others? My only advice: just do what you feel you have to do in every season to find the reason.

For me, I was right back to where I started this story, knowing there had to be another way, not just for my own personal life, but for each of us, beyond the politics, potholes and platitudes. My reaching the milestone of having given up the chase was enough of a paradigm shift for the moment. It was time to stop traveling and to sit down with the Buddha again, tend my own garden, and bloom where I was soon to be planted.

With Family of Origin on an Unfamiliar Garden Isle

Forty-Five

Transitioning

Flying from Tokyo to New Delhi on Japan Airlines let me cling to the beautiful Oriental country and its courtesies a little longer before I had to retrace some of my steps. Back in India, I closed out my bank account in Poona and purchased my New Delhi-London airline ticket. I wanted that one last stop in the UK to visit my daughter Michelle again before launching the new nesting project stateside with my mother and sister.

When I got to the airport, however, my flight to London on the Russian airline Aeroflot was overbooked. I stood there with about 30 people, stunned at the thought of being stranded for another 24 hours before the next scheduled flight. Perhaps that was why the ticket was so much cheaper than other airlines. A riot was in the making at the ticket counter with all those people desperate to get to Moscow and beyond.

"It is outside my control, and there's nothing I can do," the clerk coldly told the angry mob. "I suggest you speak with 'The Manager' in the office around the corner."

They all rushed off, each trying to be first in line. I stood practicing "accepting what is," plus trying to figure out how to lighten my overweight bag so as not to pay an extra fee, a highly unsavory deed against my principles. Everything jammed into my backpack and carry-on was important to me. So much for trying to stretch my funds.

Right after I opened my backpack and threw out the five ounce, four-tiered tiffin I treasured as a souvenir, the airline clerk at the desk addressed me.

"Excuse me, Madam, were you booked on this flight to London? I have one seat left, but you must board immediately." She tagged my overweight luggage without charging the excess fee, handed over a boarding pass, and directed me to the gate. "Hurry."

Without attempting to retrieve the tiffin, I rushed down the gangway; the jet plane doors closed behind me, and I was on my way as scheduled.

The Russian passengers all looked big to me after being with the tiny Japanese. I felt the cultural shift. Different attitudes became obvious once in the air after the "No Smoking" light was turned off. Seated on the aisle near the front of the plane, in the next row behind the smoking section, I was offended when a middle-aged man with a giant Soviet frame, standing in the aisle next to me, leaned on the back of my seat. He began conversing with the person behind me while enjoying a cigarette.

"Sir," I took it upon myself to inform him politely, "This is the non-smoking section."

The Cold War got a lot chillier as he straightened up, puffed up, glared at me, and angrily addressed me in Russian (something about being a %$!*# Americana).

Thoroughly intimidated and shaken, non-violent pacifist me didn't say another word or even glance at him. The stewardess said nothing. The man didn't move, cease talking, or stop smoking until he was good and ready to do so.

Fortunately, he deplaned in Moscow. (I also got my long-time wish to have "been to Russia" fulfilled, even if it was only a two-hour layover.) I would have been spared the rebuke had I known then, as we do now, that no matter where you were seated on the airplane in those "smoking allowed" days, all passengers were affected by the recycled air. It was also just as well that I didn't realize until after a gentle landing at London Gatwick that Aeroflot had a dubious safety record, though primarily on domestic flights.

Once grounded on English soil, sister Gini and I firmed up our new plans via phone conversations. She would take Mum from the nursing facility and meet me in late November in Atlanta, Georgia, where she had friends. From there and with their help, we would find our new dream residence on the coast. Savannah sounded nice. I felt confident that I could share Mum's care with my sweet sister. Gini, a registered nurse with a PhD in psychology, had experience in two potentially important roles on this mission.

Absolutely thrilled with the "I have to know what's next" arrangement (given my "homeless mentality"), I relished my time in London with my daughter Michelle at her Notting Hill flat with her British husband and my first granddaughter named Guinevere, who while I wasn't looking had grown into a beautiful, bright two-year-old. The toddler, whom I knew I wouldn't see often when on the other side of the Atlantic, had exceptional communication skills and I felt sure we had an incredible "first fruit" in the family tree. Not only that, Michelle was expecting her second child, another grandbaby I wouldn't be around to cuddle. My daughter seemed resigned to my future neglect while applauding my decision to take care of my mother.

Why was I so blind at that time and not see how overwhelmed Michelle was with juggling marriage, a demanding career, and a growing family. It seemed glamourous to me that she was living in Notting Hill, looked beautiful in her pregnant state, and had Guin in an excellent day care program. (I didn't approve of putting such young ones in someone else's care but convinced myself that that's what career mothers did those days. Besides, Guin had to be adaptable and was. She grew up to be very open minded after being raised with so many different colors and cultures in the childcare center Michelle had chosen.)

Thursday nights were my spiritual time whenever in London. I would accompany Tatiana, Michelle's British landed-gentry friend, to a meditation practice at the Friends of the Western Buddhist Order Center nearby. This angelic blond and I became closer as we shared the experience (which became important later). I was also a regular on Monday nights at Unity Church, for a Realization Fellowship meeting which satisfied my need for ritual; it provided almost more than enough ritual.

More family time across the Atlantic followed in Boston, where the living was easy with daughter Dianna and her husband Robert. My first-born always had great ideas of which museums to visit, gallery openings to attend, day trips to take. I also started to see movies again after five years away from that treat.

Following those reunions and that pampering, I hopped a bus and headed south to spend the winter as planned. It was my first trip to Georgia where Gini had rented a two-bedroom first floor flat, just down the street from a mall in Atlanta. It was to be short term until we manifested our dream position as property caretakers in a small coastal town. We visualized having enough time and savings/retirement monies to take care of Mum, do the work, walk the beach, and start art projects. It didn't happen. Regardless of all our efforts in that fantasy and the leads from all Gini's friends, we had to come up with a Plan B.

"What are you doing in all that December cold?" asked Monique, Gini's daughter, calling from Maui. "Come to Hawai'i where winters are mild." After her sharing about citrus fruits and tropical flowers, buildings only as tall as the highest palm tree, and how wonderful the 50th state was (in spite of being a very expensive place to live), Gini decided to fly over and check out the islands.

Meanwhile, Mum and I spent a dark, damp and drafty December getting reacquainted, which felt like something I could handle, determined as I was to "bloom where I was planted" and make the best of it. Mum was docile, didn't talk or smile, but seemed to trust me, maybe even to know who I was. We got exercise on our daily, three-block walk to purchase groceries and filtered water. Some days that was a real challenge on the black-icy sidewalks. While Mum was getting used to being outside of an institutionalized setting, I was adjusting to being responsible for someone besides myself once again. There would be time for art, however, and I planned on making a fabric wall hanging.

Before Gini left, I prepared for my project. I bused to another mall where there was a Singer store. I talked the owner into lending me a sewing machine in exchange for a wall hanging I promised to make for the store and to deliver when I returned the machine. (He was actually surprised when I came back four weeks later with the agreed-upon bartered art item.) I then collected remnant samples and fabric scraps, mostly white or off-white, from nearby Mathews Furniture Galleries. Looking back, I wonder why those merchants let me walk out with their property and goods without paying a cent. It must have been obvious that I was from another planet.

I even asked about the unfortunate young men hanging around the mall in loose garments with their pants hanging low on their hips (cracks showing), poor things. I didn't realize how utterly in fashion they were. Lots of things looked strange, including me in my four-year-old, well-worn, rayon outfit, wrapped up in shawls to keep warm.

Gini flew from the Atlantic coast to the Pacific islands. Now, only Mum and I shared the space, and my "hospital corners nurse" sister was not there to remind me to keep everything in its place. I positioned the borrowed Singer on what was usually the dining table, and spread all the fabric samples I had gathered all over the floor, leaving only a walking path clear. All this was left out day and night to facilitate my making the best choices as to which white fabric to use where, on my quilted work of art. Having made other fabric wall hangings while living with my daughters the previous two months, I knew what I wanted to create. It would be from the Tibetan tradition, similar to the Green Tara that I had recently completed while in Boston.

That particular divinity, a representation of the female Bodhisattva of Compassion, later made her home on a wall of a Tibetan Tara Temple on Kaua'i, where women held their monthly dances to honor the Goddess in each other and themselves. "Om Tare, Tu Tare, Ture Svaha."

The creation which came out of that Atlanta flat was my quilted fabric version of a painted thangka: a 3.5 x 6 sized Buddha. It was white-on-white except for the hair which turned red when the cotton fabric picked up color from our red-dirted environment. (At this point I hadn't learned that since the Buddha was a bald monk, 108 snails gave their lives to protect the enlightened one from sunstroke while meditating – hence the round knobs we see on sculptures are a cap of those martyrs.) My side-curtained Buddha sat in a lotus pose with his hands in the mystic mudra representing teaching: thumbs and fingers touching in a circular position. I copied the image as closely as I could from a Tibetan text that the artists in Dharamsala used for their wall paintings. After a few weeks of creative mess and lots of undisturbed time, since Mum and I had nothing to do and no place to go, I was almost finished.

It was New Year's Eve, and Gini was flying in from Hawai'i late the next day, the first of January, 1996. I had to complete my sewing project then and there. I stayed up all night working while Mum sat and slept in her comfortable, lounge chair covered with a couple of blankets. The radio provided the entertainment over the stitch, stitch, stitch of the sewing machine.

After midnight, as the traditional countdown of tunes from the 1930's to the 1940's, 1950's, 1960's, 1970's and 1980's progressed, I noticed Mum tapping her feet to "Hey Jude" by the Beatles. It might have been true also for "Good Vibrations" or when I sang along with "Bridge Over Troubled Waters" by Simon and Garfunkel in the 1970's Top Ten. From the 1980's, Madonna's "Like A Virgin" and "Sweet Dreams are Made of This" by the Eurythmics had me distracted and dancing. I didn't even recognize most of the popular songs from the early 1990's, having been on another continent at that time.

The white-on-white Buddha was coming together: head and halo, inked-in facial features, torso, hands and feet, clothing and side curtains. As the rising winter sun showed itself and the fabrics elevated from the floor to the thangka, I claimed well done. My mother wasn't that familiar with the Buddha and didn't appear impressed with my creation that dawn. Perhaps a Madonna might have solicited a second look. I rewarded her and myself with fig newtons and milk, assisted her with her shower, and helped her to bed before I collapsed onto mine, leaving the living room in a mess.

Later, after sweeping and dusting and detailing the flat, I admired the result of my labor of love which I had hung by a rod on the west wall of our sitting room. It looked quite feminine. This image of the teaching Buddha was to be another of my ad infinitum meditation tools meant to bring me further down the path to Enlightenment. I thought I had given up on that, but reviewed what I had been told: "See the Buddha as a guide and visualize yourself as being that deity, thereby internalizing the Buddha's qualities." Now there's a New Year's resolution for you.

Gini returned, tanned and glowing, to a perfectly ordered space around 7 p.m. with great news of a tropical island in the middle of the Pacific waiting for us. We packed a suitcase full of spirited plans for another new beginning in this year which had just been birthed. The "Go West" directions I had received long before in an I Ching reading were being fulfilled once again. This time I was going further west than California, but not planning on going so far west that I would be in the Far East again. I resolved to go to Hawai'i to float after all the strong swimming with and against the tides that I had done as a compulsive seeker.

Forty-Six

Kaua'i, Hawai'i

It was love at first sight. Kaua'i, the oldest of the Hawaiian chain, was the perfect Garden Isle for Mum, Gini and me. It was as far west as one could go and still claim living in the USA.

Eventually we settled in at the foot of the beautiful Waimea Canyon. Kekaha was the town furthest west in this westernmost state, also the hottest and driest on the leeward side of the island. This mile long, many horse town with its sweet-smoke-belching sugar mill was bordered by cane fields on the east below the Canyon, and the beautiful Pacific on the west. Gini had found a dream-come-true property for the three of us: a beachfront two-bedroom rental we could afford. It was of single wall construction, which I first learned when I drilled a hole for a hook in the wall and saw daylight. It had a two-burner propane stove, a big refrigerator, and a bathroom with a tub, better than a shower for our mother. A lovely cottage by the beach.

"It's hot, for sure, but I have thin blood after all that time in Asia. The temperature suits me fine," I wrote to my children. "And I'm living near Japanese, Filipino, Chinese, Portuguese and Hawaiian families. No chance of getting homesick for the Far East in this community of sugar mill workers. Not only that, there is a huge mango tree in the backyard, and the Haydens are ripe and delicious. Looking forward to your visits."

Since each of us had arrived with two suitcases only, there was a lot that we needed in order to make the house we shared into a home. First stop was the Salvation Army Thrift Store, top priority being a bed for Mum.

The second thing I did was hang my Buddhist thangka from a bamboo pole on a living room wall. No need for curtains, as the cottage was wrapped with tropical plants. The huge Hayden mango tree shaded the picnic table below it, and most of the back yard. This giant fruit-bearer generously provided mangos for drying, freezing and sharing for many months of the year-and-a-half that we resided there.

Mummy was such a joy to me, even though sometimes it was hard because of her unresponsiveness. Nevertheless, being off all the drugs except for her thyroid pills (Registered Nurse Gini's idea with Mum's new doctor's approval), she became more and more aware as the days drifted by on balmy Kaua'i. She had never been much of a talker even when we were growing up, busy as she was raising six children, while Daddy worked 24/7 on the same Coast Guard Station property where we lived. I remembered her humming as she lit the coal stove, cooked for the eight of us, washed clothes in a wringer washer, cleaned the house, and sewed or retrofitted many of our outfits. I missed those comforting vocalizations, her smile, and the turkey dinners she prepared for our too many to count family reunions over the decades. In retirement, she and Daddy shared the fruit from the mature trees and the vegetables they grew with the neighbors, landscaped with flowers, and hosted lawn parties for relatives.

Mum, even if confused, still appreciated men. We do have a rare picture of her grinning slightly, once, when one of Gini's men friends came to visit and started paying attention to her. Her eyes always lit up when our Kekaha landlord would stop and chat with us. Although perfectly ambulatory, Mum would take Joel's arm, feigning imbalance, and lean against him as they walked together.

As a slight, straight-postured, five-foot-tall woman, she was no problem as she could care for her basic needs and knew where her bed and the bathroom were. She loved to eat, especially sweets. Once she wandered over to the landlord's family home, entered their kitchen and stood at the counter enjoying some treats from their cookie jar. Upon discovering her there, Joel asked, "Do you want to take some brownies home?" He prepared her a baggie full, offered his arm, and walked her back to our door. She was happy, after close contact with that hunk and chocolate to boot.

"Come outside, Mum," I would say on many mornings. "It's time to collect the mangoes." She liked gathering the fallen fruits, then would sit across the picnic table from me, take out her false teeth, and happily gum the pits as I peeled and sliced up the Haydens.

"Have these bits too," I encouraged her, passing a plate of pieces too small to sun-dehydrate on a repurposed screen. When I was distracted or away from the table, our Ms. Sweet Tooth would slide the big bowl of choice slices over in front of her and really start feasting.

It was a bountiful and beautiful life. Sunset was our favorite time of day. We crossed the few hundred feet to our primarily private stretch of beach, where Mum immediately took off her shoes as soon as we approached the sand. We walked barefoot on the shoreline, our tabby cat following behind.

"I'm tired," Mum would say, always just at the point where we usually turned around to go back to our staked claim near an ironwood tree.

Gini and I had created a large, airy fence book-ending our 24' x 50' beach encampment by interlocking long and short, monster or pygmy sized, unique one of a kind sculpted pieces of wave-smoothed driftwood. We decorated this enclosure with various sizes, colors and shapes of floats and fishing nets to create a cozy conversation area around our rock-rimmed fire pit, complete with a semi-circle of curious chairs we discovered washed up on our shores. Two of these sit-upons were three legged and had to be jerry-rigged with rocks or wood to be secure, but Mum's was sturdy. Seated in her plastic throne with a comfortable pillow after our beach walk, our dear mother would spend many minutes carefully toweling the sand off her feet and from between her toes before putting her white socks and soft sneakers back on and tying them securely.

We ate supper before our nightly walks, and spent the hours of dusk in front of a driftwood campfire, sipping tea or enjoying an occasional marshmallow roast when we had company. One night on our walk back to the cottage long after sunset, Mum slowed down even more than usual, dropped Gini's arm, and stopped in protest because it was new moon time and black as black can be. We never used a flashlight. Gini assured her that it was no problem, adding that the Indians always walked in the dark without artificial light.

"I'm not an Indian," Mum replied.

◇ ◇ ◇

Sometimes as we watched the sunset from that perfect western view of the ocean with the forbidden island of Niihau off our coast, our bewitched mother would ask, "Are we in Hawai'i? I don't know why people live in all that ice and snow." Both she and Daddy, who'd had a 30-year career in the US Coast Guard after being a lighthouse keeper, had always wanted a transfer to Hawai'i. Those orders never came through, only an offer to move the family of eight to Ketchikan, Alaska, which they turned down. It would have been even colder than the Great Lakes Erie and Michigan Coast Guard Stations, where we six children grew up in the snow belts of Pennsylvania, Michigan and Ohio. Brrr!

Decades later, when our brother Captain Greg, successful entrepreneur of his own three boat sail, snorkeling and tour boat company in Puerto Rico, took his siblings on a cruise to Alaska, we checked out that particular Coast Guard Station. We learned that Ketchikan would not have been a good post to raise six children in those war years. It was notorious as a favorite R&R port, as we noted when visiting some of the historical watering holes and dance halls along a salmon river-run. How's that for proof that things work out for the best?

Our life on Kaua'i was a beautiful example of getting what one asked for. Mum got her wish to move to Hawai'i, and I got my many dreams come true. More than once I told my mother that I loved her and thanked her for staying alive while I was on my spiritual journey.

"I needed that time to find myself and to be ready to spend this time with you, Mummy. Even though I felt guilty leaving you in a nursing home, I did what I felt I had to do for myself. I am so grateful that you waited for me to return. It's wonderful to be with you and Gini now after my 'homeless by choice' five years on the road."

It had been eight years since we six well-intentioned siblings, busy with children and professional lives, had found it impossible for any of us to give our widowed Mum the attention she needed at her most difficult and confusing time. We did the best we could as we attempted to care for her in our family homes on a rotating basis, only to find it was disconcerting to her as well as disruptive to our families. She needed professional care in a more consistent assisted living situation. At the time I agreed with my siblings to place her there – and began to displace myself; you have heard the story.

It was most difficult to move Mum out of the beautifully furnished three-bedroom, ranch house that our newly retired father and brother Greg had built over a period of nine years. It was on seven acres from the estate of our dear Grandpa K. which was a working farm complete with chickens. How we loved going into the coop and collecting eggs when visiting as children. Our grandfather's gentle manner and smile reinforced our behavior as he leaned on his rake watching us gleefully play on his haystacks. He spoke only Polish, which we children never learned, just as we had never learned German from my mother's side of the family. Parents of their generation usually wanted their offspring to act and sound as American as possible.(I was in fact a bit embarrassed by my bilingual Polish cousins' accent, diet and customs until we related as adults.)

Our parents loved the house they built for their retirement, the only home they ever owned, after living in government housing at Coast Guard Stations for Daddy's entire career. When retired, he moved from lakeside to farmland for sustenance and enjoyed the role of pruning the mature fruit trees and invigorating the vegetable garden. Mum landscaped with flower beds, called 2532 Saltsman Road the "hermitage," and hosted many reunions there. We were lured back again and again with the aromas from her kitchen and the treat of eating the backyard organic apples that she sliced up for us as we sat in front of the granite-fronted fireplace.

"One day each of you will have an acre to build your home here," our parents dreamed, a fantasy none of the six of us shared. But Mum suffered from dementia a decade after Daddy died, and the life we all loved ended. Helen Catherine had to be moved, against her wishes, heartbroken and angrily protesting, from her beloved home and farm into bedroom #29 in the Cozy Comfort Nursing Home where she could not go outside beyond a courtyard. The location was chosen because it was near where our younger brother David, who had Power of Attorney, lived with his family in mid-state Indiana.

When our mother settled into the assisted living facility, after being put on medication to control the symptoms of the disease (a euphemism for being drugged into complacency?), she appeared to forget about the trauma and stopped asking to "go home." When we family members came to visit and take her for outings, like a special haircut or shopping, Mum would get agitated and anxious around well-established mealtimes. She wanted to go back for meals. It was lining up for dinner outside the dining hall a half hour before serving time that interested her most.

Now, all these years later, I give Gini credit for walking Mum away from her lock-down. The staff there loved her.

"Helen is soft and quiet," they said, and gave her a hearty farewell party. Still abroad, I was not part of any of that. But I was certainly an equal partner in caring for Mum, now in her 90th year, on Kauaʻi, a lifestyle that was good for each of us.

I recall the trips to the grocery store where Mum would fill the cart with all her favorite candies and cookies, which I had to manage to leave at the checkout counter. I attempted many times to get her to sit at a café table and enjoy a cup of soup and crackers while I scurried to make purchases without her help. A couple of times I wasn't fast enough, and returned to find her missing. Each time I was frantic, until I tracked her down, walking down the block towards our bus stop or standing on the curb outside watching the world go by.

It was hard getting her to stay put for long. Even on the beach, when I had her comfortably seated under the ironwood tree with milk and cookies, she would eat fast and walk away as soon as I got distracted while attempting a short swim. At home it was funny, maybe a little sad, but clever of her to go and sit in the passenger seat of whatever car was in the yard when she felt bored and in need of an adventure. She knew what being on wheels meant: she loved trips.

Twice a week, Mum went to scheduled-activity-time for the elderly at the Adult Care Center located at Wilcox Hospital in Lihue, an hour away. We had to get her out of bed earlier than usual on those days to get her dressed and fed before the Paratransit arrived to take her to town. Late in the afternoon she returned tired yet peaceful. It was more R&R for us than for her, we learned, as Mum was not interested in the projects. This was surprising as she had always loved crafts and decorated everything within reach. The staff said she stayed off by herself.

Gini and I took these few hours as personal time to work on art projects, created most often with found objects from the beach. It wasn't long before I completed a seven-foot-tall "Gardening Angel" for the front yard. I also started using my sewing machine after repossessing her from storage at our brother's. Ms. Singer worked just fine after a good oiling.

My sister likes to tell the story of when Mum went missing on her watch, and how she had to go to the police station to fetch her.

"She obviously remembered hitch-hiking with you, Laurel, to get to town as you two did sometimes. I never dreamed she would do it on her own when my back was turned. The couple who picked her up said they saw this elderly woman almost in the center of the road. After stopping and observing from a short distance, they decided to turn around and pick up this unusual hitch-hiker and take her to the Waimea Police Station three miles east. When any car passed without stopping, they said, she would just go out further into traffic and put her thumb out." Gini continued with the story, "When I finally went to the Police Station to inquire about our missing mother, I found her. After thanking her rescuers, I asked Mum if the cops had given her ice cream while she was waiting. We made up for that lack by stopping at Ishihara Market to get her favorite ice cream, chocolate covered bars on a stick. We shared all six bars before they melted, three for her and three for me."

Gini and I always slept on the beach because some guest, whether a sibling, daughter or friend, was usually occupying the second bedroom of our rented cottage. We used that as an excuse because we found it more ideal to be outdoors on all those beautiful nights, resting by the rhythm of the sea. I set up a bamboo-framed teepee from an old poleless tent, and Gini built a sleeping platform up in the ironwood tree. It didn't feel at all strange to us to do so.

We'd been told to expect company when we moved to Hawai'i. We not only anticipated it; we encouraged visitors. Our first guests were our two older sisters, who came together. Esther, called the "pick of the litter" by her second husband, and JoAnne, the religious one with seven children, set up tents borrowed from their off-spring next to ours on the beach. Being blessed with a dry summer, a camper's delight, we were only waterlogged by all the swimming we did. We never toured the island; we siblings just hung out with our mother. After being together for this first time in decades, we four sisters decided to make it a yearly tradition to vacation as a foursome. We followed through and, over the years, rubbed each other in ways that eventually made us most compatible.

For most of the first year that Mum was with us, I thought of her as an example of an ideal way of Being, living in such a neutral manner that nothing disturbed her equilibrium. She appeared neither excited nor agitated to any notable degree, only responding to everything as "just what is," quite like the man with the horse in the Buddhist story. Maybe being at a dessert table or having a man's attention were the exceptions. (I related to that also.)

Shortly after our sisters left for home, I got a long-distance call from London. I was always delighted to hear from my daughter Michelle, who had just had her second child, another daughter.

This time the tale was upsetting. "I'm leaving my husband," she said, "I'll tell you the story later. May I come visit you on Kaua'i?"

Now that was a surprise, but without a moment's hesitation, I said of course.

"Thank you so much," sighed Michelle, and added, "I have five more months of paid family leave with lovely newborn Skye, you know that English benefit, so I can contribute. Are you sure it's all right with Aunt Gini too, having me and two babies there as well as Grandma?"

It was soon settled. Michelle, month-old Skye, and 2 ½-year-old Guinevere made flights over the Atlantic, the continental US, and halfway across the Pacific to join us the next week. It was just enough time for us to acquire a crib, a little bed, and a child's front bar seat to put on my bicycle.

We became Michelle's "city of refuge," a traditional Hawaiian custom, a place of safety. There were now four generations (plus one auntie) in our household: great grandmother, grandmother, mother and daughters. I was delighted with having my life line under one roof. Actually, we spent more time outside under the mango tree or at the beach.

Guin loved the seaside. "I'm going to work," this toddler would say, as she picked up her bucket and shovel. She would glance back to the cottage to see if we were watching before doing her job of moving sand from one pile to another on the shore. However, being accustomed to structured time and challenging activities in daycare, it was obvious this very bright child needed more than just playtime as much as Michelle needed respite from the demands of mothering two daughters. The only nearby possibility was a preschool for 3-to-5-year-olds at St. Theresa's School, close enough to reach by bicycle. The problem was that Guin was only 2½.

We came up with a rather unethical solution: we would observe her birthday six months early. We reasoned that when we were asked her age, we could reply, "We just celebrated her third birthday." When this precocious child was asked how old she was, we programmed Guin to answer "three" and hold up three fingers as children do. (A child less bright would not have survived keeping up with the assignments given to the class of mostly five year olds.)

She continues to be ahead of her time, as well as relating beautifully with other cultures, having been exposed so early to peers of Japanese, Filipino, Portuguese, Chinese and Hawaiian heritage at the preschool and even more nationalities when back in London. (As an adult, Guin studies radical economics, volunteers at southern European refugee camps, and educates all of us on the hardships the displaced face.)

Newborn Skye now received more attention. Even her great grandmother appreciated holding this beautiful baby... for a while anyway. That never happened again unsupervised, after Mum once placed the two-month-old gently on the ground by her chair when she felt like doing something else. Perhaps as a mother of six, she had had her share of child care, while Michelle was adapting to a totally different lifestyle.

My professional daughter's business suit apparel, highrise office career and challenging development assignments as a Chartered Surveyor were on hold while halfway around the world to get away from it all and heal from her divorce. For the five months spent at her mother's home, Michelle was occupied with breastfeeding her new baby, coping with an energetic toddler, living in a mill town without a car, and oh so privately wrestling with decisions made and yet to be tackled. (She believed and told me that there wasn't anything else I could do to help her deal with her stuff. Life was boring, yes, but at least far away from a threatening husband.)

Perhaps to get her mind off of her own life, and circumstances that I felt helpless to resolve, Michelle started thinking about mine, which at least was a distraction she desired.

"Mum, I think you should write a memoir. I have so many friends who, when hearing of your travels, wish their mothers were inspired to do the same. Older women need to know that there is another way to live, and that there are infinite possibilities like the ones you explored after going through menopause and a divorce. You really have a unique story to tell." Michelle would hear none of my protests.

"So, what if you're not a writer. It will flow once you start. I'll get pencil and paper. Just start talking and I will take dictation." So began this book, dictated while sitting on a blanket oceanside.

When my daughter, now a single parent, and granddaughters moved back to Notting Hill in London months later, she typed up the notes and mailed it to me. Less interested but grateful, I boxed the beginning script away and left it to gather dust. (If in a parallel universe, had I carried on with the project and gotten it published before *Eat, Pray, Love*, dare I fantasize that Julia Roberts might have been playing me instead of Elizabeth Gilbert in the movie? Or perhaps not; I didn't get the man in the last chapter, even though both books end in love.)

Michelle continued to encourage my writing even when returning to her demanding but flourishing career, going through with the painful post-divorce period, juggling the demands of getting the girls to daycare daily, and managing the flat and the tenant in the extra bedroom (for necessary pounds needed to help pay the mortgage). I applauded her resilience knowing she had the right stuff to keep her act together and find happiness once again.

Soon after the family left, Tatiana, Michelle's friend and mine from London, moved in with us. We had shared the meditation practice at the Friends of the Western Buddhist Order whenever I was in the big city. This gorgeous woman had had a marvelous life before health challenges changed everything. She took me up on my invitation to come to Hawai'i after hearing Michelle speak of her healing time. It was like having another daughter in the house because she related well to Helen, as she called our mother, and adjusted well to our simple lifestyle. She inspired me with her Ayurvedic diet and yoga practices as she healed herself.

Journal Entry:
June 21, 1997

The 1997 Summer Solstice was so exceptional a day that I recorded a special journal entry about Mummy. I wrote of how I came back from my walk at 8:15 a.m. and was surprised to find Mum dressed and sitting outside on the porch chair. She greeted me with a smile, was happy as we picked mangoes for our breakfast, and commented that the fruit was beautiful as we prepared slices for drying. After enjoying lunch, Mum said that she didn't want a nap and went out to the backyard, busying herself breaking up branches and twigs for our evening fire. When friends came by to work on driftwood art, this observer wanted to help and even laughed at jokes. Mum seemed to enjoy her evening walk on the beach more than usual.

"How nice to be here with you," she said. "What lovely water. The sun must be very hot for the water to be so warm. The clouds are so beautiful."

Later we talked about her age and she commented, "'I feel old."

We agreed that she should feel old at 91 and how lucky she was to be so active, but she added, "Living so long is good as long as you don't look too old – that's not good."

Reminded of her birth year of 1905, Mum thought reaching the year 2000 "would be really something." When my dear mother finished her bath that evening before bed with another thank you and appreciative comment, I too was very grateful for having shared such a magnificent day.

Less than a month later...

Forty-Seven

Hospice on the Beach

7 a.m. July 12th, 1997: "Oh Mummy, God bless."

Entering my mother's bedroom, I gasped, finding her unconscious and struggling for breath. Gini joined me immediately by her bedside and recognized the signs of a stroke. We hugged each other in those moments of shock and then snuggled next to our dear mother who was never to wake to full consciousness again. We took her hands in ours and glanced at each other, being fully present with her and with our own soul-searching thoughts and prayers. In a period of timeless time, Gini verbalized the life-death decision made long before this: "We will not call 911."

I had known this moment might come. Had I been alone, my gut reaction could have gone against my mother's will, and I might have ordered the "extraordinary means" in an attempt to hold our lives together a bit longer.

We didn't dial 911. It took trust and a thoughtful response not to do so, but rather to honor this 91-year-old's advance directive, a Living Will declaring "Do Not Resuscitate."

I thanked my sister, a nurse with much hospice experience, who replied, "It's not the same when it is your own mother who is dying. This is much more difficult when it is so upfront and personal."

She paused, tears running down her face. "I'll call Mum's doctor for palliative medication to make sure that she doesn't suffer in these final hours."

I turned back to our beloved mother who was having another moment of agitation and attempting to sit up as she struggled for breath. I held her gently and whispered The Lord's Prayer in her ear, hoping that would give her some solace.

"It's all right to let go," I told her, only half believing it myself. I then recited the Holy Mary prayer (when I finally remembered it, as it had been years since I had last recited it.) As she settled down, I realized that we could also call the priest and request his prayers. He said he would come right over. We prepared: cleared off the side table by Mum's bed, freshened up the flowers there, and brought out a candle and matches.

Father Frank from St. Theresa's Catholic Church soon arrived. He mentioned he had seen us at church a few times and remembered our mother. He first reviewed how the Last Rites of Extreme Unction would give health and strength to the soul: that it was "a preparation for immediate entry into heaven." First was an absolution of sin for those who had not made their last confession. Mummy would not have had anything to confess anyway. Certainly St. Pete would have no problem flicking off any mistakes she may have smudged on her page in his book. (But I couldn't help wondering if I wanted to add a request for Extreme Unction on my own Advance Directive.)

"Please light the candle. I will now administer the Last Sacrament," Father said. "Let us pray." Offering traditional prayers of comfort, peace, and courage, he made the Sign of the Cross each time as he applied the "Final Anointing of Holy Oil" first to Mum's forehead, then to her eyes, ears, nostrils, lips, hands and feet. Truly sanctified during and after the ceremony, the blessed body was calm.

"Peace be with you," the priest said as he left us. He might have added, "May God have mercy on your souls" or "Keep the faith." I don't really remember; maybe I imagined it.

Gini and I agreed that the ritual was comforting for us even though we had never really talked with our mother, or each other, about those kinds of last wishes. Receiving the end-of-life sacrament was what Catholics did, yet Mummy had been unhappy with the Roman Catholic Church during those semi-cognitive years when she felt God had forsaken her. How could a loving Deity have allowed her children to move her out of the home that she and Daddy and son Greg had so lovingly built? What kind of God would permit her to be put away with "all those old people?" It was hurtful for all of us as her unhappiness turned to rage against us, as we struggled and failed to care for her in our homes on a rotating basis.

That was regrettable, but being present for the past year and a half and these final three days of our mother's life on Kaua'i was the biggest blessing. We trusted that it was "all for the best" at the end. We made her as comfortable as we could, one of us always by her side that first very long day.

Dr. Williamson made a house call, and applied the transdermal morphine patch to alleviate her suffering. He promised to return the next day. Word spread and friends dropped by to pay their respects with flowers and homemade bread, poke (a popular Hawaiian raw fish dish), cheese, and coconut water.

The hours passed as did the day.

"It's time. We always go to the beach to catch the last rays and the green flash of the setting sun. What shall we do?" Mum was unconscious, but she was alive, and tradition is tradition.

"We can make a stretcher of sorts and carry Mum to our camp, can't we?" It may have been unusual, certainly unprofessional, but the lawn recliner worked as a transport to our encampment. We gently set the fully reclined chair down on the sand and pondered what to do next. Sitting on each side of Mom, we meditated until the last rays of this mid-July sunset subsided. We agreed that we trusted the weather to remain in its present drought condition, and chose to follow through with the idea of having Mom sleep on the beach with us that night. Giving up our normal sleeping spots, we took turns preparing the bedding, first spreading a tarp, and then arranging three mattresses side-by-side on the sand embankment at the edge of the calm Pacific sea.

Thus began our watch: hospice on the beach. We rested side-by-side: Mum in the middle with a daughter to the north and south of her, the ocean to the west and the canyon to the east. The campfire burned down to embers; the moon waxed; the stars did their thing, something that if it only happened once in a lifetime, could not have been more appreciated. We paid close attention to our Mother's breath and movements to guide us as to when we felt drawn to whisper prayers and encouragement whenever she appeared agitated. I was very impressed with my sister's nursing skills. She wiped Mum's mouth out periodically with a wet cloth to keep it from becoming too dry. "Giving the patient liquids only extends their dying," Gini said. She knew about turning the bedridden. She was the one who wiped Mum's bottom, as well, to keep her clean, and was aware of a patient's comfort level and medication needs. I could not have done this without my sister, and she kindly thanked me also for being there.

It was a glorious sunrise on day two. As the ball of fire rose higher and grew hotter, we pulled the tarp and mattresses up under the ironwood tree for the cooling shade. We positioned a white mosquito net over a driftwood frame to create a sacred space over our loved one. There was also room for whoever attended her to rest by her side under the netting. Sometimes it was Tatiana who, having adopted our mother after living with us all for a few months, kept watch after carefully placing crystals around the site.

Feeling elevated by the prayers we witnessed the day before, we invited our dear friend and neighbor Caroline Carr, a minister at the United Church of Christ, to make an offering.

"I was expecting that you would ask," she said, putting her ceremonial stole over her head and around her shoulders. After her prayers, she sat with us and told stories of our family life as she had observed it and been a part of in the past year. She especially appreciated having befriended my daughter Michelle and her babies during their stay with us. I told her how glad I was to receive her wise counseling and an introduction to the Science of Mind monthly magazine.

Later, Reverend Nori, the Buddhist priest from the Waimea Hongwanji Temple, made us laugh when he came by to offer blessings from the sangha.

"Helen was most welcome and seemed to enjoy festivals; plenty mochi ice cream and daifuku for her," he mentioned in his Japanese-accented English. We would never forget his having been so attentive to her, and how often he kept slipping her extra desserts.

Quite the heavenly send-off it was for our loving mother, by three diverse clergy: Catholic, Protestant and Buddhist, because we couldn't get enough of that wonderful stuff.

Friends came by on what turned into three hospice days. Mum was loved and respected as a mother of six, grandmother of 20, great-grandmother of

29. We basked in that love as well, when visitors spoke of how impressed they were with our care and attentiveness. Dr. Williamson came by after work each day as he had promised, saying he had never made house calls on the beach before, but that he was glad to do it, and to be of assistance in regulating palliative medicine.

Predawn, after the three days of gathering and nights of rest at the calm oceanside, I awoke to find Mum breathing even more faintly. I gave her a good morning kiss and momentarily basked in the beauty of the pink and purple waking sky. When I looked back, I realized my mother had just died. I had never been with anyone at the moment of death before, and I was not prepared for the change in countenance. Mum had never looked more beautiful; her expression was absolutely angelic. I felt it was a sign that she was at peace, and was being greeted by Daddy and other family members who had gone before. I sat holding my dearest one's hand in the glow of the sunrise at that precious ending. I asked a passing fisherman to call my sister, who had gone up to the cottage before I awoke. Then I flashed on Mum's false teeth and thought of rigor mortis, of which I knew very little. If I didn't put her teeth in now, would it be too late? She surely would want to look her best when meeting her husband again after so many years. Our mother had always wanted to look good for Daddy.

Gini returned soon after and sat in silence with Mum. After a while, we started the ceremony, a celebration of life and death. We had prepared for this moment by having bells and sparklers and a steel drum on hand. Having spent so much time in India, I loved the fire rituals and bell ringing so prominent at a Hindu puja. We used the last embers of the previous night's campfire to light the sparklers, and started ringing the bells and sounding the steel drum. All seemed proper for a proper send-off.

As the smoke cleared, we silenced the instruments and sat in contemplation, the three of us side-by-side. We agreed that this was indeed a perfect place to leave the planet, being as close as it was to the famous Kaua'i beach called Polihale, "House of Spirit," a name with a strong basis in Hawaiian mythology. Some translated it as the "afterworld," the place where souls would jump from its cliffs into the next reality deep in the sea. Believing this, Hawaiians buried the bones of their royalty there high up on the cliffs.

Others believed Polihale represented birth, the source of life. Either way, it felt auspicious. Mother and two daughters were each going to give birth to different lives after this event.

It also felt right to prepare and wash the body, and we both knew without speaking that it would be in the ocean. Gently, we carried Mum's body into the calm sea and floated her lovingly.

"There is a baptism at birth," I said, "Why not one also at death?" At first, we just scooped water over our mother's head, before deciding to do the St. John the Baptist thing and submerge the body. Must admit, we got a bit giggly then and frolicked some.

By this time, Tatiana was on the beach with her camera taking pictures of the event, vacillating between being enchanted and shocked by our behavior, proper landed-gentry Englishwoman that she was. After coming out of the water and drying the body, Gini oiled Mum's torso while I paid final attention to her feet, which would never again walk this beach. We dressed Mum in a purple and white Hawaiian muumuu, and moved her body once again under the shade of the ironwood tree where we created a shrine-like setting.

Our friends again stopped by all day to offer their sympathies, bring fresh flowers, and sit and snack with us. Dr. Williamson returned once more to make out the death certificate. It was a beautiful full 11 hours before we called the pre-arranged funeral home. It was dark when an unmarked white windowless panel truck pulled up to the beach and two men went about their business. It was hard to watch, but impossible not to, as they zipped our precious matriarch into a body bag, slid her into the back of the vehicle and drove away.

Our siblings, Esther, JoAnn, Greg, and David, made the funeral arrangements and scheduled it in three weeks' time when we would all meet again in Erie, Pennsylvania, where Helen Catherine was to be laid out and buried next to her beloved husband, our sweet father Capt. Walter John, who had died decades before.

The next day, I was surprised to see a policewoman at our door.

"Whenever someone dies at home, it is a procedure to investigate," she said. It was her job to check for possible foul play, but it turned out to be a long sentimental conversation instead. Her mother had passed a month earlier, and this public servant took this opportunity to share that part of her life with me. Only after she left did I start to worry that if they did an autopsy, we might be accused of drowning our mother because of the dunking. I later was relieved to learn that a dead person cannot take water into their lungs. It is safe to re-baptize the dead. Whether it is politically correct or not is another issue. Gini and I spent the next three weeks at home, adjusting to the emptiness, and creating a scrapbook of our time together with our mother at this last chapter of her life. We also were packing, as our move from the cottage was imminent.

We flew into our Great Lakes hometown well prepared for the ceremony and the reunion that funerals turn out to be. We had decided to make it as Hawaiian a viewing as we could. Gini purchased dozens of shell leis to be presented to family and friends. After contacting my gardening tribe on island for advice about flowers for the funeral home and gravesite, Elaine generously led me into her garden and we gathered tropical flowers for floral arrangements. We cut heart-shaped anthuriums, heliconia lobster claw, blue cat's whiskers, Japanese tumbleweed, birds of paradise, torch ginger, pink pineapple flowers, squirrel's tail, and the mysterious protea flower of the gods. (Hopefully nobody would test me in identifying the other blossoms or the accompanying greenery by name.)

After the agricultural inspection at the airport, we were able to cold-storage ship them to Erie, Pennsylvania, along with our luggage, easily accomplished shortly before we boarded our flight.

The wake at the funeral home was a most loving occasion, one in keeping with the traditions of her generation, and all according to our mother's wishes. Mum was laid out dressed in her favorite purple and white flower-printed muumuu in a beautiful casket, surrounded by the Hawaiian tropical flowers. Relatives and friends; some old, some new, most curious, each now wearing a lei, gathered at the Mulcahy Funeral Home for visiting hours, saying the right things, sharing memories, and commenting on how good Mum looked.

After the Catholic funeral mass at St. Anthony's the next morning, Mum was buried next to Daddy in the Presque Isle Cemetery, not far from the Coast Guard station where we children were raised. The tribes of siblings, great grandchildren, and our parents' surviving neighbors from the previous decade, then had lots of cabbage rolls at a nephew's Polish restaurant. Gini and I spent a few days with our sisters and brothers before returning to Kaua'i, and life without our mother.

Forty-Eight

Tending My Own Garden

Had Mum known that the cottage was to be sold after our rejection of our option-to-buy lease? Did she feel our anxiety about having to find another place to live? Could she have chosen the time to die based on recognizing the difficulty a move for the three of us could be? We would never know, but we gave her credit for such consideration anyway.

Our mother had died, our home was being sold, and Gini was moving on to caretaking another elder, now that our shared mission had been accomplished. I admit I felt a bit abandoned for a while. Oh, such crazy issues. What shall I do now?

Tatiana decided to stay on Kaua'i, not move back to London. A year later, she married a local man who mirrored her spiritual nature. I was very fortunate to find a funky studio space for rent. It had served as a large classroom, with high screened openings as windows, in an ancient Japanese one-story, school building. The lot buffeted the Kekaha sugar cane fields and was a block from the mill, four blocks from the beach.

"It's still standing," my landlord said, "because the termites are holding hands." The rent was cheap since it was not legal as a residence, even though it had a toilet and shower, hot running water, and a laundry sink, around which I set up a kitchen.

"No problem with not being allowed to sleep here," I told Ray and his wife, "I plan to continue to sleep on the beach anyway. I'm just delighted to have the studio space to make sculptures. Figure if I am renting a studio from a fine woodworker and a potter, I must be an artist too."

When Ray asked what I would make first, I told him that I wanted to create a huge chair out of driftwood, floats, nets and sections of surfboards, a kind of King Neptune throne.

"That's timely," the artist replied. "You'll have a piece to enter in the upcoming Kaua'i Society of Artists (KSA) 'To Sit or Not to Sit' chair show."

Excited about being invited to participate in my first-ever art exhibit, I got busy attempting to create a chair, one level and strong enough to earn the noun. It took me months. I had to purchase a heavy drill to implement incorporating the ¾ inch dowels to hold it all together. After lots of starting over, my project was complete. It was arty as well as functional. Then, as a new member of the KSA organization with beginner's luck, I won the "Best in Show" award of $250 for my nine-foot-tall creation which was big enough to seat three children. I was ecstatic when "Neptune's Beach Chair" also sold for $300 to the owner of a surf shop. Now that was auspicious. So began my rebirth on Kaua'i as an artist.

◇ ◇ ◇

While living in Kekaha for three more years after Mum died, I continued to sleep out under the stars on the same dry leeward side beach of Kaua'i, and to work in my art studio by day, until making two moves further north on this westermost paradise. A change in emphasis came with each new P.O. Box address, along with day and night roofs over my head.

My sculptures from repurposed objects, all found materials, grew a bit more sophisticated over the years. After starting with abundant flotsam and jetsam, I took some welding classes and began creating sculptures using dismembered bicycle parts and odd tools, a modality that didn't last long. I soon found the fire and fumes from welding to be health threatening.

Driftwood-bodied birds with fabric wings became a theme, then make-believe musical instruments. Assemblages got smaller and more intricate, as I continued to enter most Kaua'i Society of Artists shows. It was always exciting to be called an artist as part of that cool community. I found it a big deal to serve on the KSA board, and ego inflating to place or win an award.

One top prize was for a two-part piece called "Player Piano Revisited." It came to life after I had rescued some parts from a piano which was headed for the dump from the ReStore. No problem for me, being the island equivalent of a dumpster diver. With my head full of ideas and storage space full of stuff,

I received another first-place award for a whimsical donkey and rider sculpture which took form upon my finding a well-aged brass teapot to serve as the beast. A wooden figure became "Don-na Quixote," a revised "Don" when a feminist friend asked, "Why not a female?" This foot-tall, now fashionable Mz. character armored with a lance and riding her stallion sold for $375.

Another big sale ($500) was titled "Creature Comfort for the Dog-Tired" and winner of a People's Choice award: a huge bamboo framed chair comfortably sculpted with around 75 stuffed toy dogs of all sizes (with the "Big Red Dog" placed to fit below the recliner's right shoulder ready for a hug.) There were only a few times I actually received sizable currency for my craft. All I need is love...

After winds destroyed my tented art studio space, and I had too big an inventory to fit all my creations into my most recent home, I gifted more art and let my website (www.KauaiFoundArt) expire. Large metal pieces were allowed to "rUst in peace" in the yard; the driftwood birds with jeweled crests flew off to other neighborhoods. My life-size seated "Lady In Waiting" sculpture was stolen from the back of the truck that was transporting her home from a show. I still miss her, but imagine this iron and driftwood lady living with a beautiful ocean view.

Artwork left my life; writing walked in. I consoled and challenged myself by joining a couple of writers' groups. After practicing with prompts and being encouraged by friends, I was finally motivated to get this memoir into the computer and now in print. It feels like a rite of passage (do they ever end?) to complete this writing assignment that my daughter Michelle inspired me to start over two decades ago.

These added decades have brought physical and financial challenges along with the "arctic blonde" hair color. Like many, my life savings were depleted by medical bills. Gratefully the doctoring was for the removal and radiation of a rare tumor in my thigh, instead of a vital organ (not to belittle my legs meant for dancing). There was the downer of side effects, but an uplift from social services. Thanks to all who pay taxes, I fell into the safety net of a HUD Section 8 Housing voucher, which covers about 60% of the cost of my one-bedroom rental. I also feel great appreciation for my children, who find that arranging for me to visit them is more reasonable than flying to Hawai'i as they have a few times. My son Christopher has treated me to abundant Christmas reunions at his palatial home in California (and on the islands) with lovely daughter-in-law Stacey and my two talented youngest granddaughters. Being that we all have gyspy blood in our German-Polish veins, we share adventures in different time zones as my five granddaughters progress from grammar school to post-grad.

Loving the earth as we islanders do, a group of us interested in starting a permaculture commune met for a couple of years. We attempted to pull together the dream of sharing land and building tiny homes, but had to move on from our fantasy to handle even smaller goals. Now I am blessed with the opportunity to keep my thumb green and my fridge full of organic produce by volunteering at the community farm across the street.

Whether my hands are in the soil or attempting African drumming, my body is blissed by yoga stretches, Qi Gong moves, morning ocean laps and acupuncture. My kind of church consists of singing both with the Sacred Earth Choir and the all-women Voice Weavers, or dancing with the Sufis. Finally, I have even gotten my wish to take ballroom dancing and tango lessons, although the older I get, the scarcer the male partners. A good time to take up Ecstatic Dance.

Thinking about the future, there is a ConsciousLivingAndDying.com study group that has met once a month for four years to take the dread out of dead, and to stop acting as if death is contagious. An outreach website called DeathDinnerAndMe.org offers opportunities for those who are willing to take death out of the closet and put it on the coffee/coffin table. Here is a space to talk about birth, life, and end-of-life issues. I've researched conservation burial grounds which are like parks, where trees replace the traditional headstones, planted over ashes or unembalmed bodies. Many of us are interested in manifesting a Home Funeral and Green Burial movement on Kaua'i. (GreenBurialCouncil.org has a comprehensive website.) I've even fantasized about becoming a funeral director to get such a green cemetery established on this island. I am willing to do more for ecology than compost food scraps and recycle trash and cardboard.

◇ ◇ ◇

While relishing the joys of being alive, thoughts of Infinite Possibilities arise. Attempting to follow my bliss as Joseph Campbell suggests, while living in the reality of duality with two sides to everything, I feel called to put my energies towards correct action for the highest good. I have no desire to stick my head in the sand when the earth is poisoned, or to ignore political malfunctions. How to stay informed and take action while letting go of the image of an enemy?

Answer: the Serenity Prayer. "Grant me the serenity to accept the things I cannot change, the courage to change the things I can, and the wisdom to know the difference."

One does not have to be a Buddha to know that all is impermanent: marriages end; Cambodia has moved beyond The Killing Fields; old age doesn't last long. One does not have to be a Buddha to know that "life is suffering": unsatisfactory, as transitory as both pleasures and pain are. I endeavor to BE Buddhist enough to remember that there is an END to Suffering.

And what kind of Buddha have I attempted to emulate? First attracted to the contemplative Bodhgaya Buddha to escape unhappiness and the Blue Medicine Buddha to heal, I then joined the Buddha on the Battlefield to promote peace; and now want to be a socially engaged Buddhist. Will I ever be the laughing Buddha who sees the humor in the movie we humans act in, produce, direct, share, and take so seriously? There are as many teachers and ways to heaven (the here and now?) as there are trails to a mountaintop, and I continue trekking. Even Robert Frost said he had miles to go before he slept. Didn't he, too, want to rest in totally unified perception?

I like this quote from my long-term study of *A Course In Miracles*: "The Bible says that a deep sleep fell upon Adam, and nowhere is there any reference to his waking up."

Ask my advice, and I suggest they do what they feel called to do, noting that a divorce need not be part of the script. Be evolved enough to trust each day's new dawn and make each birthday a celebration (especially in one's eighties). Know it to be true that when the pupil is ready, a new teacher appears – now, more than ever, on the internet.

It's no longer necessary to go to India for the gurus – they're on YouTube and in podcasts, with as much inspiration as you can handle.

Rupert Spira is my go-to Advaita teacher at the moment. His quote "When the journey TO God ends, the journey IN God begins" is found on YouTube labeled "It's Not Enough to Discover What You Are Not." My journey IN God has begun as I trade in my rolling stone search in exchange for memoir sharing (with maybe a bit more wandering in wonder).

Jon Kabat-Zinn says, "It is time to finish the job and be aware that I am aware." In that awareness, I think about death and dying, a boat we're all in together, along with the perception of being in a body (the cycle "from the maternity ward to the crematorium" as Alan Watts calls it). I have taken hospice and death doula training. Physical birth was not the beginning of my life, and death is not the end, except in material form.

I didn't do anything to make my birth happen, yet have the opportunity now to make some preparations regarding the "non-ending." Isn't that like rearranging furniture on the Titanic while practicing non-resistance? I'm getting used to the idea of planting my dead body in a meadow with a GPS tracking number to mark the grave (if / when we have a green cemetery on the island at that time.)

So, I come to THE ENDing with one final reminder to myself to give up attachment to the fruit of any of my actions, including these stories, and surrender willingly.

I believe that there is no finish line in the great unknown. As Abraham-Hicks says, "You can't get it wrong because you never get it done."

Epilogue

The potential within each of us to BE:
From bourgeois for me, to Buddha for all
meant steps out of a marriage and a quest for consciousness
then 24 more years often forgetting
"what I am looking for is what I am looking from"
still on the stage playing roles
while ingesting less melodramatic morsels:
no more appetizers of infidelity
far fewer treats in New Age communes
yet just as savory as sitting sharing with gurus
and less heavy than banquets hoping to satisfy the hunger
for peace on the pilgrims' process...
like a checked-off Christmas list:
1 Vitamix, 2 Dell computers, 3 second hand cars,
4 new food plans, 5 granddaughters,
and an obsession with an avocado tree...
a half-dozen embraced and liberated lovers
2 surgeries and 5 weeks of radiation
8-mile walking marathons
9 Na Pali boat trips
10 gifted retreats
and lotsa coconuts to eat.

Life flowing rowing this life-boat of mine
more gently down the dream-stream
correcting my course, feeling the Force
journaling and journeying
seeing few auras, fewer visions
more like ordinary folk
looking to be "woke"
and content...
free to Be.

As Rumi said,
"Whoever brought me here
will have to bring me home."
On my pine box
planted under a mountain laurel bush,
please print *Return To Sender*.

About the Author

Laurel Ann Francis grew up with five siblings on the Great Lakes. She graduated from Boston University, studied in Denmark, raised a family, and received a Master's degree from the University of New Hampshire. A retired educator, she now lives in Hawaii and swims every day.

You may contact the author at: Lafxoxo@yahoo.com.

Selected Bibliography

__ *Ashes & Light: Auschwitz to Hiroshima.* Nipponzan Myohoji, Leverett, MA, 1996.

Bach, Richard. *Illusions: The Adventures Of A Reluctant Messiah.* n.p. of Dell Publishing Co, Inc.,1997.

Bly, Robert. *John, A Book About Men.* Addison-Wesley, Boston, 1990.

Campbell, Joseph, Kudler, David ed. *Pathways To Bliss: Mythology and Personal Transformation,* New World Library, Novato, CA., 2004.

Clark, Ramsey. *War Crimes: A Report of U.S. War Crimes Against Iraq.* n.p. of Maisonneuve Press, 1992.

Eddy, Mary Baker. *Science And Health With Key To The Scriptures.* Christian Science Publishing Co. Boston, 1875.

Forward, Susan & Torres, Jean. *Men Who Hate Women And the Women Who Love Them: Why Loving Hurts and You Don't Know Why.* Bantam Books, NY, 1980.

Gilbert, Elizabeth. *Eat, Pray, Love: One Womans Search for Everything Across Italy, India, and Indonesia.* n.p. of Riverhead Books, 2007.

Griffiths OSB, Bede. *The Golden String: An Autobiography.* Fontana Books, London, 1954.

Hart, William & Goenka, *S.n. The Art Of Living: Vipassana Meditation As Taught by S.N. Goenka.* n.p. of Harper & Row, 1989.

Johnson, Robert. *We, Understanding The Psychology Of Romantic Love,* n.p. of HarperCollins, 1985.

Karma Lingpa. (Translated by Thurman, Robert A. F.). *Tibetian Book Of The Dead.* Bantam Book, N.Y., 1994.

Katie, Byron. *Loving What Is, Four Questions That Can Change Your Life.* n.p. of Harmony Book, 2002.

Kopp, Sheldon B. *If You Meet The Buddha On The Road, Kill Him.* Bantam Books, N.Y., 1982.

Krishnamurti, Jiddu & Lutyens, Mary ed. *Freedom From The Known.* Harper, San Francisco, 1969.

Levin, Stephen. *A Gradual Awakening.* n.p. of Knopf Doubleday Publishing Group, 1989.

Maharshi, Sri Ramana & Goodman, David ed. *Be As You Are: The Teachings of Sri Ramana Maharshi.* Penguin Books, New Delhi, India, 1992.

Ninedita, Sister. *The Master As I Saw Him: Pages From the Life of Swami Vivekananda.* Udbodhan, Calcutta, 1997.

Osho. *Nirvana: The Last Nightmare: Learning to Trust in Life.* Osho Media International, New York, 1975.

Pilgrim, Peace. *Peace Pilgrim: Her Life and Work in Her Own Words.* n.p. of Ocean Tree Books, 1994.

Poonja, H.W.L. (Papaji). *Wake Up And Roar: Satsang with H.W. L. Poonja,* n.p. of Gangaji Foundation, 1992.

Ram Dass. *Be Here Now.* n.p. of Harmony/Rodale, 1971.

Roach, Mary. *Stiff: The Curious Lives of Human Cadavers.* n.p. of W.W. Norton & Co., 2004.

Rodegest, Pat & Stanton, Judith. *Emmanuel's Book: A Manual for Living Comfortably in the Cosmos.* Banton Press, New York, 1987.

Sargeant, Winthrop. Christopher Kay Chapple (ed.). *The Bhagavad Gita.* State University of New York Press, Albany N.Y., 1994.

Schucman, Helen (Scribe). *A Course In Miracles.* n. p. of The Foundation for Inner Peace, 1975.

Spira, Rupert. *Being Aware Of Being Aware (The Essence of Meditation Series)*, Sahaja Publications, Oxford, U.K., 2017.

Spira, Rupert. "It's Not Enough to Discover What You Are Not" Oct 22, 2020, uploaded by scienceanddality.com https://youtu.be/gmDTwg8fAlE.

Spira, Rupert. "The Essence of Non-Duality" Feb 20, 2020, uploaded by scienceand-nonduality.com, https://youtu.be/WV-naO9ULp8.

Westling, Annabelle ed. *Handmade Lives, A Collective Memoir.* Canyon, California: Firefall Press, 2002.

Wheeler, Tony & Wheeler, Maureen. *Lonely Planet Guide To India.* n.p. of Lonely Planet Publisher, 1981.

Williams, Robert Carl. *Low Sweet Notes.* Mellon Poetry Press, Lewiston, Maine, 2002.

Yogananda, Paramahansa. *Autobiography Of A Yogi*, n. p. of The Philosophical Library, 1946.

CPSIA information can be obtained
at www.ICGtesting.com
Printed in the USA
BVHW041435221221
624600BV00009B/1045

9 781737 093701